Eat Your Way Across the U.S.A.

Eat Your Way Across the U.S.A.

500 Diners, Lobster Shacks,

Farmland Buffets,

Pie Palaces, and Other

All-American Eateries

Jane and Michael Stern

Broadway Books, New York

BROADWAY

Broadway Books titles may be purchased for business or promotional use or for
special sales. For information, please write to: Special Markets Department,
Bantam Doubleday Dell Publishing Group, Inc., 1540 Broadway, New York,
NY 10036.

BROADWAY BOOKS and its logo, a letter B bisected on the diagonal, are
trademarks of Broadway Books, a division of Bantam Doubleday Dell
Publishing Group, Inc.

Library of Congress Cataloging-in-Publication Data
Stern, Jane.
Eat your way across the U.S.A. : 500 diners, lobster shacks, buffets, pie palaces,
and other all-American eateries / Jane and Michael Stern. — 1st ed.
p.   cm.
ISBN 0-553-06711-7 (pbk.)
1. Restaurants—United States—Directories.
I. Stern, Michael, 1946–   . II. Title.
TX907.2.S837   1997
647.9573—dc21   96-51032
CIP

FIRST EDITION

Designed by Kathleen Herlihy-Paoli, Inkstone

97 98 99 00 01 10 9 8 7 6 5 4 3 2 1

CONTENTS

★ ★ ★

Great Plains

☆

Southwest

☆

West Coast

☆ ☆ ☆

Acknowledgments

★ ★ ★

One nice thing about our job is how many people want to help. The more we write about our favorite places to eat, the more enticing suggestions we get. Tipsters via U.S. mail, E-mail, and word of mouth have helped us build a database of good eats prospects that make every road trip an appetizing adventure.

It has been especially exciting to be associated from the start with Broadway Books, where we know once again the steady hand of old friend and publisher Bill Shinker. John Sterling's enthusiasm has inspired us all along the way, and editor Harriet Bell has made our life as writers all too easy. As ever, Binky Urban, our four-star agent, manages to take the worry out of publishing.

Some of the choicest places in this book were discovered while researching "Two for the Road," our column that appears in *Gourmet* magazine. It is inspiring to be part of *Gourmet*, an oasis of civility and high spirits in the publishing world, where every month we have the pleasure of working with a team of brilliant editors. In particular, we thank Gail Zweigenthal for her unfailing support and Alice Gochman, the world's best dining companion.

Finally, heartfelt thanks to Bunny Kyle and Jean Wagner, who care for our beloved Lewis, Minerva, and Clementine when we are on the road, as well as to John Porto and Karen Rue, who mind our equine pals Piegan and K.T. every day.

Introduction

✯ ✯ ✯

Eat Your Way Across the U.S.A. is a guide to the best food in America. Whether your goal is to explore regional specialties all across the country in neighborhood cafés, seaside shanties, and backwoods supper clubs, or simply to find something decent to eat while on a road trip or in an unfamiliar city, this book is designed to be your appetite's favorite travel companion.

It will lead you to unforgettable (but often unsung) restaurants, delicious (but mostly inexpensive) meals, and the kinds of culinary roadside experiences that can transform breakfast, lunch, and dinner into the high points of any trip. We intend for this book to be a way to know the diversity of America through its food: Texas beef parlors, Yankee shore dinners, Creole gumbo lunchrooms, Great Lakes fish fries, High Plains farmers' cafés, the Basque dinner halls of the Rockies, Georgia soul food buffets, bordertown chile cheeseburgers, Milwaukee milk shakes, and Seattle seafood.

Although we hope that armchair gourmets will find pleasure in merely browsing through the national bounty reflected herein, our primary goal in writing and designing the book has been to create a traveler's tool as useful as a road map or Swiss Army knife. We want *Eat Your Way Across the U.S.A.* to be easy to consult when you need a dining tip anywhere in the country—a valued resource to be packed in briefcase, knapsack, or automobile glove compartment, to be consulted in small towns and big cities, along interstates, back roads, and blue highways.

A vast majority of the 500 places reviewed are very inexpensive, for the simple reason that in most parts of this country, the truly wonderful food is *not* the pricey fare sold in linen-tablecloth dining rooms. From the po'boys of Cajun country and the pig pickin's of the Carolinas to the pie palaces of the upper Midwest and the old-time pizza parlors of the Northeast, America's most distinguished food tends to be of-the-people fare, eaten without pomp and circumstance and fine wine, but with a large stack of paper napkins and a tumbler full of iced tea or a cold beer on the side.

We have indeed included a handful of the very best fine and expensive restaurants in this book—cattle country steak houses, lobster shore dinners, high-fashion dining rooms in big cities—because these special places do serve glorious meals and provide the kind of unforgettable deluxe dining experience that we travelers often crave. In every case, the top-dollar meals we have included are, in their own way, true reflections of local culinary character. For each region of the country, we have listed these places as "splurges." And every restaurant in the book has been rated with from one to three dollar signs. $ = an average meal is under $10. $$ = a meal is between $10 and $25. $$$ = a meal is over $25.

We should state a point that we hope is obvious to any reader: This is a very personal book. We really love the places we have included, and we hope you love them, too. This is not the kind of guidebook that is compiled by committee or survey. For us, eating is a passion, and reading about it—whether for vicarious pleasure or to get some practical advice—ought to be inspiring.

Although we depend on (and are profoundly grateful for) tips, suggestions, and advice we get from readers of our previous books and our "Two for the Road" column in *Gourmet*, as well as from net-surfers who log onto our *Epicurious* postcards, we have always done all the eating and traveling and writing ourselves. When considering restaurants for inclusion in this book, we used no stringers and no hired eaters. We personally ate everywhere. We dined anonymously and we paid for the meals out of our own pockets. And perhaps one out of ten restaurants we visited was good enough to include.

Since we started traveling around the country looking for good food in 1974, we have driven more than three million miles and we have eaten in tens of thousands of restaurants. *Eat Your Way Across the USA* is the culmination of that quest, reflecting what we have learned in nearly a quarter century of American meals. A few of the restaurants listed here are old favorites that we have returned to dozens of times over the years; many are recent discoveries. Each and every one has won our hearts, and never just because it serves delicious food. For us, the joy of eating our way across the USA has been something more than sustenance. It has shown us the soul of a nation. It is our hope this book will help readers find—and savor—that soul.

How to Use this Book

☆ ☆ ☆

☛ If you are planning a special trip to any restaurant in this book, please call ahead to make certain it is open. Hours of operation change and proprietors sometimes go fishing. Many heartland restaurants do serve dinner, but you should be aware that dinner hour can end as early as six or seven o'clock. Also, some specialties are seasonal.

☛ Most of these restaurants require no reservations and are come-as-you-are. Some pricier ones do have a dress code and a few require a reservation. We've tried to note which ones get insanely crowded and what you can do about it. But again, if in doubt, please call ahead.

☛ Our approximate cost guide is as follows:
- $ = one full meal is under $10
- $$ = one full meal is between $10 and $25
- $$$ = one full meal is over $25

☛ We use the abbreviations B (breakfast), L (lunch), D (dinner) throughout.

☛ We welcome tips for inclusion in future editions, comments, and even complaints. Please address any such correspondence to us c/o Broadway Books, 1540 Broadway, New York, NY 10036. Or E-mail us: KTDoll@AOL.COM.

Eat Your Way Across the U.S.A.

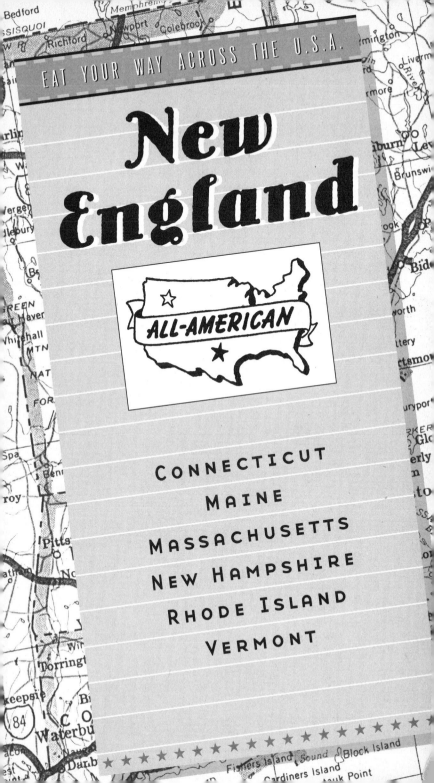

EAT YOUR WAY ACROSS THE U.S.A.

New England

ALL-AMERICAN

CONNECTICUT

MAINE

MASSACHUSETTS

NEW HAMPSHIRE

RHODE ISLAND

VERMONT

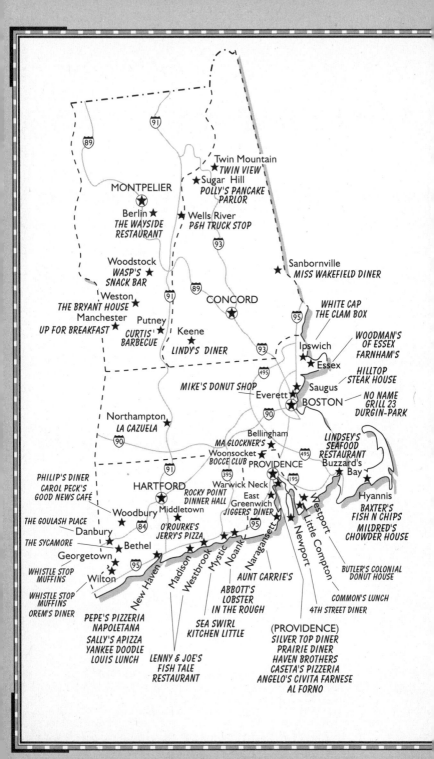

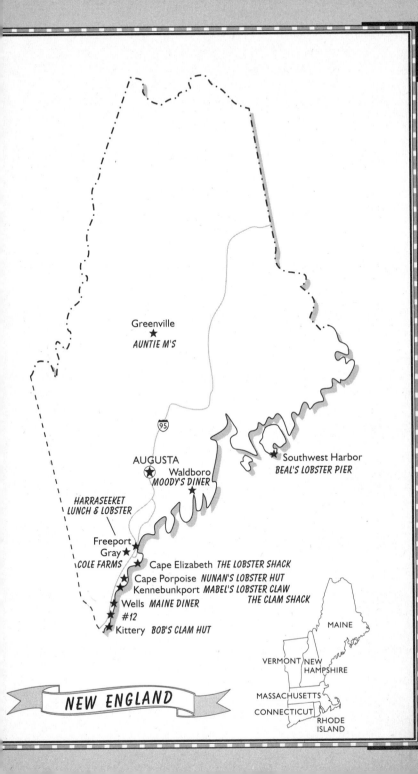

Greenville
★
AUNTIE M'S

95

AUGUSTA
★
Waldboro
MOODY'S DINER

Southwest Harbor
★
BEAL'S LOBSTER PIER

HARRASEEKET LUNCH & LOBSTER

Freeport
Gray ★
COLE FARMS

Cape Elizabeth *THE LOBSTER SHACK*
Cape Porpoise *NUNAN'S LOBSTER HUT*
Kennebunkport *MABEL'S LOBSTER CLAW*
THE CLAM SHACK
Wells *MAINE DINER*
#12
★ Kittery *BOB'S CLAM HUT*

NEW ENGLAND

MAINE

VERMONT NEW
HAMPSHIRE

MASSACHUSETTS

CONNECTICUT
RHODE
ISLAND

CONNECTICUT

Abbott's Lobster in the Rough

117 Pearl St., Noank, CT (860) 536-7719	$$
(May to Labor Day, then weekends through Columbus Day)	£D

The chowder is bracing—briny and loaded with clams; the steamers are plump and luscious; there are pearly pink littlenecks and steel-gray oysters on the half shell; and the hot lobster roll sandwich is swoonfully buttery; but the prime lure of Abbott's is a big, whole lobster. Order any size you like (once you make it to the head of what can be a long, long line); then, twenty minutes later, crack, pick, suck, and pluck your way through a timeless pleasure of the Yankee shore. Dining is al fresco at picnic tables and utensils are plastic, but it is a million-dollar meal. BYOB.

Carol Peck's Good News Café

694 Main St., Woodbury, CT	$$
(203) 266-4663	£D

The menu at this artistic roadside bistro has something for all tastes, whether you favor a wickedly luscious fried onion bundle, healthy vegetarian pasta, or a handsome coconut cake inspired by the ones they used to serve at HoJo's (but better!). You can have square-meals pork chops or a Mediterranean seafood salad, a BLT sandwich or fried alligator nuggets. For spud-hounds like us, Carol Peck's is heaven. Ms. Peck, who has referred to potatoes as "the perfect food," bakes them and garlands them with vegetables, uses them to make mushroom hash to accompany grilled fish at dinner, and serves a "smashed potato" lunch of whipped Yukon golds combined with blue cheese on a bed of greens.

The Goulash Place

42 Highland, Danbury, CT	$
(203) 744-1971	L D

Just minutes off the interstate in a pleasant residential neighborhood, the Goulash Place is an oasis of Old World home cooking. It is a paper-napkin lunchroom, run by the same couple since the 1970s (he cooks, she waits tables), during which time the prices have stayed firmly in the single-digit range. Loyalists come for satisfying plates of such Hungarian classics as chicken paprikash, pork-stuffed cabbage, goulash (three varieties), or roast duck (on weekend evenings) with all the trimmings including either squiggly little nockerli dumplings or tasty seasoned mashed potatoes. Soups are definitively comforting; the best dessert is palacsinta—Magyar crepes folded around sweet apricot filling.

If you go, tell Magda we sent you. She's a nice person—been feeding us well for twenty years.

Jerry's Pizza

885 Washington St., Middletown, CT	$
(860) 346-5335	L D

This little storefront in a shopping center is an unlikely looking source of grand food, but since 1968 Jerry Schiano has been our main man for breathtaking pizza in central Connecticut. He makes all kinds of fine thin-crust ones, as well as hot oven sandwiches and spaghetti with red sauce; but his triumph is a specialty he calls the white Sicilian. It is a medium-thick pie heaped with a mishmash of anchovies, garlic, parsley, oregano, and hot red pepper plus olive oil; and it is *strong*. Its crust is elegant: crunchy at its edges, yet cream-soft within, and with a yeasty dignity that offsets the giddy topping. Just as it takes a full ninety minutes to make, you must allow a good long while to savor this pizza, then more time afterward to bask in its afterglow.

Kitchen Little

Rte. 27, Mystic, CT (860) 536-2122	$
(later hours on summer weekends), D Thur–Sat	**BL**

Tiny isn't a little enough word to describe this cute breakfast shop, where the seats are so close together that private conversations are virtually impossible. We once accidentally shared mugs (inscribed IS THERE LIFE BEFORE COFFEE?) with our neighbor at the counter. Weekends year-round and every day in summer, throngs wait outside to be called for a precious table or stool. Once inside, happy eaters plow into pancakes, omelets, and such elaborate egg concoctions as a "S'medly," which is two scrambled eggs atop home fries, sausage, mushrooms, and onions, all blanketed with melted cheese, or a "Portuguese fisherman," scrambled eggs with sausage, peppers, and jalapeño cheese.

Lunch is mostly sandwiches—there is a meaty lobster salad roll—and the wonderful clam chowder unique to southern New England, which is clams and bits of potato packed into a bracing clear broth.

Lenny & Joe's Fish Tale Restaurant

1301 Post Rd., Madison, CT (203) 245-7289;	$$
and at 86 Boston Post Rd., Westbrook	**LD**
(860) 669-0767	

Lenny & Joe's is famous for its whole-belly fried clams—big, hefty mouthfuls with brittle crusts—and its crunchy onion rings and just about any other summertime shoreline food that fits in a fry kettle: shrimp, scallops, oysters, scrod, and calamari. But there are many superlative nonfried things to eat in this pair of happy-go-lucky joints, foremost among them a lobster roll, which is nothing but chunks of lobster meat sopped with butter in a hot dog bun. Chowder is delicious—Yankee-style with plenty of clams—and there is a full repertoire of such virtuously cooked seafood as broiled swordfish steak and filet of sole, even Connecticut River shad in the spring, served with boiled redskin potatoes.

Louis Lunch

261–263 Crown St., New Haven, CT	$
(203) 562-5507	BLD

Whether or not the hamburger was invented in this tiny cook shop in 1900 (as some historians contend) has no real bearing on the fact that the burgers served at Louis Lunch today are delicious. What fun it is to watch them made, one by one, from balls of ground beef dusted with salt and flattened on the carving board, then broiled in an antique cast-iron implement that suspends patties sideways in a grate (so grease drips away). To sink your teeth into one of these lovely hunks of beef with dark crusts and juicy pink insides is a timeless joy. Ask for "works" and onions are grilled right along with it; sliced tomatoes are available (but not ketchup), as is a schmear of Cheese Whiz. Instead of buns, Louis Lunch sandwiches its burgers in toast made in a vintage assembly-line toaster.

Orem's Diner

209 Danbury Rd. (Rte. 7), Wilton, CT	$
(203) 762-7370	BLD

For us, Orem's is old reliable—the local diner where we go whenever we're home and too lazy to cook. It is a comfortable place with a counter and booths and a gigantic menu that has something for everyone. Our favorites are the crusty hash browns that come with morning eggs, hearty homemade soups, gravy-bathed hot turkey sandwiches with drifts of creamy mashed potatoes, and a chicken souvlaki plate served with killer-garlic cream on the side.

There is nothing fancy about the old wooden-sided hash house, which has been dishing out honest eats since 1921, when Route 7 meandered north through bucolic farmland. Now the road is crowded with businesses, and there is usually too much traffic, but Orem's remains the kind of quick-service, decent-food stop that takes you back to simpler times.

A Passion for Fried Dough

New England loves fried dough. It has the most and the best nonfran-chised donut shops; deep-fried clam fritters are a common compan-ion for chowder in Rhode Island; doughboys accompany fish dinner in southern Massachusetts; and country fairs feature fried dough wag-ons, where flaky-crusted disks of dough are dished out hot from the fry kettle, topped with either cinnamon-sugar or maple butter, or even sometimes with pizza sauce, as if ordinary baked pizza weren't wicked enough.

Some essential places for eating fried dough in New England in-clude

- ☛ Aunt Carrie's (for clam cakes), Narragansett, RI (p. 32)
- ☛ Butler's Colonial Donut House, Westport, MA (p. 21)
- ☛ Mike's Donut Shop, Everett, MA (p. 25)
- ☛ Phillip's Diner (for donuts), Woodbury, CT (p. 10)
- ☛ Rocky Point Park Shore Dinner Hall (for clam cakes), Warwick Neck, RI (p. 37)
- ☛ Woodman's of Essex (for clam cakes), Essex, MA (p. 27)

O'Rourke's

728 Main St., Middletown, CT	$
(860) 346-6101	BLD

Tucked among the storefronts at the north end of Main Street, O'Rourke's 1946 diner is a silver jewel in the rough. Proprietor Brian O'Rourke started working here for his uncle as a potato peeler in 1958, when he was seven. He has kept the best diner traditions, and added many of his own, including a tremendous repertoire of home-made breads (Norwegian rye, Portuguese sweet bread, potato bread, pain noir, banana bread, and muffins) and spectacular Sunday breakfasts, including seasonal garden omelets and Irish soda bread pancakes topped with cream, sabayon, and fruit.

O'Rourke's menu ranges from sophisticated chili (Brian grinds the peppers himself) to Connecticut shad and shad roe in season, but there is one local specialty better here than anywhere else on earth: the steamed cheeseburger. The steamer, a central Connecticut passion, was invented in Middletown about a half century ago at Jack's Lunch (now defunct). It is a medium-thick burger cooked to ultimate juiciness in a small metal steam box. The meat is topped with an oozing blob of melted cheddar that has been prepared in its own separate steam box tray. The drippy duo are set forth upon a fluff-centered hard roll and garnished with a thick slice of crisp raw onion and yellow mustard. Not to be missed!

Pepe's Pizzeria Napoletana

157 Wooster St., New Haven, CT	$$
(203) 865-5762	D

Crust is what makes a Pepe's pizza our food-god. Cooked at high temperature on the brick floor of an ancient oven, it is brittle, especially around its edges, which are burnished gold and occasionally blistered black, and yet there is a profound resilience in every bite. The pizza men aren't persnickety about scraping the oven floor, so it is likely the pizza's underside will be speckled with burnt grains of semolina and maybe even blotched by an oil spill where another pizza leaked, all of which give the mottled oval a kind of reckless sex appeal that no tidy pie could ever match.

The best of the menu is white clam pizza, for which the crust is dotted with freshly opened littleneck clams, a scattering of grated sharp Romano, a salvo of coarsely minced garlic, and a drizzle of oil. Mozzarella with onion (but no tomatoes) is another long-time favorite, as are the more traditional sloppy configurations with tomato sauce, cheese, pepperoni, and sausage. Broccoli and spinach recently have been added to the kitchen's repertoire; on a white pie with mozzarella and garlic, they're delish.

Phillip's Diner

Rte. 6, Woodbury, CT	$
(203) 263-2516	BLD

Chicken pie is a nearly lost tradition in Connecticut. Time was, farmers' wives made them to sell out their back doors, and they were on the menu in neighborhood cafés throughout the state. Phillip's still makes and serves these time-honored beauties, with big chunks of tender chicken in well-seasoned gravy, accompanied by great flakes of crust.

The other overpowering allure to this humble town diner is donuts, which are eat-'em-by-the-dozen fine. They are pure, fresh, and sweet, eminently suitable for dunking. The ones that send us into ecstasy are the basic round brown ones, unfilled and unfrosted, with a faintly chewy crust gilded with a sandy coat of cinnamon-sugar.

Sally's Apizza

237 Wooster St., New Haven, CT	$$
(203) 624-5271	D

New Haven pizzaphiles debate whether Sally's or Pepe's is better, but we are not so fussy about these two Wooster Street culinary landmarks. Either place we can get a table is fine with us (seats at both are extremely scarce at mealtime). Cooked on the brick floor of an ancient oven, Sally's pie has soul. Sally's does have some things Pepe's does not, most notably a photograph on the wall of Sally's brother Tony standing with Frank Sinatra, as well as two outstanding specialty pizzas: fresh tomato pie (made only in the summer) with thick circles of tomato, creamy mozzarella, garlic, and chopped basil; and broccoli rabe pie, heaped with bitter greens when they are available at the Long Wharf produce market.

Sea Swirl

Rte. 1, East of Mystic, CT (860) 536-3452	$
closed from late fall to late spring	£D

Sea Swirl's whole-bellied fried clams feel debonair, light, and lithe when you heft them from their cardboard container; and yet their taste belies their elegance. They are luscious and briny—assertive seafood, not for sissies or nutritional prigs, but pure delight for clam cognoscenti. Sea Swirl, which is a soft-serve ice cream stand, also offers impeccable clam shack atmosphere, with its picnic tables sandwiched between Route 1 and an auto supply store, and its best seats providing a view of giant drums of Eat-It-All Twinkle Cote topping that is used on sundaes.

The Sycamore

282 Greenwood Ave., Bethel, CT	$
(203) 748-2716	BLD

A Dagwood burger (two griddle-cooked, lush-crusted patties with the works), French fries, homemade root beer: that's all you need to know about the Sycamore, a neon-ringed drive-in where service at counter and booths is speedy, and car hops are available for those of us who prefer to dine off window tray and dashboard.

Whistle Stop Muffins

20 Portland Ave. (Branchville Station), Georgetown, CT	$
(203) 544-8139; also in the Wilton train station,	ℬℒ
7 Station Rd., Wilton (203) 762-9778	

In a charming little wood-slat waiting room, over the counter where the station master once sold tickets, muffin makers now serve hot-from-the-oven pastries and coffee to commuters (the train still stops here). There are crusty scones, swirly cinnamon sweet rolls, coffee cake, and about a dozen kinds of muffins made every day. It is all first-rate stuff; we like the caramel sticky buns, banana walnut muffins, and weekend-only apricot scones best of all, especially very early in the day when they are almost too hot to hold. Most customers get breakfast to go; veterans know how to make their own change from piles of coins and dollar bills strewn across the counter during the busy rush hour; but there are also a few cozy seats where those in no hurry can sip, munch, and dunk while enjoying the morning papers at their leisure.

Yankee Doodle

260 Elm St., New Haven, CT	$
(203) 865-1074	ℬℒ

At the ancient stove and griddle in a short-order hash house, eggs are scrambled at lightning speed every morning and pigs in blankets (hot dogs wrapped in bacon, accompanied by hot relish) and Dandy Doodle Double burgers sizzled in the blink of an eye at noon. Checks are issued with the food; and it feels quite normal to be in and out, with a satisfying meal under your belt, in under five minutes. Twelve stools at a counter are the only accommodations, so the place gets crowded at mealtime, when people-watching is superb. Clientele includes a curious mixture of eccentric townies and culturally adventurous Yalies, for whom these good cheap eats are a great equalizer.

MAINE

★ ★ ★

Auntie M's

Main St., Greenville, ME	$
(207) 695-2238	BLD

Auntie M's folksy dining room is where locals come for breakfast and to fiddle with the communal jigsaw puzzle when it's still dark outside in winter months. Donuts are freshly made, the egg platters are piled with crusty fried spuds, and the coffee keeps coming. At lunch, summertime treats include good fried clam platters; and year-round, you can count on soups and chowders and such daily specials as meat loaf with (genuine) mashed potatoes, tuna casserole, lobster rolls, and chicken à la king, followed by handsome hunks of pie—chocolate cream, pecan, peanut butter, banana split, apple, or blueberry.

Beal's Lobster Pier

Clark Point Rd., Southwest Harbor, ME	$$
(207) 244-7178 or 244-3202	LD

Picnic tables overlook the harbor; from them, you can see the mountains of Acadia National Park in the distance and listen to the water rippling against the hulls of berthed fishing boats.

Inside, select a lobster from the tank; while waiting for it to boil, eat your way through a bucket of steamer clams or dip into a cup of chowder. If a handsome whole lobster is too challenging a proposition, you can also get a lobster roll—tightly packed, with plenty of fresh, sweet meat atop a cushion of shredded lettuce.

Chowder Variations

Genuine New England restaurants offer soup, stew, and chowder, all on the same menu. Soup needs no explanation, but stew and chowder have unique regional meanings. *Stew* (oyster, fish, clam, or lobster) is warm milk or cream seasoned with salt and pepper, pooled with melted butter, and containing nothing but large morsels of seafood: no potatoes, no vegetables of any kind. You'll get soda crackers on the side. *Chowder* always has potatoes in addition to its featured ingredient, which may or may not be seafood, and it can be milky, creamy, or clear.

New England–Style Chowder

A milk or cream-based gallimaufry, rich with the flavor of salt pork and thick with chunks of potato. Clams are the usual main ingredient, but farmhouse chowders can be made with corn or even root vegetables. As a rule, this is a rib-sticking dish, traditionally served as a meal unto itself.

Rhode Island–Style Chowder

A creamy bisque made with just enough tomatoes to turn it blushing pink, traditionally served with crusty clam cakes on the side. (This is not to be confused with "Manhattan-style" chowder that is basically a vegetable soup with clams in it and no cream or milk whatever.)

Southern New England–Style Chowder

This very popular but seldom-documented variation on the theme is frequently served at clam shacks and lobster pounds in Connecticut and into Rhode Island. Made without any milk or cream but with a scattering of potatoes and onions and plenty of minced clams and their nectar, it is a bracing, steel-gray brew made to pique appetite prior to a grand shore dinner.

Bob's Clam Hut

Rte. 1, Kittery, ME	$
(207) 439-4233	£ⅅ

Bob's Clam Hut is an eat-in-the-rough stand by the side of the road that makes a specialty of seafood baskets: shrimp, haddock, oysters, and clams (whole bellies or strips). A basket includes French fries, which are fine pale twigs, but pay extra for a side of onion rings, which are huge and crunchy—a perfect complement for fried seafood. Bob's lobster roll is also top drawer, cool and expensive (about two dollars more than a fried clam roll), in a bun that is buttered and grilled until toasty golden brown on both sides.

The Clam Shack

Dock Sq., Kennebunkport, ME	$
(207) 967-3321	£ⅅ

Here they are: the best fried clams in Maine and the best lobster roll on earth. A ebullient hut no bigger than a newsstand with nowhere to sit inside or out, the Clam Shack is perched at one end of the Kennebunkport Bridge and is crowded all summer long. Customers cluster in the sun devouring clam baskets, chowder, and lobster rolls off the hood of their car or leaning against the whitewashed bridge rail. Either way, you must contend with greedy birds eyeing unattended onion rings (crunchy hoops with luscious warm insides). A posted sign warns: BEWARE OF SEAGULLS. THEY LIKE OUR FOOD AS MUCH AS YOU DO.

When you sink your teeth into a Clam Shack lobster roll, you know instantly you are tasting greatness. Six to ten big pearlescent chunks of fresh-from-the-shell tail and claw are arranged in the bun; some are so succulent you can hear the juices ooze when you bite them. You have a choice of mayonnaise or butter; what that means is the meat is assembled on the bun and only then is the condiment spooned on. The result is an array of pure pink lobster merely frosted with a dollop of mayonnaise or veiled in a shimmering mantle of melted butter. One July afternoon as we ate from the hood of our car, a lawyer visiting from Idaho polished off a lobster roll and an order of onion rings and stood on the sidewalk announcing to travelers and Kennebunkporters who ambled past, "We've got nothing like this in Boise! Nothing at all!"

Cole Farms	
Rte. 100, Gray, ME	$
(207) 657-4714	**BLD**

Off the coastal tourist trail, Cole Farms is a big, informal restaurant that locals have frequented for decades. They come for honest inland food: hot muffins in the morning, farmhouse corn chowder, good fish chowder with clam cakes on the side, hot dogs and baked beans, American chop suey, and old-fashioned puddings (Indian, Grape-Nuts, tapioca, etc.) for dessert. It is honest food, freshly made, satisfying and cheap.

Harraseeket Lunch & Lobster	
Town Landing, Freeport, ME	$
(207) 865-3535	**LD**

One summer afternoon at a picnic table under the striped blue tent outside Harraseeket Lunch & Lobster, we looked down at our trays of food and sighed with the sheer joy of the moment. Here before us were a couple of irresistible shoreline meals: a mountain of crisp fried clams, a lobster roll overstuffed with great chunks of pink meat, crusty clam cakes, and a curious fry-basket delicacy called onion middles (little sweet nuggets that are deep-fried along with the more traditional rings). Plus, homemade whoopie pies for dessert—big, gooey devil's food discs sandwiching marshmallow creme. We ate slowly, listening to gentle waves lap against the wharf and to an American flag flapping crisply overhead in the July breeze. All the money in the world could not buy a culinary experience more purely pleasurable than this cheap-eats boon.

The Lobster Shack

246 Two Lights Rd., Cape Elizabeth, ME (207) 799-1677	$
mid-Apr to mid-Oct	£🍴

A gorgeous setting for summer seafood, the Lobster Shack has a picturesque indoor dining room as well as picnic tables that overlook a rockbound coast, perfumed by ocean breezes. Pick your own whole lobster from the tank, or if you are too impatient to wait twenty minutes for it to boil, have a bowl of the Shack's delicious lobster stew, a milky-orange brew loaded with big hunks of meat. There is a full eat-in-the-rough menu: chowder and lobster stew, boats and plates and sandwiches of fried clams, plus puddings for dessert and strawberry shortcake during strawberry season in July. It is an unassuming place to eat but it has found a spot in our thoughts as a perfect taste of Maine.

Mabel's Lobster Claw

124 Ocean Ave., Kennebunkport, ME	$$
(207) 967-2562	£🍴

Mabel Hanson's wood-paneled walls are decorated with autographed pictures of the many celebrities who favor her restaurant, including local householders George and Barbara Bush (he likes baked stuffed lobster; she goes for eggplant Parmesan). You don't have to be famous to feel at home in this comfy dining room, which has an old-fashioned, summer-resort ambiance and a staff of swift waitresses in rubber-soled nurse shoes who just naturally suggest that any piece of pie you order ought to be had à la mode.

The bread, cakes, and pies are made by Mrs. Hanson every morning; her peanut butter ice cream pie with hot fudge topping is rapturous; and however you like your lobster, Mabel does it right. Her lobster stew is legendary; if you want a really large whole lobster for dinner, she will go next door to the Port Lobster Company and fetch you a five-pounder. The lobster roll is as deluxe as they come, served with fries and slaw on an actual china plate (although the roll itself is sheathed in a cardboard case). The meat in the roll is juicy, fresh, and copious, some chunks so large that you feel a little embarrassed picking it up and eating it out of hand; a knife and fork seem more suited to the task.

Maine Diner

Rte. 1 N, Wells, ME	$
(207) 646-4441	BLD

This ship-shape blue-and-white eatery is a landmark on the lobster trail. It is best known for lobster pie, an ambrosial family recipe in which big chunks of lobster meat are mixed with the lobster's own tomalley and some buttery stuffing, then baked in a casserole. The Henry Brothers, who run the place, have won awards for their seafood chowder, but it is that luxurious pie and the lobster rolls that keep us coming back.

Two kinds of lobster roll are listed on the menu: the traditional one made with big chunks of knuckle, claw, and plenty of succulent tail meat with mayo in a toasted, grilled bun, and the "hot lobster roll," which is nothing but unadorned warm lobster meat piled into the toasted bun, accompanied by a cup of drawn butter. "Somebody from Rhode Island suggested the buttered roll many years ago," proprietor Dick Henry said. "But we found that if we served the meat already buttered, the bun fell apart." So you can either pour the butter on the sandwich, risking bun disintegration, or you can simply pick chunks of meat and shreds of toasted bread from the plate and dip them in the cup of butter as you wish.

Moody's Diner

Rte. 1, Waldoboro, ME	$
(207) 832-7468	*BLD*

The Formica counter is the same, as is the old wooden phone booth, but Moody's counter stools have been reupholstered, and the expanded diner, which first opened as a roadside stand in 1935, now seats a hundred people—a welcome change for those of us who have spent time waiting to get inside for breakfast. Corned beef hash, home fried potatoes, and blueberry muffins are the choice morning foodstuffs in this roadside landmark, which exudes plenty of quirky downeast character despite its sprucing up. At lunch, count on such staples as meat loaf, franks 'n' beans, American chop suey, and stew. The many regional specialties include what connoisseurs consider the finest fish chowder in the state. Whatever you eat, top it off with pie—mincemeat, custard, or irresistible walnut cream.

Nunan's Lobster Hut

Rte. 9, Cape Porpoise, ME	$$
(207) 967-4362	*D*

A practical restaurant made for lobster eating: tables with ribs around the edge so debris doesn't fall off, big wash-up sinks and paper towels in the dining room, and marine paint on the floor for easy swabbing. It isn't in any way pretty, but there is a certain utilitarian charm about it, like an old army Jeep or vintage coffee grinder.

Lobster dinners—the only thing to eat—are presented on large metal pans. The perfectly boiled crustacean is accompanied by uninteresting rolls and a bag of potato chips. For dessert: brownies or blueberry pie.

That's all you need to know, except the fact that Nunan's is extremely popular and can be maddeningly hard to get in. We recommend going at 5 pm when they open, or very late, preferably on a weekday.

MASSACHUSETTS

Baxter's Fish N Chips

177 Pleasant St., Hyannis, MA (508) 775-4490	$
closed from Columbus Day until early spring	LD

Overlooking the Hyannis harbor, Baxter's is an ultracasual fish-fry where customers call out their order and tote their food to picnic tables indoors and out. Clams are grainy-textured, luscious, and oily with a nice ocean savor; fish is tender; scallops are sweet; and the clam fritters, served with syrup for dunking, are superb. To drink, get your own tonic (Massachusettsese for soda) at the bar, where a sign warns: NO CHECKS, CHARGES, CUFFING.

Yankee Drink Lingo

North of New York City (in which a "coffee, regular" means coffee *with* cream), soda fountains have strange terms for familiar drinks, especially confusing because the slang varies from place to place.

What the rest of America knows as a *milk shake* (ice cream, milk, and syrup blended smooth) is known throughout Rhode Island as a *cabinet,* and farther east along the coast as a *frappe* or *velvet.*

A *milk shake,* in most downeast sweet shops, means milk and flavored syrup, but no ice cream.

A *soda* is a soft drink (what the Midwest knows as *pop),* except in eastern Massachusetts, where soft drinks are known as *tonics.*

Butler's Colonial Donut House

461 Sanford Rd., Westport, MA (508) 672-4600	$
only on Fri, Sat, Sun	BL

Weekends only, starting at seven in the morning and until the day's supply is gone, here's a little place on the road to Rhode Island Sound that is a donut-eater's delight. Glazed or raised, circular with holes or long and filled with jam and whipped cream, they're probably not what you need to eat before going swimming; but after too much time doing healthy things in sun and surf, nothing quite fills the bill as nicely as a half dozen of these handsome sinkers.

The Clam Box

206 High St., Ipswich, MA	$
(508) 356-9707	LD

A roadside marvel in business since 1935, the Clam Box is shaped exactly like a trapezoidal cardboard clam box, but thirty feet high. Its clams are some of the North Shore's finest, their sea-salt smack sheathed in a frail crust that blends perfectly with the plump clam inside. A Clam Box platter features shatteringly crisp onion rings and fried potatoes as well as cole slaw so finely chopped you want to eat it with a spoon.

Durgin-Park

Faneuil Hall Marketplace, Boston, MA	$$
(617) 227-2038	LD

Durgin-Park is an antique mess hall mobbed by tourists and locals who come for unaffected Yankee fare dished out by brusque Yankee waitresses. It is a raucous place where food gets slapped onto plates without concern for how it looks, then slammed down on long communal tables with no regard for etiquette; but the disdain for dining nicety only adds to the sense of authenticity. Beantown standbys, all served in abundance, include blocks of downeast corn bread, oyster stew made with milk and cream, stone-crock baked beans, wondrously dark Indian pudding, and strawberry shortcake made with fresh berries on an old-time biscuit. For many regular customers, the only thing to eat is prime rib—thick as the Boston Yellow Pages and oozing juice—and we wouldn't think of ending a meal without hot apple pan dowdy with ice cream on top, along with a dish of Durgin-Park's own weird, wonderful coffee Jell-O.

Farnham's	
88 Eastern Ave., Essex, MA	$
(508) 768-6643	*BLD*

A cute little roadside diner with flower boxes in its windows and a pleasant marshland breeze wafting over the short counter and high-backed wood booths, Farnham's is the kind of place favored by locals more than tourists. Regulars help themselves to coffee refills; we've seen friends of the house bus their own tables after breakfast.

Fried clams are positively ethereal—tender, light-crusted, easy to eat, and with a faint nut-rich flavor; and the snapping-firm, sweet-fleshed fried shrimp are equally inspired. A plate of either is a mountain, and the onion rings are great—big and meaty with ragged crunchy crusts. To accompany such feasts, Farnham's offers all the usual brands of tonic (Massachusettsese for soda pop), plus sarsaparilla and Moxie.

Grill 23	
161 Berkeley St., Boston, MA	$$$
(617) 542-2255	*LD*

The Morton's and Ruth's Chris chains in major cities all across the country have made steak houses into top-dollar McDonald's; and while we have had decent meals in some of the franchises (and bad meals in others), none offer the real satisfaction of a good, independent steak house, like Grill 23, featuring succulent sirloins and strong martinis (and terrific seafood, too), all dispensed with polish to a powerhouse clientele. Yes, it is costly and you have to dress politely to get in the door—strictly a splurge for the likes of us—but there are times in life when the pleasures of cold gin and sizzling red meat, served on thick white linen cloths with heavyweight silverware, are worth the price.

Hilltop Steak House

855 Broadway (Rte. 1), Saugus, MA	$$
(617) 233-9520	£©

Not an elegant restaurant, not a great restaurant, the Hilltop is nonetheless an adventure that all American-food aficionados need to have at least once. It is a daily feeding frenzy that happens to be the world's largest and busiest restaurant, dishing out two-dozen semi-truck loads of beef every week to 1400 customers at a time in a half-dozen cavernous, western-themed dining rooms. The beefsteaks, cut extra-large, are pretty darn good, and the lobster pie is a regional dish worth eating. For dessert, choose Grape-Nuts pudding, a Yankee passion done particularly well.

At busy mealtimes the wait can be exasperating, and the walk from the far edges of the 1000-car lot, overseen by life-size plastic cows, can be a trek. But such travails are all part of the full Hilltop experience.

La Cazuela

7 Old South St., Northampton, MA	$$
(413) 586-0400	©

Mexican food, like Memphis barbecue and Chicago-style pizza, doesn't travel well. Generally speaking, the farther away you get from the source, the worse it is; and in the Northeast, good Mexican food is as rare as fresh lobster in El Paso. La Cazuela is one wonderful exception. The fashionable second-story restaurant, with decor reminiscent of upscale Santa Fe and chilies imported from Hatch, New Mexico, is a colorful outpost of red chilies, blue corn enchiladas, and pollo verde. No tacos à la Alpo in this swank establishment. Instead, savor the autumnal special called *chilies en nogada,* made of roasted poblanos stuffed with pork and spices, topped with walnut sauce and pomegranates; or taste the smoky wonder of chipotle chilies in seafood Colorado sauce, made with Gulf shrimp and sea scallops.

Incidentally, La Cazuela happens to be a fine place for vegetarians, featuring several meatless meals, including zesty spinach enchiladas and burritos pico de gallo with hot jalapeño relish on top.

Lindsey's Seafood Restaurant

3138 Cranberry Hwy., Buzzards Bay, MA	$$
(508) 759-5544	£Ɗ

Years ago, Lindsey's sold clam baskets to beach-goers, and although it has grown from a roadside shack into a large, modern clamatorium, it still serves lovely platters of fried seafood, with crunchy clams a specialty. Start your meal with milky-sweet New England chowder and end with warm Indian pudding. For fish frowners (who have no business on Cape Cod to begin with), there are actually some fine farmhouse suppers on the menu, including turkey pot pie and roast beef, with tasty mashed potatoes on the side.

Ma Glockner's

151 Maple St., Bellingham, MA (508) 966-1085	$$
(closed several weeks in winter)	Ɗ

"Berch-frying," Ma Glockner's claim to glory, is a mysterious cooking process the details of which are known only to the kitchen staff, but we can tell you that the result is a crisp-skinned half-bird that fairly drips buttery flavor. It is served with French fries, cranberry sauce, and delectable hot rolls, swirled with cinnamon-sugar. This well-nigh perfect meal has drawn crowds to the old-fashioned family restaurant with the neon hen roosting on top since the 1930s.

Mike's Donut Shop

115 Broadway, Everett, MA (617) 389-9415	$
Always open except from midnight to 6 am, Fri and Sat	𝓑

Here is beantown in the raw, 'round the clock. Frequented by truckers, cabbies, insomniacs, and fried-dough addicts, Mike's is a pleasure of the soul that only culinary outlaws really understand. The donuts are hand-cut and freshly cooked, but they aren't elegant. The plain ones have a dense, cakey texture just right for dunking; and the French crullers are airy enough to eat a half dozen at a shot, easy. Boston creams, loaded with cool whippo and blanketed with chocolate, are just the kind of sweet treat the nutrition police are always warning us about, so it is only natural to break out into a mischievous smile as one scarfs down a bunch of them in this rogues' gallery of a donut shop.

Mildred's Chowder House

290 Lyanough Rd., Hyannis, MA	$$
(508) 775-1045	𝓛𝓓

Once a roadside clam shanty, now an immense eating hall, Mildred's continues to serve the simple Cape Cod cooking that made it famous. Chowder, of course, is the house specialty, and it is a classic: creamy, vaguely porcine, generously dotted with clams and little tender chunks of potato. A Mildred's seafood stew is well worth spooning into, simplicity itself. Lobster stew, for example, is nothing but a broad bowl of warm cream and melted butter in which float large, tender pieces of lobster meat. What could be more comfortable than that? There is plenty of good local fish on the menu, and there are some fancy-pants casseroles, but we suggest travelers in search of Yankee flavors stick to basics. For dessert, of course, that means pudding. There is good, old-fashioned Indian pudding, made of long-cooked cornmeal and molasses, as well as a fine Grape-Nuts custard, gentle as baby food.

No Name	
15¹/₂ Fish Pier, Boston, MA	**$$**
(617) 338-7539	**£Đ**

No Name isn't an undiscovered haunt of fishmongers and mariners anymore. In fact, it's quite a tourist attraction. The old lunch room on the pier among the fish warehouses and lobster companies has become a large institutional restaurant. But the transformation has not changed the fact that this is still a fine place to eat fresh Boston seafood at reasonable prices.

The chowder is superb, thick with fish but not overly rich. Scrod is served simply broiled in a pool of butter on a silver plate, its surface faintly crusty from the broiler. Poke it with a fork and it falls into big, sweet hunks, pure as fish can be. Fried clams, scallops, shrimp, or fish are all exemplary, served with milky cole slaw and an especially tasty tartar sauce. Our exuberant waiter, who barks out orders amidst the clatter of this overgrown luncheonette, gleefully explained why the tartar sauce is so good, holding his fingers to his lips and puckering up with an air kiss aimed at the chef back in the kitchen: "The Greek touch!"

White Cap	
141 High St., Ipswich, MA	**$**
(508) 356-5276	**£Đ**

Of all the first-rate clamatoria on the North Shore, White Cap is our favorite. In a low, flat building set back from the road, it has a worn pink Formica counter where you place your order and a functional dining room cooled by noisy fans.

Its clams are golden blistered squiggles, rich and satisfying, melt-away light. There are various sizes on the plate, and they are impossible to stop eating until they are gone. The onions are lovely, too; by the time they and the clams and the French fries are polished off, a paper plate is all that's left. Amazingly, there isn't a drop or stain of oil on the paper. This fried food is that clean.

We must also alert you to White Cap clam chowder. Served in a cardboard vessel either coffee-cup-size or pint-size, this is Yankee-style clam chowder at its best: milky-smooth more than creamy-thick, it is sweet as a sea breeze and deeply satisfying. There are some pieces of potato in it, but what is amazing is how many chunks of diced clam each spoonful yields.

Lobster Rolls, Hot and Cold

Lobster rolls are a glory of New England's shore, served at roadside stands and in sit-down seafood restaurants; we actually ate one once at a McDonald's in Maine. (Never again!) Most are lobster *salad* rolls: cool picked meat bound with mayonnaise inside a toasted hot dog bun. Good as that configuration is, hot lobster rolls are even better. Made with warm, fresh-picked meat sopped with butter rather than mayo, they are messy eating, because the butter makes the bun disintegrate, but their sheer luxury cannot be denied. The Clam Shack of Maine (p. 15) serves its own excellent version of both kinds of roll. Fine hot rolls can also be found at the Maine Diner (p. 18), Lenny & Joe's Fish Tale Restaurant (p. 6), and Abbott's Lobster in the Rough (p. 4).

Woodman's of Essex

121 Main St., Essex, MA	$
(508) 768-6451	£𝔇

Woodman's is a raucous enterprise, a helter-skelter complex of eating areas including a tent for clambakes, a raw bar, and a sprawling enclosed dining room where wooden booths and tables are almost always packed with carefree eaters. There are signs taped and tacked everywhere. Some announce menu items: LOBSTER ROLL SPECIAL, CLAM STRIPS. One near the take-out window says, ATTENTION: ALL COLE SLAW, TARTAR SAUCE, AND BUTTER MONEY GOES TO THE L. DEXTER WOODMAN SCHOLARSHIP FUND, THANK YOU. Another near the order window alerts customers: OUR FRIED CLAMS ARE RUNNING BIG TODAY.

The fried clams, which were invented here in 1916 by Lawrence Woodman, are beauties: light gold with a suave crunch to their surface and a velvety interior that is pure pleasure on the tongue. You can buy them by the pint or—better choice—as a clam plate, piled so ridiculously high that it would seem impossible for it to hold one more clam, onion ring, or French fry. Besides impeccable fried seafood, Woodman's sells beauteous whole lobsters. It is also well worth sampling Woodman's clam cakes and chowder . . . although not at the same time you are eating a clam platter. Either choice is a full meal, and then some.

NEW HAMPSHIRE

★ ★ ★

Lindy's Diner	
19 Gilbo Ave., Keene, NH	$
(603) 352-4273	*BLD*

You have probably seen Lindy's many times, but always in the background. It's the all-American Main Street diner across from the bus station where candidates for president of the United States come to be seen hobnobbing with ordinary citizens and enjoying such of-the-people meals as bacon and eggs for breakfast, and franks and chili, creamed chipped beef, or pot roast for lunch. During primary season, the place is frequented by an inordinate number of out-of-town journalists, politicos, and campaign camp followers, but once the citizens of New Hampshire have cast their ballots, Lindy's reverts to being an honest, blue-plate diner that deserves your vote.

Miss Wakefield Diner

Rte. 16, Sanbornville, NH	$
(603) 522-6800	฿ £

"We are NOT a fast-food operation," warns the menu in this lovely 1949 diner resuscitated by the Benner family a few years ago. That's a fact: no fast-food outlet serves mashed potatoes like this, piled into a mountain with gravy cascading down the side, to accompany excellent meat loaf; and the warm bread pudding is diner fare *par excellence*. Indeed, you will wait a bit if you order your corned beef hash extra well done; and a burger with bacon, mushrooms, and blue cheese takes a while to assemble. But service is brisk enough; and the taste and quality of Miss Wakefield's homey food is a quantum leap beyond anything mass produced.

Breakfast is especially right—handsome blueberry or cranberry pancakes with real maple syrup, Texas French toast, giant muffins, tawny home fries with eggs—but we must also thank traveling epicure Dorothy S. O'Connor for alerting us to the fine grilled cheese sandwich at lunch, served with homemade soup. Such comfort food cannot be franchised.

Polly's Pancake Parlor

Rte. 117, Sugar Hill, NH (603) 823-5575	$
(seasonal)	฿ £

Ever since "Sugar Bill" Dexter and his wife, Polly, converted the carriage shed of their farm into a tea room in 1938, this rustic White Mountain eatery has been a showcase for maple products at their finest. Pancakes are the specialty of the house; they are made from stone-ground flours or cornmeal, accompanied by crystalline maple syrup and maple butter spread. You can also get maple muffins, maple Bavarian cream, and a wondrous slivered apple and maple syrup ice cream topping known as Hurricane Sauce (named after the hurricane of '38, which blew so many apples off the trees that they had to figure out a way to use them up fast). Polly's opens after mud season in the spring, when many of the surrounding maple trees are hung with taps and buckets; the spectacular time to visit is autumn, during the sugar-bush's chromatic climax. (Warning: during tourist season, you will wait for a table.)

Twin View	
Rte. 3, Twin Mountain, NH	$
(603) 846-7736	ℬℒ

Friday at lunchtime in the summer, this little outpost at the far reaches of the White Mountains is the place to go for a north country fish fry. Dine at a picnic table outdoors and inhale the bracing aromas of crisp golden white fish, fresh from the Fryolator, accompanied by mountains of delicious potatoes. Other times, count on Twin View for hearty breakfasts with plenty of home fries and lunches with honest sandwiches accompanied by a freshly made soup du jour.

RHODE ISLAND

☆ ☆ ☆

4th Street Diner	
184 Admiral Kalbfus Rd., Newport, RI	$
(401) 847-2069	ℬℒᕲ

The jonnycakes Trish Warner makes at the 4th Street Diner are nearly see-through thin, just the way people in this part of Rhode Island like them (and spell them—without the *h*). Served alongside just about any meal—but especially at breakfast—the elegant corn cakes are reason enough to find a seat in this mid-century diner that provides a reality check for anyone overwhelmed by the rich people's "cottages" that attract tourists to Newport. In this joint, you rub elbows with locals and eat such of-the-people fare as biscuits with sausage gravy, Portuguese soup made with kale and beans, chorizo sausage–stuffed quohog clams, and freshly roasted turkey made into hot sandwiches and Thanksgiving-style suppers every day.

New England Splurges

Expensive, fancy, and/or fashionable regional restaurants that are worth it.

- ☛ <u>Carol Peck's Good News Café</u>, Woodbury, CT (p. 4)
- ☛ <u>Durgin-Park</u>, Boston, MA (p. 21)
- ☛ <u>Grill 23</u>, Boston, MA (p. 22)
- ☛ <u>La Cazuela</u>, Northampton, MA (p. 23)
- ☛ <u>Mabel's Lobster Claw</u>, Kennebunkport, ME (p. 17)
- ☛ <u>Al Forno</u>, Providence, RI (p. 31)

Al Forno

577 S. Main St., Providence, RI (401) 272-7980	$$$
Tues–Sat	D

A modern culinary legend, Al Forno can be hard to get into (no reservations) and the staff can seem harassed, especially on a busy weekend night, but no one we know has ever walked away from this breezy trattoria without a smile on his or her face. Inventive Italian/Provençal food is the order of the day. Al Forno's grilled pizzas are one of the finest foods in all the East. In fact, anything grilled is divine: herbed split chicken, duck, lamb, veal tenderloin, and steaks cooked directly among the coals. There are many wonderful desserts, including dizzyingly good lemon soufflé, but the one you will remember best is the cookie assortment, served still-warm from the oven.

Angelo's Civita Farnese

141 Atwells Ave., Providence, RI	$
(401) 621-8171	ℒⅅ

Atwells Avenue is the main artery of Federal Hill, one of America's most delicious Little Italys, a brick-street neighborhood of aromatic bakeries, pizzerias, cheese shops, and sidewalk cafés. Among the many good restaurants, Angelo's stands out for its southern Italian home cooking: honest pastas, braciola (Tuesdays and Wednesdays only), veal or eggplant parmigiana, and utterly comforting pasta e fagiole soup. It is an unassuming place with large tables shared by strangers, friendly service by waiters in well-worn aprons, and good cheap wine by the jugful.

Aunt Carrie's

Point Judith, Narragansett, RI (401) 783-7930	$
June through early Sept	ℒⅅ

This breezy beachside dinner hall and clam shack takes you back a half century to carefree days along the ocean shore. Salt breezes blow in across the parking lot, where barefoot sun worshipers eat crunchy fried clams, shrimp, and scallops by the plate or pint, then head down toward the sand and surf. There is also a lovely wood-paneled dining room where contemplative customers enjoy bounteous soup-to-nuts shore dinners that include clam cakes, chowder, steamer clams, brown bread, filet of sole, corn on the cob, lobster, and Indian pudding. In early summer, look for rhubarb pie, an Aunt Carrie's specialty for decades.

Bocce Club

226 St. Louis Ave., Woonsocket, RI (401) 762-0155	$$
Wed–Sun	D

Gigantic dinners of roast chicken and pasta, served family-style, are a Rhode Island custom and the specialty of at least a half-dozen institution-sized eating halls around the state. The Bocce Club, a modest restaurant in a homey Woonsocket neighborhood, is where the tradition began in the 1920s when a group of Italian-Americans gathered for supper after their afternoon bocce game. The chicken, seasoned with rosemary and bathed in butter and olive oil, is succulence incarnate. It is preceded by antipasto, accompanied by crusty bread, pasta in a meaty red sauce, and a motley heap of French fried *and* oven-roasted potatoes. Pass the platters, and eat until you cannot move: that is the Bocce Club way.

Caserta's Pizzeria

121 Spruce St., Providence, RI	$
(401) 272-3618	£D

If you have any doubt that New England is Pizza Central, come to Caserta's in Providence, Rhode Island, and you will achieve blissful certainty. On a side street just off Atwells Avenue in Federal Hill, Caserta's is an old-world godsend. Here the pies are built upon thick, yeasty crusts, spread with fragrant tomato sauce and luxuriously creamy cheese or topped with whatever round-the-world hodgepodge you favor. One locally liked interpretation of the flat pizza pie is known hereabouts as a popeye (elsewhere, a calzone), in which the dough is folded over to make an immense sandwich. Caserta's own variation on this theme is called the Wimpy: spinach, mozzarella, and disks of pepperoni, all folded inside a big pocket of the flavorful crust. It's pizza paradise.

Common's Lunch

The Commons, Little Compton, RI	$
(401) 635-4388	BLD

There are many good things to eat in this comfy town lunchroom, which is the kind of place where the day's newspapers are passed along from one bunch of morning coffee hounds to the next. Stuffies—quahog clams with oceanic cracker-crumb stuffing—are moist and satisfying. Buttery clam chowder is accompanied by crusty clam cakes. We once had a prune apple pie here that was grandmotherly good. But the main culinary lure is jonnycakes, corn griddle cakes made the way cooks in the eastern part of the state prefer them: light and lacy, and so thin you can practically see through them. They are served for breakfast, just like ordinary pancakes with bacon or sausage and syrup on the side, but their slightly gritty texture and steamy corn flavor is a unique Yankee taste experience to remember.

Haven Brothers

Fulton and Dorrance sts., at Kennedy Plaza,	$
Providence, RI (no phone)	
5 pm–3 am Mon–Thur, until 4 am Fri and Sat, closed Sun	

Love it or leave it, Haven Brothers is not for the culinarily squeamish. It is a movable lunch truck that comes to this spot and parks every night, six nights a week, just as it has done for more than a century. An old-time dog wagon par excellence, Haven Brothers sparkles with sass and attitude as hash slingers dish out hot dogs and baked beans, cheap sandwiches with "coffee milk" on the side, and beef patties that loyal customers know, with affection, as murder burgers. Seating is limited—there are three stools—but that doesn't stop crowds from gathering around in the middle of the night to consume their meals on foot and partake of New England's most colorful late-night junk-food binge.

The Best Fried Clams

Fried clams are summertime fun food—served "in the rough" from an order window on paper plates or in trapezoidal cardboard clam boxes, eaten by hand at picnic tables or off your dashboard.

Serious clam-o-philes prefer a *whole-belly* clam, which is one great mouthful of briny mollusk enveloped in a wickedly crisp crust that melts in your mouth. *Clam strips* are chewier, with a less assertive clam flavor. Whichever you order, French fries and/or onion rings are the essential side dishes.

The very best ones are found on the North Shore of Massachusetts, where clam-frying was invented in 1916, at Woodman's of Essex, and where the sweetest ones are still harvested from the pure waters of the Essex River.

- ☞ Aunt Carrie's, Narragansett, RI (p. 32)
- ☞ The Clam Shack, Kennebunkport, ME (p. 15)
- ☞ Farnham's, Essex, MA (p. 22)
- ☞ Harraseeket Lunch and Lobster, Freeport, ME (p. 16)
- ☞ Lenny and Joe's, Madison, CT (p. 6)
- ☞ Sea Swirl, Mystic, CT (p. 11)
- ☞ The Clam Box, Ipswich, MA (p. 21)
- ☞ White Cap, Ipswich, MA (p. 26)
- ☞ Woodman's of Essex, Essex, MA (p. 27)

Jigger's Diner

145 Main St., East Greenwich, RI (401) 884-5388	$
(𝔇 Fri only)	𝓑𝓛

Jigger's had been neglected for ten years when chef Carol Shriner restored the vintage 1950 dining car in 1992. She varnished wood booths until they gleamed, she polished stainless steel in the open kitchen, she buffed the green-and-white tile on the walls and found matching pale valances for the windows, and she crafted a menu of blue plate specials and regional delights way above ordinary diner standards.

Fine-textured meat loaf is accompanied by genuine mashed potatoes or hefty steak fries and (for a dollar extra) tart homemade applesauce. There are gravy-topped turkey croquettes, cheese steaks on good torpedo rolls, even trendy specialty sandwiches such as pesto chicken and deluxe turkey (with roasted red pepper). Start with a cup of comforting soup, conclude with baked-here pie, cake, or a stellar bread pudding with rum sauce; you can even accompany the meal with a tall milk shake (known in these parts as a cabinet) served in a silver beaker.

Breakfast is grand, too (especially so on weekends): hot muffins, chunky home fries, hand-crafted sausage patties, and jonnycakes, which are Rhode Island's unique style of cornmeal griddle cakes, made here the South County way—plump and moist inside with a fine sandy crust.

On Fridays only, this convivial place stays open for dinner, serving fish and chips, clam cakes, and chowder.

Prairie Diner

416 Public St., Providence, RI (401) 785-1658	$
Mon–Sat	BL

There is one good reason to come to the Prairie Diner, a weathered eatery in a less-than-lovely part of Providence, and that reason is snail salad. Since mid-century, chef Albert Iannone's zesty mélange of thin-sliced snails in a marinade with onions, chopped celery, and olives has built a loyal clientele of diners and take-out customers who savor this only-in-the-Ocean-State salad as an antipasto before hot Italian platters, alongside cornucopic sandwiches and quohog chowder, and as a cool meal unto itself.

Rocky Point Shore Dinner Hall

Rocky Point Park, just off Rte. 117, Warwick Neck, RI	$$
(401) 737-8000	£D

Shore dinner has been a tradition at the Rocky Point Amusement Park since long before the hurricane of '38 destroyed the original Rocky Point Shore Dinner Hall. Today's restaurant, the largest shore dinner hall in the world, seats 4000 people at one time, and the cacophony at the long, paper-topped tables can be deafening. Meals are enormous, served fast. You are seated depending on what you want to eat, either the smaller all-you-can-eat deal of clam cakes, chowder, and watermelon, or the full-bore dinner of lobster, chowder, clam cakes, steamers, baked fish, bread, spuds, corn, and warm Indian pudding. We actually like the "lesser" of the two meals: the clam cakes, which are crisp, clam-dotted fritters, are impossible to stop eating; and the chowder is a fetching bisque, made with both cream and tomatoes.

Silver Top Diner

13 Harris Ave., Providence, RI (401) 272-2890	$
11 pm to 6:30 am daily	

For night owls only, Silver Top is a genuinely old wooden dining car in the working part of town. Recently refurbished, it specializes in big, simple meals that appeal to peripatetic appetites with middle-of-the-night munchies. The omelets are massive, the char-cooked steak sandwiches are served on good buns, and the "Caveman" burgers are a guaranteed half pound of beef, served with good garlicky home fried potatoes. Of course, the true appeal of this intensely lively place is people-watching. The clientele is a fascinating mix of club-hoppers, tattoo collectors, cops on and off the beat, and insomniacs on the prowl, all doing their own thing along the counter as the jukebox throbs and the grill sizzles until dawn.

VERMONT

The Bryant House	
Rte. 100, Weston, VT	**$**
(802) 824-6287	**LD**

A t a wooden table in the Bryant House, you can order a bowl of crackers and milk: good old cracker-barrel crackers, a bowl of milk

Yankee Arcana

Most of America's regional cuisines have enjoyed a certain vogue in recent years—California, Cajun, Tex-Mex, Gulf Coast, etc. One that never was chic, and likely won't be, is New England. In this part of the world, the fuddy-duddy ways of the kitchen don't lend themselves to high-fashion interpretation by trendy chefs. But they sure make for interesting eating along the road. These are some of the tasty regional oddities still fairly common at ordinary cafés, diners, and roadside stands:

<u>American chop suey</u> A parsimonious school-lunch-type meal of elbow macaroni mixed with ground beef, and tomatoes.

<u>Boiled dinner</u> Corned beef boiled with cabbage, beets, carrots, and new potatoes. Look for this at the table of an old inn.

<u>Brown Betty</u> Cracker-crumb pudding sweetened with molasses or maple syrup.

<u>Fried dough</u> Disks of quick-fried dough topped with cinnamon-sugar or tomato sauce and eaten on the stroll at Grange fairs and draft horse competitions. Similar items, but not so flat, are often served with seafood along the southern shore in Massachusetts, where they are known as doughboys.

to crumble them in, and a hunk of local cheddar on the side. There's a forthright meal for you! Other Yankee treasures on the menu include chicken pie topped with a broad, flaky biscuit, apple crisp redolent of maple syrup, and Indian pudding as respectable as adult breakfast cereal, not too sweet, served warm with vanilla ice cream melting fast on top.

This tidy little café is affiliated with the adjacent Vermont Country Store (of mail-order fame), which is itself a bonanza of such local culinary peculiarities as five-pound bags of mush cereal, cans of fiddlehead greens, and penny candy by the piece.

Grape-Nuts pudding A sweet custard in which the cereal softens to create streaks of grain.

Indian pudding Cornmeal and molasses, cooked forever, to become a dark, spicy samp like breakfast cereal, but eaten for dessert. Served hot with ice cream on top.

Jonnycakes Little corn cakes made from hard flint corn. On the eastern side of Narragansett Bay, they tend to be broad and thin. To the west, they are silver-dollar size, moist, and plump. Eaten for breakfast, but also as a side dish with supper.

Red flannel hash Made from leftover boiled dinner, named because the beets make it blush.

Sugar on snow During maple sugaring season, warm syrup is poured on fresh-fallen snow, forming chewy maple candy. Sugar on snow (also known as frogs or leather aprons) is so intensely mapley that it is customarily eaten with dill pickles, which help revive an exhausted sweet tooth. Not served in restaurants, but sometimes available at sugar houses in the spring.

Whoopie pie Snack cakes made of two disks of chocolate cake with sugary white goo between them.

Curtis' Barbeque

Rte. 5 (exit 4 off I-91), Putney, VT (802) 387-5474	$
Wed—Sun, Apr through Nov	LD

There are picnic tables but no dining room at Curtis Tuff's unusual roadside attraction, which he bills as the "Ninth Wonder of the World." Mr. Tuff has transformed a couple of immobilized school buses into a kitchen and built a smoke pit to the side. Here he sells delicious barbecued pork ribs and chicken, accompanied by zesty baked beans or baked potatoes. The air smells of burning wood and sizzling pork, and if you are lucky, you will meet Isabel, Mr. Tuff's pet pig, who roots around the woodpile or the tables looking for a snack.

P & H Truck Stop

Exit 17 off I-91, Wells River, VT	$
(802) 429-2141	BLD

The aroma in the P & H is not of axle grease and diesel fuel, it is of fresh-baked bread and pot roast blanketed with gravy. The moment you walk in, past shelves of white and cinnamon-raisin bread for sale, you know you have found a kitchen that means business.

Soups and chowders are especially inviting: tomato-macaroni soup is thick with vegetables, ground beef, and soft noodles; corn chowder is loaded with potatoes and corn kernels and flavored with bacon. We love the falling-apart pot roast and any kind of sandwich made using thick-sliced P & H bread, but the mashed potatoes (*purée de pommes de terre* on the bilingual menu, written for French-Canadian truckers) taste like they were made from powder, and the meat loaf is strictly for die-hard diner fans.

The homemade dessert selection is huge, including fruit pies, berry pies, custard pies, meringue pies, Reese's pie (a peanut-cream), a few types of pudding, and maple-cream pie thick as toffee and topped with nuts.

Up For Breakfast

710 Main St., Manchester, VT	$
(802) 362-4204	B L

Green Mountain pancake paradise! Three kinds are available, with or without blueberries in the batter: buttermilk, buckwheat, and sourdough. Good muffins, too: tender-textured quick breads with broad-risen tops and cream-colored insides, the best of them chock-a-block with blueberries and nuts. More elaborate breakfasts include multi-ingredient fritattas, omelets filled with goat cheese and avocado, French toast made using big slabs of marvelous applesauce pecan spice bread, and chicken-duck-cilantro sausage. Wild turkey hash—wildly assembled, not made from wild turkeys—is a cook's tour de force that combines big shreds of roasted turkey with peppers, onions, potatoes, and pine nuts, all griddle-cooked until crusty brown on the outside and topped with poached eggs and a film of fine Hollandaise.

Beware: seats in this café can be mighty scarce, especially on weekends or during leaf-peeping season, when an hour's wait is not uncommon.

Wasp's Snack Bar

67 Pleasant St., Woodstock, VT	$
(802) 457-9805	B L

Many sightseers visit Woodstock for its Green Mountain charm, quaint shops, and rarefied gourmet meals (at the Woodstock Inn and the Kedron Valley Inn). But few of them find their way to the ten-stool counter in this shoebox-shaped, wood-shingled diner. "The Wasp" is a hangout for townsfolk—workers, housewives, dowagers, artists, and eccentrics—who come for eggs, hash browns, and coffee at 6 am, for hot dogs and hamburgers at lunch, and for bull sessions and to catch up on local gossip any time. Although it took down its sign several years ago so as not to encourage accidental tourists, the Wasp has always seemed a friendly place to us, and we love the grilled cheese sandwiches and chicken soup at lunchtime, with chocolate cake for dessert. It's an honest meal for a couple of dollars, with a taste of old Vermont thrown in for free.

American Breakfasts

Breakfast on the road is an opportunity to eat good things not available back home, such as red-eye gravy in a Shenandoah Valley ham house, beignets in New Orleans's French Quarter, *huevos rancheros* in a bordertown café, or grade-a maple syrup in a White Mountains sugar shack. It is also the best time of day to soak up local color. In small town cafés and urban diners, regular customers come to trade news and gossip at the counter; cops stock up on donuts; truckers fill thermoses with forty-weight java to get them through the day.

These are some of the country's most colorful breakfast spots:

- Al's Breakfast, Minneapolis, MN (p. 203)
- Café du Monde, New Orleans, LA (p. 141)
- Chatter Box Café, Sutter Creek, CA (p. 315)
- Clarksville Diner, Decorah, IA (p. 191)
- Classen Grill, Oklahoma City, OK (p. 284)
- The Diner, Yountville, CA (p. 317)
- Doidge's, San Francisco, CA (p. 317)
- Durango Diner, Durango, CO (p. 264)
- Hob Nob Hill, San Diego, CA (p. 322)
- Ina's Kitchen, Chicago, IL (p. 171)
- Jigger's Diner, East Greenwich, RI (p. 35)
- Kitchen Little, Mystic, CT (p. 6)
- Lou Mitchell's, Chicago, IL (p. 176)
- Loveless Café, Nashville, TN (p. 100)
- Otis Café, Otis, OR (p. 335)
- Polly's Pancake Parlor, Sugar Hill, NH (p. 29)
- Romney Coffee Shop, Lafayette, IN (p. 186)
- Silver Spur, Sheridan, WY (p. 251)
- Up For Breakfast, Manchester, VT (p. 41)
- Whistle Stop Muffins, Georgetown, CT (p. 12)
- Wolfie Cohen's Rascal House, Miami Beach, FL (p. 129)
- Yankee Doodle, New Haven, CT (p. 12)

The Wayside Restaurant

Barre-Montpelier Rd., Berlin, VT	$
(802) 223-6611	*BLD*

An oasis of genuine regional cooking in a state with too many mediocre "gourmet" inns, the Wayside is a place to sample salt pork and milk gravy (Thursday), fresh native perch (during ice-fishing season), old-fashioned boiled dinner (when it's cold out), and several kinds of hash, including red flannel hash, made with beets.

We especially like the Wayside on Wednesday, which is chicken pie and meat loaf day. What a feast the chicken pie is, piled into a big crockery boat with dressing and a crusty biscuit, with a great heap of gravy-dripping mashed potatoes on the side. Wayside meat loaf is outstanding, too: a two-inch-thick slab with a sticky red glaze along the rim and rivulets of stout brown gravy dripping down its sides.

Homespun desserts include Grape-Nuts custard, mince pie, apple pie in a fork-crimped crust, and a radiant maple cream pie that comes dolloped with whipped cream.

Mid-Atlantic

ALL-AMERICAN

DELAWARE

D.C.

MARYLAND

NEW JERSEY

NEW YORK

PENNSYLVANIA

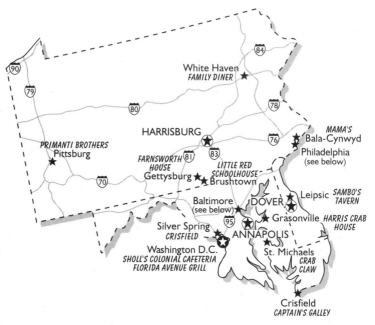

White Haven
FAMILY DINER ★

HARRISBURG ★

PRIMANTI BROTHERS
Pittsburg ★

*FARNSWORTH
HOUSE*
Gettysburg ★

*LITTLE RED
SCHOOLHOUSE*
★ Brushtown

MAMA'S
Bala-Cynwyd ★
Philadelphia
(see below)

Leipsic ★ *SAMBO'S
TAVERN*

Baltimore
(see below)

DOVER ★

Silver Spring
CRISFIELD ★

ANNAPOLIS ★

★ Grasonville *HARRIS CRAB
HOUSE*

Washington D.C.
*SHOLL'S COLONIAL CAFETERIA
FLORIDA AVENUE GRILL*

St. Michaels
*CRAB
CLAW*

Crisfield ★
CAPTAIN'S GALLEY

Philadelphia
*JIM'S STEAKS
OLIVIERI'S PRINCE OF STEAKS
PAT'S KING OF STEAKS
SHANK AND EVELYN'S*

Baltimore
*WOMAN'S INDUSTRIAL EXCHANGE
OBRYCKI'S
ATTMAN'S DELICATESSEN
GUNNING'S CRAB HOUSE*

NEW YORK

PENNSYLVANIA

NEW JERSEY

MARYLAND   DELAWARE

WASHINGTON D.C.

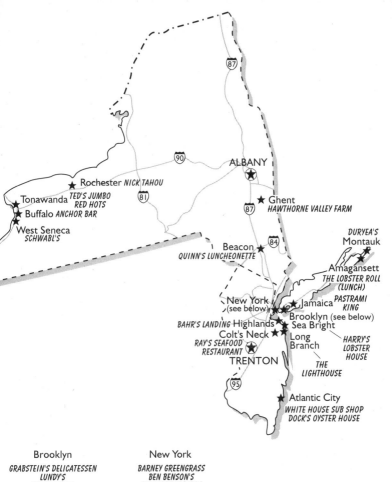

87

90

ALBANY

★ Rochester *NICK TAHOU*

81

Tonawanda *TED'S JUMBO RED HOTS*
★ Buffalo *ANCHOR BAR*

West Seneca
SCHWABL'S

★ Ghent
HAWTHORNE VALLEY FARM

87

84

DURYEA'S
Montauk

Beacon
QUINN'S LUNCHEONETTE

Amagansett
*THE LOBSTER ROLL
(LUNCH)*

New York
(see below)

★ Jamaica
*PASTRAMI
KING*

Brooklyn (see below)

BAHR'S LANDING Highlands
Colt's Neck
*RAY'S SEAFOOD
RESTAURANT*
TRENTON

Sea Bright
Long
Branch

*HARRY'S
LOBSTER
HOUSE*

*THE
LIGHTHOUSE*

95

Atlantic City
*WHITE HOUSE SUB SHOP
DOCK'S OYSTER HOUSE*

Brooklyn

*GRABSTEIN'S DELICATESSEN
LUNDY'S
PETER LUGER
TOM'S LUNCHEONETTE
TOTONNO PIZZERIA*

New York

*BARNEY GREENGRASS
BEN BENSON'S
BENNY'S BURRITOS
EISENBERG'S SANDWICH
THE FOUR SEASONS
OYSTER BAR
SPARKS*

MID-ATLANTIC

DELAWARE

★ ★ ★

Sambo's Tavern	
Front St., Leipsic, DE	$$
(302) 674-9724	LD

rab feast! Newspaper tablecloths, paper-towel napkins, piles of hard-shelled crabs, radiating peppery spice: all the elements of the Delaware Bay delectation are at the ready in this family-friendly crab house with a view of the slow-moving Leipsic River. If pick and hammer and bib are not your favored tools for dining, Sambo's Tavern also makes fork-and-knife fine crab cakes and platters of tasty fried fish.

DISTRICT OF COLUMBIA

★ ★ ★

Florida Avenue Grill	
1100 Florida Ave. NW, Washington, DC	$
(202) 265-1586	LD

Taxi drivers originally staked out this modest corner café near Howard University back when it opened in the mid-1940s. It has since been discovered by *everybody*, high and low, black and white, famous and unknown. The midday menu is a roster of soul food classics including stuffed pork chops, fried fish, and chitterlings, but the great meal to eat in a ramshackle Grill booth or at the scenic counter (where staff and customers trade hash house repartee) is breakfast. Country ham is sizzled to perfection and served with eggs, grits, and gravy, and heaps of sinfully sweet fried apples, hot biscuits on the side.

Sholl's Colonial Cafeteria

1990 K St. NW, Washington, DC	**$**
(202) 296-3065	**£ D**

No power tables here, no lobbyists or politicians or trendy foodies, either. Sholl's is a rare enclave of culinary democracy in the heart of Washington, DC. An old-fashioned cafeteria serving three square meals a day, it is plain, simple, and cheap. And the food is good, extraordinarily so when it reflects the southern-rural kitchen traditions that surround the capital, such as crisp fried chicken, savory greens, and a repertoire of creamy-sweet pies. Our favorite meals are the squarest ones: meat loaf with real mashed potatoes, beef stew with corn bread on the side, chicken and biscuits. And for dessert, when we can pass up the rainbow selection of Jell-Os, the rice pudding is superb.

MARYLAND

☆ ☆ ☆

Attman's Delicatessen

1019 E. Lombard St., Baltimore, MD	**$**
(410) 563-2666	**£ D**

When the craving for good corned beef (or brisket or pastrami) on rye strikes you in the Baltimore area, go to Attman's in the part of town once known as Corned Beef Row for all its delis. The neighbor-

Diner Slang 101

"Adam and Eve on a Raft" . . . . Poached eggs on toast
"Barn paint" . . . . Ketchup
"Bird seed" . . . . A bowl of cereal
"Cat's eyes" . . . . Tapioca pudding
"Crow slab" . . . . Chocolate pie
"Dog soup" . . . . A glass of water
"Gob stick" . . . . Spoon
"Hounds in hay" . . . . Hot dogs with sauerkraut
"Slippery Joe" . . . . Coffee with cream
"Whiskey toast" . . . . Rye toast

hood, and even Attman's itself, is a bit run-down, but the culinary experience is axiomatic. Grab a tray and holler your way along a cafeteria line of fragrant Jewish fare, all tended by a staff of good old cranks behind the counter. In addition to piled-high hot sandwiches, blintzes, pickled herring, and matzoh ball soup, Attman's serves wonderful oversized all-beef hot dogs.

Captain's Galley

1021 W. Main St., Crisfield, MD (410) 968-1636	$$
in summer, shorter hours off-season	BLD

The Captain's Galley is a pleasant, polite restaurant that serves much delicious seafood native to the mid-Atlantic region, including sautéed soft-shelled crabs and luxurious oyster fritters. But the one thing you need to eat in Crisfield is crab cakes, and there are none better than the Captain's. Served two-by-two, creamy-sweet and fresh as ocean spray, tender but with a nice little snap to their golden crust, they are the best along the Chesapeake Bay, *ergo,* the best on earth. The house crab seasoning is sold to take home, but the real secret, of course, is the utter freshness of the local backfin crabmeat.

Crab Claw

Navy Point, St. Michaels, MD	$$
(410) 745-2900	£🔴

Overlooking the harbor and outfitted with open-air tables for sunny-day dining, the Crab Claw has been a favorite fixture of the Eastern Shore for decades. Locals and vacationers alike crowd into the nautically themed dining room to eat piles of hot-spiced Maryland blue crabs, crab cakes, and soft-shells accompanied by pitchers of beer and stacks of paper napkins. It is an informal place, boisterous and fun. If you arrive by boat, there is a house dinghy to help you get ashore.

Crisfield

8606 Colesville Rd., Silver Spring, MD	$$
(301) 588-1572	£🔴

No longer a dump with shower-room ambiance, in its new location Crisfield is a plain and polite fish house that continues to serve consummate mid-Atlantic seafood, including Chesapeake Bay striped bass, luscious stuffed shrimp, and wantonly creamy crab imperial in the shell, as well as Norfolk-style sautéed-in-butter crabmeat. Don't come here to eat the kind of lean, meager seafood the nutrition police are always telling us we ought to eat. Even the broiled fish seems impossibly rich: huge fillets of flounder, moister and sweeter than anywhere on earth. Nor is this the restaurant for gracious amenities—don't expect fawning service—but for a good ol' fish feast, Crisfield cannot be beat.

Gunning's Crab House

3901 S. Hanover St., Baltimore, MD	*$$*
(410) 354-0085	*£D*

Steamed crabs, highly spiced and served by the dozen with plenty of beer on the side, are the essential Maryland meal; and no one presents it with more panache than the impertinent staff of Gunning's. With deep-fried pepper rings, faintly sugar-sweetened, to put a twist on the luscious marine feast, it is a culinary adventure not quite like any other, and one all adventurous eaters need to know about. Dine near the bar or in the open-air crab garden when weather permits, and be sure to wear clothes you can wipe your hands on. No amount of napkins are ever sufficient.

(There is a newer Gunning's, operated by the family that opened the original one but sold it, at 7304 Parkway Dr. in Hanover [410] 712-9404. The crabs and fried green pepper rings are every bit as good, and the staff is every bit as sassy.)

Harris Crab House

433 N. Kent Narrows Way, Grasonville, MD	*$$*
(410) 827-9500	*£D*

The long tables are covered with brown wrapping paper. The sound in the big, airy dining room and on the outdoor deck is of crab shells cracking and people slurping up the sweet pink meat. Buy 'em by the dozen and feast, the Chesapeake Bay way. There are ribs and chicken on the menu for crab-frowners, as well as a good array of fresh, local seafood, but steamed crabs are the primary lure to this family-oriented crab house on the waterfront.

Obrycki's

1727 E. Pratt St., Baltimore, MD (410) 732-6399	$$
(closed Nov through Apr)	£Đ

You'll pay handsomely to eat in an old row house now spruced with Colonial trim (brass chandeliers, wall sconces), but no matter how much the management turns on the fine-dining charm, the great Obrycki's meal is a sloppy one. Hard-shell crabs, steamed and brilliantly spiced, can only be eaten with sturdy hammers and picks like the tools of a combat engineer. So wear a bib . . . and prepare to feast. On days when Obrycki's can get no good Chesapeake Bay crabs (call ahead if that's what you have your heart set on), they serve a mighty fine pan-fried soft-shell crab sandwich. And we even like the crab imperial—a creamy, goopy comfort-food concoction utterly at odds with today's cruel lite-is-good nutritional dogma.

Woman's Industrial Exchange

333 N. Charles St., Baltimore, MD	$
(410) 685-4388	ßℒ

There isn't a nicer restaurant anywhere for an old-fashioned ladies' lunch: chicken aspic, deviled eggs, and biscuits, for example, served by a staff of uniformed, kindly waitresses in a dining room unchanged for decades. Or you can choose a mild chicken salad sandwich on white bread, meaty croquettes with gravy, or fine-spiced crab cakes. Accompany the dainty fare with a glass of lemonade, top them off with layer cake or meringue pie. Then, when you're done, you can buy jams, jellies, and handwork made by deserving local women, who have been beneficiaries of this stalwart institution since it started serving meals in 1882.

NEW JERSEY

Bahr's Landing

2 Bay Ave., Highlands, NJ	$$
(908) 872-1245	£D

When the Bahr family started serving soup to fishermen from their Highlands houseboat in 1917, the New Jersey shore was a string of little villages and long, sandy beaches. The villages have sprawled but the beaches are still beautiful, and Bahr's has become a big barn of a place catering to hungry families. With a picture window overlooking the Shrewsbury River, a museum's worth of nautical decor, and a long menu of shore dinners, it is the quintessential vacation-time seafood restaurant. Start with "famous chowder" made with tomatoes and vegetables and mountains of chopped clams, or a big bowl of steamers served with broth and butter. Then move on to lobster, flounder, or maybe fried clams. Keep it simple—the stuffed, sauced preparations are best ignored—and you can have a fine, familiar, and satisfying tourist meal.

Dock's Oyster House

2405 Atlantic Ave., Atlantic City, NJ (609) 345-0092	$$
Wed–Sun, late Mar to mid-Nov (reservations advised)	D

For impeccable seafood in civilized surroundings at reasonable prices, Dock's is Atlantic City's best bet. You can have freshly opened clams and oysters or a good-sized boiled lobster, but don't ignore preparations that require more formidable kitchen skills. Fried seafood is gorgeous, sheathed in a frail, savory crust; oyster stew is lush and comforting; and there isn't a finer linguine with garlicky, *freshly chopped* clam sauce this side of Hoboken.

Jewish Deli Lexicon

W aiters in the urban delis of the Northeast are crabby all the time, but they treat you even worse if you act like a greenhorn. So here are ten basic terms you should know before ordering:

Blintzes: sweet pot cheese rolled in crepes and fried in butter

Chicken-in-a-pot: a stew/soup in golden broth with tender vegetables

Kasha varnishkes: bow-tie noodles with buckwheat groats

Knish: a potato dumpling with the atomic weight of lead

Knoblewurst: garlicky salami

Kugel: noodle pudding that can be either sweet or savory

Latkes: potato pancakes, served on the side of sandwiches or as a meal

Novie: short for "Nova Scotia lox," meaning sliced smoked salmon that isn't too salty

"Oy vay": an expression of exasperation; the waiter's mantra

Schmaltz: rendered chicken fat, often spread on dark bread like butter

Harry's Lobster House

1124 Ocean Ave., Sea Bright, NJ (908) 842-0205	$$$
(reservations advised)	𝔇

T he Jersey shore has many, many places to eat steamers, lobsters, clams, and crab. Most are breezy and casual and serve decent-enough food. Harry's Lobster House is deluxe (no beachwear allowed!) and serves excellent food. There isn't a better stuffed lobster anywhere, loaded with pearly hunks of sweet crabmeat, and the flounder, either simply broiled or crab-stuffed, is a delight. Start with a dozen raw oysters and/or clams and you have an unimprovable mid-Atlantic feast. The pleasure of a Harry's meal is due in great part to the charm of the place itself, open since 1933 and located in a plain wood-sided building on the main drag of an old vacation town. In its simple, white-walled dining room (without the usual nautical jim-crack decor), loyal customers enjoy a kind of resort-town luxury that has faded away nearly everywhere else.

The Lighthouse

65 New Ocean Ave., Long Branch, NJ	$
(908) 229-1222	£D

For quick refreshment along the shore, the Lighthouse is a dandy place to know about. It is a small stand with no seating other than three picnic tables in the parking lot and a menu of hot food limited to hot dogs and meatball sandwiches. But the reason everybody stops here is Italian ice: cool, not too sweet, the perfect summer pick-me-up during a hot day at the shore. Flavors include chocolate, vanilla, cherry, orange, and lemon.

Ray's Seafood Restaurant

29 Rte. 34 S., Colt's Neck, NJ	$$
(908) 758-8166	£D

Located in the lovely green New Jersey that interstate travelers do not see, Ray's is a civilized country restaurant surrounded by horse farms and orchards. And yet it is just miles from the shore, and its forte is seafood. Plain (baked flounder in lemon butter) or fancy (salmon in puff pastry with crabmeat and brie), the fish on Ray's menu is always fresh and delicious. We particularly like the mussels—marinara or bathed in garlic and wine—and anything with crabmeat. Crab cakes with sweet mustard sauce, flounder stuffed with crab, or crab imperial are all four-star meals . . . not cheap, but worth every penny.

After a meal at Ray's, go across the road to Delicious Orchards, a u-pick-'em apple stand and stupendous country market that is proof positive New Jersey deserves its sobriquet, the Garden State.

White House Sub Shop

2301 Arctic Ave., Atlantic City, NJ	$
(609) 345-1564	£D

The White House invented the submarine sandwich. Apparently, the great moment occurred during World War II when the sandwich hereabouts known as a hoagie was rechristened as an ode to the men in the Navy who served in loaf-shaped underwater boats. Today's edible White House subs set the gold standard for gigantic sandwiches. They are piled into bakery-fresh lengths of crusty bread, and their configurations range from the White House Special (a sheaf of Italian cold cuts well-oiled and decorated with lettuce and sweet pepper) to messy hot boats loaded with meatballs. Ambiance is Americana in the raw: the walls are plastered with pictures of celebrities who have come to gobble down the gorgeous sandwiches, and the counter help is full of Jersey sass.

NEW YORK

☆ ☆ ☆

Anchor Bar

1047 Main St., Buffalo, NY	$$
(716) 886-8920	£D

In the kitchen of the Anchor Bar in 1964, Teressa Bellisimo invented the Buffalo chicken wing. For years, the fried-crisp, hot-sauced little munchies remained a local obsession, but in the early 1980s, they went national in a big way. Anchor Bar wings, which are part of an otherwise unexceptional menu in this corner tavern, are served just the way they were in 1964, in the now-classic configuration with celery stalks (to relieve the palate from their heat) and a bowl of creamy blue cheese dressing to dip them in. They are available hot or mild; the former really is hot, and will set your lips tingling and reaching for a beer. That, of course, is the idea of bar food, of which these zesty wings are a definitive mouthful.

Barney Greengrass	
541 Amsterdam Ave., New York, NY (212) 724-4707	**$$**
until 6 pm	**BLD**

Smoked sturgeon is a staple at good delicatessens everywhere; nowhere is it better than at Barney Greengrass, a family business since 1908. Each cool slice of sturgeon is firm and white, lean and luscious, the sweet flesh insinuated with a whisper of smoke. Have it on a sandwich between slices of rye bread, or on a smoked fish platter with silky pink salmon, pickled herring, and sable. Other good things to eat include whitefish salad, flamingo-pink borscht served in a glass, excellent chopped liver, and triple-decker masterpieces of tongue, pastrami, brisket, and/or corned beef. Perhaps the greatest single dish at this old Formica-table West Side luncheonette is scrambled eggs laced with nuggets of Nova Scotia salmon and oily onions.

Beware of long lines to get in, especially on weekends.

Ben Benson's	
123 West 52 St., New York, NY	**$$$**
(212) 581-8888	**LD**

Midtown Manhattan has many steak houses where a meat-and-potatoes meal for two can easily top $100. Although the prices can be eye-popping (eight-pound lobster, anyone?), these establishments are not really fancy places; they have manly staffs who are so efficient they verge on brusque; and the food they serve, made from the finest groceries available, is simply prepared and bluntly served. If such a forthright meal appeals to you, we recommend Ben Benson's, where the dark wood walls are decorated with clubby pictures of horses and dogs (some owned by Mr. and Mrs. Benson), and where the steaks and chops are magnificent and the chilled martinis are dreamy.

Dive into an extraordinary basket of raisin bread and hard-crusted dinner rolls while you peruse the long, interesting menu, which includes a strange "prime rib steak," cut like a slab of prime rib, but marinated and then grilled like a steak; heavenly chicken pot pie every Monday and roast beef hash on Thursday; lots of fine, fresh seafood; and an array of complex salads big enough to be dinner. First-time visitors, though, probably ought to stick to the basics, which are as good as you'll find in any restaurant in this land: oysters on the half shell to start, sirloins and filets mignon accompanied by plates piled with thick cakes of crisp, onion-flavored hash brown potatoes, and maybe some spinach or other green thing on the side.

There is dessert—you see samples of it on the way in the door—but we have never gotten to the end of a Ben Benson meal with a shred of appetite remaining.

Benny's Burritos

113 Greenwich Ave., New York, NY (212) 727-0584;	$
also at 93 Ave. A (212) 254-2054	£D

You might not think of burritos as a real New York food, but they are, thanks to Benny's. When this boisterous joint opened about a decade ago, it started a major eating trend, and now burritos are as much a part of the city's culinary scene as pizza by the slice and hot dogs from a cart. The two Benny's and their uptown sibling, Bertha's (at Broadway and 76 St.), are rightly famous for delicious behemoth burritos loaded with high-quality ingredients ranging from classic meat and cheese to spinach and even tofu. The margaritas are immense, the setting is hip, the people-watching is a gas. It all adds up to a dining experience that is downtown New York at its most beguiling.

Duryea's

Tuthill Rd., Montauk, NY	$$
(516) 668-2410	£D

Eat in the rough: choose what you want from a photocopied menu, place your order by the cash register, then wait until your name is called. Tote your own plastic tray full of food (on paper plates) to a table on the lobster deck with a lovely view of Montauk Bay. Then, feast on an absolutely simple but expertly prepared shore dinner: whole lobsters, fresh and sweet, are served with good baked potatoes and rugged cole slaw; big lobster rolls come on toasty buttered buns. Bring your own beer or wine, and it will be a summertime meal to remember.

Eisenberg's Sandwich

174 Fifth Ave., New York, NY	$
(212) 675-5096	BL

What's not to like at this neighborhood luncheonette, famous for its tuna sandwich on rye toast? There are other good things to eat—chicken salad, egg salad, corned beef and pastrami, as well as a hot entree each day—but it's the tuna that has attracted repeat customers since the 1930s. A few years ago, *New York Eats* author Ed Levine secured the sacred recipe: one can of Bumble Bee solid white tuna and Hellmann's mayonnaise (plenty of it), *mixed with a big spoon, not a fork.*

Like its impeccable tuna, Eisenberg's charm is all about simplicity. One narrow room with a long counter on one side and minuscule tables-for-two along the other, it is a guileless taste of old New York, with a big bowl of pickles on every table.

Four Seasons

99 East 52 St., New York, NY (212) 754-9494	$$$
(reservations required)	LD

It is impossible to imagine the Four Seasons anywhere other than in its exalted position overlooking Park Avenue and 52 St. The quintessence of high style when it opened in 1959, it remains the absolute New York dining room—grand and classy, it's a landmark that is always up to date, home equally to captains of industry who lunch in the Grill Room daily and to celebrants who come for a special-occasion

Mid-Atlantic Splurges

Expensive, fancy, and/or fashionable regional restaurants that are worth it.

- ☛ Obrycki's, Baltimore, MD (p. 53)
- ☛ Harry's Lobster House, Sea Bright, NJ (p. 55)
- ☛ Ben Benson's, New York, NY (p. 58)
- ☛ Four Seasons, New York, NY (p. 60)
- ☛ Lundy's, Brooklyn, NY (p. 63)
- ☛ Oyster Bar, New York, NY (p. 64)
- ☛ Peter Luger, Brooklyn, NY (p. 66)
- ☛ Sparks, New York, NY (p. 67)
- ☛ Farnsworth House, Gettysburg, PA (p. 71)

supper in the lap of luxury. We favor the airy expanses of the Pool Room with its rippling gold-bead curtains, a magical setting for happy toasts and great banquets to commemorate life passages. The menu is broad, ranging from debonair spa cuisine for weight-watchers to fine old gourmet classics such as Dover sole meunière and a mesmerizing tableside preparation of steak tartare. Our favorite meal—utterly atypical of this kitchen, yet tastebuds' siren call—is grilled calves' liver with onions and potatoes and creamed spinach on the side, followed by chocolate velvet cake. Accompanied, of course, by plenty of champagne.

Grabstein's Delicatessen

1845 Rockaway Pkwy., Brooklyn, NY	$
(718) 251-2280	£Đ

When Grabstein's opened in Canarsie in 1960, there were hundreds of kosher delicatessens in New York. Last year, the *New York Times* reported that they were fading fast, and that Grabstein's was one of the few remaining old-time delis that still held high the banner of pastrami-on-rye with big, crunchy pickles on the side. It is a piece of work all right, complete with waiters who carry cold cuts, chicken soup, and knishes in their hands and the weight of the world on their shoulders. Dine at worn Formica tables with a view of glass cases filled with smoked fish; plow into salami, pastrami, corned beef, tongue, or brisket piled high between slices of fresh bread slathered with coarse mustard; give the gents behind the counter a hard time about the fat content of the pickled meats they slice: it adds up to a spicy culinary experience that long ago defined delicatessen dining.

Hawthorne Valley Farm

Rte. 21C, Ghent, NY (518) 672-7500	$
seasonal hours	

Known for fine-textured Swiss cheese and maple vanilla yogurt, Hawthorne Valley is a biodynamic farm, as close to self-sufficient as a farm can be. Its cows eat hay grown on the premises, and grains grown here find their way to the farm's bakery, where specialties include loaves of nubby-textured multigrain bread. The farm store also carries raw milk and quark (like cream cheese, but better for you) and a good supply of organically grown vegetables. For quick picnics-on-the-fly, it's a treasure.

Katz's Deli

205 E. Houston St., New York, NY	$
(212) 254-2246	BLD

A vintage lower East Side dining experience, Katz's (since 1888) is a line-up-and-order delicatessen where the size of your sandwich and even the quality of meat in it is determined by your rapport with the counterman. Tipping is supposedly not allowed, but if you manage to slip your man a little something as he forks the corned beef onto the cutting board, he'll give you fat or lean, whichever you prefer; he may even offer a few forkfuls to nosh while he slices. Pastrami, corned beef, and brisket on fine, fresh rye bread are all deli paradigms, as is the garlicky salami known as knoblewurst, and the all-beef hot dogs are New York's best.

A sign above the cash register on the way out advises SEND A SALAMI TO YOUR BOY IN THE ARMY.

The Lobster Roll	
Rte. 27, Amagansett, NY	$$
(516) 267-3470	£D

On any sunny day, you will wait too long in line, and the wood-benched tables scarcely provide a view of the highway let alone the ocean. But despite these hardships, the Lobster Roll is one of the essential seafood shacks in the Hamptons. It has been here forever, operated by a family that settled on Long Island in the seventeenth century, and the menu is traditional family-fun vacation food. Chowder, steamers, plump lobster rolls, and fried puffers are the staples; but it is dessert that is great, pie in particular. It is glorious pie, pie that reminds you of Long Island's farmland heritage, with a fine flaky crust and bounteous filling. Midsummer, when the sky is blue and the waves lap against nearby sands, what could be better than a lunch of chowder and lobster followed by a slab of fresh strawberry-rhubarb or raspberry pie?

Lundy's	
1901 Emmons Ave., Brooklyn, NY	$$$
(718) 743-0022	£D

For seafood feasting the old-fashioned way, Lundy's is tops. Opened in 1918, known as the largest restaurant in America into the postwar years, it closed in 1979 and reopened in 1995, one-quarter of its former size, now seating a mere 800 customers at one time. It remains a boisterous Brooklyn dining hall, staffed by hordes of white-jacketed waiters toting warm baking powder biscuits, bowls of chowder, and giant tureens full of steamer clams to start a meal, then the great, juicy lobsters that star in the house's famous shore dinners, followed by enormous wedges of pie and cake for dessert. Portions are big, service is brash, customers are loud, and the good times roll just as they did fifty years ago. It is possible to have a downscaled, less-expensive meal in Lundy's clam bar or in an adjoining sidewalk café.

Nick Tahou

2260 Lyell, Rochester, NY (716) 429-6388	$
always open	

Western New York is America's wiener world, and Nick Tahou of Rochester dishes out some of the wickedest. Upstate franks are not slim aristocrats like you might get from a cart in New York City, nor are they crowned with baroque bouquets of condiments like the all-beef red hots of Chicago. Tube steaks in this part of the world tend to be raunchy but irresistibly seductive. Nick Tahou, a round-the-clock eat place where the air is redolent of spice and oil, dishes out several good varieties: red hots, Texas hots, pork hots radiating pepper, and regular pink weenies that are split and grilled to attain maximum lewd character before they are loaded into buns and heaped with a fine-grained chili. *Specialité de la maison* is the garbage plate: baked beans, home fried potatoes, macaroni salad, a pair of grilled dogs, raw onions, and chili sauce all heaped upon a thick cardboard plate. At sunrise, after a long, hard night, a garbage plate at Nick's just might be what you need.

Oyster Bar

Grand Central Terminal, New York, NY	$$$
(212) 490-6650	£D

Noisy and swarming with customers (especially at lunch), the Oyster Bar is a vast, beauteous catacomb underneath midtown Manhattan where it is possible to eat some of the freshest and tastiest seafood on the East Coast. Many kinds of oysters are always available, of course—pricey but impeccably fresh and opened as you watch if you perch at the counter. The other thing you see created at the counter is pan roasts, which are creamy stews instantaneously brewed in gleaming vessels that look like something from Diamond Jim Brady's kitchen. The menu changes daily and always lists varieties of seafare rarely served elsewhere: Virginia spots, anyone? Fried sea squabs? Solianka (sturgeon stew)?

We stick to oysters, pan roasts and stews, and more basic fish such as grouper, striped bass, and Montauk bluefish. With the Oyster Bar's warm baking powder biscuits on the side and the clatter of Gotham all around, such dishes are the ingredients of a unique and delicious Manhattan banquet.

Pastrami King

124-24 Queens Blvd., Jamaica, NY	$
(718) 263-1717	BLD

Most American cities have restaurants that serve pastrami sandwiches, but they pale by comparison to the lean, dark red brisket made by this old deli across from the county courthouse. The Pastrami King of Queens sets the cured-meat benchmark. Its meat is sultry, well-peppered, and heavily garlicked, so aromatic your mouth will begin watering as the waitress carries it to your Formica table. What sheer joy it is to sink teeth into a sandwich full of these lean, firm slices, accented by grainy mustard, wrapped in fresh-baked, seeded rye bread!

Pastrami is the great meal to eat, but there is much other good Jewish deli fare on the menu, too, including house-cured corned beef or tongue sandwiches, brisket platters, and motherly chicken-in-the-pot. All are served with appropriate crabby attitude by a squadron of waitresses as sour as the pickles in the silver bowls on every table.

Peter Luger

178 Broadway, Brooklyn, NY (718) 387-7400	**$$$**
(reservations required) (only Peter Luger credit cards are accepted)	**LD**

Peter Luger is the archetypal neighborhood restaurant of a bygone New York. Although the neighborhood is now moribund, the heavy oak tables of this robust tavern are packed every night with happy carnivores quaffing dry martinis and gliding knives into butter-tender slices of prime beefsteak. White-aproned waiters, most of them seasoned veterans, seldom bother to let customers know that lamb chops and prime rib are also available (a written menu is given only if you ask for it) because nearly everyone comes for porterhouse, which arrives sliced on a platter to which all at the table help themselves. The meal starts with freshly baked onion rolls and tomato and onion salad (tasty in tomato season). On the side, you want crusty hash browns and creamed spinach; then cheesecake or apple strudel for dessert. It is a classic meal, well-nigh perfect.

Quinn's Luncheonette

330 Main St., Beacon, NY	**$**
(914) 831-8065	**BL**

People sometimes forget that there is more to New York than New York City. There are plenty of small and medium-size towns up-state, where the livin' is easy and the restaurants are homey and af-fordable. Such a place is Quinn's of Beacon, where for many years now, locals have congregated at lunch for bowls of soup (turkey noodle is especially excellent), oven-fresh bread, and made-from-scratch maca-roni and cheese. At Quinn's, the waitresses call you "Hon" and give you their honest assessment of the day's repertoire of pies. The hustle of the Big Apple seems light-years away.

Schwabl's

789 Center Rd., West Seneca, NY	$
(716) 674-9821	£ⅅ

One of the essential things to eat in the Buffalo area, other than fried chicken wings and charcoal-cooked hot dogs, is the sandwich called beef on weck. Several places make a specialty of it. Schwabl's, an old leather-table beef house, is the one we like best. The beef is roasted to the pink, sliced thin, and piled high inside a salty-topped roll that is infused with caraway seeds (known as kummelweck). Unless you want it dry, the man who carves the beef and assembles the sandwich behind the bar dips each half of the roll in natural gravy—not so deeply that the sturdy bread falls apart, but long enough for juice to ooze when you heft the sandwich from the plate. Horseradish, the preferred condiment for beef on weck, is provided at each table and at the bar.

Sparks

210 East 46 St., New York, NY	$$$
(212) 687-4855	£ⅅ

Sparks can be the most satisfying steak house on earth. The quality of food is above reproach: glistening prime steaks are accompanied by mountains of delicious hash brown potatoes or fried onion rings. Start with clams or oysters on the half shell—freshly opened, sweet and briny—along with a few icy martinis, and you'll likely be singing "New York, New York" by the time the cheesecake comes.

The revelers who frequent Sparks are part of the dining experience. They include mobs of suburbanites, genuine wiseguys from the outer boroughs and overcoiffed wiseguy wannabes, insolent city politicians and sports stars, and innocent young couples on big-splurge dates. The people-watching is sensational, a quintessential Gotham experience, but it can be maddening to sit next to a party of twelve from Great Neck singing "Happy Birthday" or a table of preferred regular customers who monopolize your waiters' attention. Much as we love Sparks, there have been times—weekend nights in particular—when we have stormed out wishing we were eating steak in Omaha or Oklahoma City. It all depends on who you sit near and your ability to tolerate the impertinence of New York's big spenders.

As you leave, the limo drivers waiting outside for clients are happy to point out the exact spot on the curb where Gambino family mob boss Paul Castellano and his bodyguard fell when they were bumped off by Gotti henchmen after eating at Sparks on December 16, 1985.

Ted's Jumbo Red Hots

2312 Sheridan Dr., Tonawanda, NY	$
(716) 836-8986	£D

Not to slight the great weenies of Chicago or Detroit, nor of New York City's kosher delis, but the fact is that western New York is probably more fanatical about frankfurters than any other place in the country. From the pale "white hots" of Rochester to the charcoal-grilled red hots of Buffalo, tube steaks are an upstate passion. We think some of the best are dealt by Ted's of Tonawanda (and about a half dozen other locations in the Buffalo area). Ted's dogs come smothered in powerful, peppery relish and sided by hard-crusted onion rings, but what makes them great is the way they are cooked: over coals that infuse each link with pungent smoke flavor and burnish its taut skin with a seared crust. The locally favored drink to accompany a grilled red hot is a loganberry-flavored beverage that tastes like bug juice at sleepaway camp.

Tom's Luncheonette

782 Washington Ave., Brooklyn, NY	$
(718) 636-9738	BL

Last year, Tom's was declared New York's best breakfast restaurant by New York magazine, which praised its "festive atmosphere" as the basis of good karma that make bacon and eggs transcendent. A 1930s-vintage, Formica-clad diner, Tom's attracts Prospect Heights residents early in the morning for banana walnut pancakes, egg sandwiches, grits 'n' eggs, and hot oatmeal. Customers rub elbows and nurse cups of coffee while exchanging pleasantries with the kindly staff. At noon, the place smells of good hot lunch: burgers frying, cheese sandwiches grilling, slabs of meat loaf and slices of beef brisket on plates with swirls of mashed potatoes. Wash down these satisfying meals with fresh lemonade, a cherry-lime rickey, or the classic New York egg cream, made by swirling together just the right amounts of milk, chocolate syrup, and seltzer water.

Totonno's Pizzeria

1524 Neptune Ave., Brooklyn, NY (718) 372-8606	$
Wed–Sun (but may close early)	£ D

In a neighborhood that has disintegrated all around it, Totonno's (pronounced "T-t-own's") remains a true and good neighborhood pizzeria. Dough made fresh each morning is pounded out and topped with slices of creamy mozzarella and fresh tomato sauce. It emerges from the coal-fired brick oven crisp and chewy, with a savor no franchise can touch.

Note the limited hours of this eccentric place. When the day's dough runs out, it closes. Another tip: it is possible to get there by subway, but we recommend driving; and if you take a cab, have the cab wait. Few hacks cruise these war-torn streets.

Submarine-Spotter's Guide

The "hero" sandwich, piled high on a crusty loaf, has variants coast to coast, from the oyster Po' Boy of New Orleans to the lamb-stuffed Fresno sandwich of the San Joaquin Valley. You can eat a "Cuban" in Miami or a "Garibaldi" in Wisconsin, Italian beef in Chicago or French dip in Los Angeles.

Such sandwiches have the most aliases between the Delaware Valley and New London, Connecticut. These are a few names for the jaw-stretching pleasures you'll find along the roads of the Northeast:

LOCAL NAME	WHAT IT IS, WHERE IT'S FOUND
Hoagie (or Hoagy)	Usually signifies cold cuts, lettuce, and tomato, in Pennsylvania
Submarine	Served hot—meatballs or veal Parmesan—with tomato sauce
Wedge	A sub in Westchester County, New York; usually hot
Torpedo	A sub in the Bronx; hot or cold
Zep or Zeppelin	A sub in western Pennsylvania; hot
Grinder	A sub in New England
Bomber	A sub in western New York; hot or cold

PENNSYLVANIA

★ ★ ★

Family Diner

302 Main St., White Haven, PA	$
(717) 443-8797	BLD

A gem just minutes off I-80. There is something for everyone at the Family Diner, from liver and onions or ham steak with a pineapple ring to short-order sandwiches and a giant-size, dolled-up "diner hamburger with a college degree."

The great meal is breakfast, served until 2 pm. Inelegant, ribsticking pancakes are as big as their plate, heaped with hot blueberry or apple topping. Creamed chipped beef is sided by home fries or bite-size potato cakes. Eggs are available any way (including soft-boiled and poached) with a choice of five different kinds of pig meat. In addition to the usual bacon, ham, and sausage, there is luscious pork roll and the even more luscious Pennsylvania treat—scrapple, sizzled to a crisp.

Farnsworth House

401 Baltimore St., Gettysburg, PA	$$
(717) 334-8838	£𝔇

Game pie, country ham, peanut soup, and crocked spoon bread are some of the vintage savories on the evening menu in this old brick home at the most famous battlefield in America. Farnsworth House was in the thick of the fight; more than 100 bullet holes in its south wall bear testimony to the hostilities of the three days in July 1863 during which Confederate snipers occupied what was then the Sweeney family home.

As Civil War–era tunes play (quietly), you dine by candlelight at walnut tables set with heavy pewter service plates and glasses, surrounded by paintings and Matthew Brady photographs of the battle's heros and framed letters written by Generals Lee and Pickett. The game pie is not actually gamy, but a robust melange of shredded pheasant, duck, and turkey mixed into a casserole with mushrooms, bacon, and wild rice and topped with a disk of pastry crust. Pumpkin fritters are an ideal side dish: plump, crunchy fried orbs with melting sweet insides.

Pennsylvania Dutch Delights

Good restaurants that serve Pennsylvania Dutch food are rare. The best place to find many of the local baked goods and preserves is a roadside stand in farm country.

Chicken pie	Stew, not pie, made with large noodle dumplings
Chowchow	Sweet, pickly relish made of corn, beans, onions, etc.
Fastnacht	Raised donut
Funnel cake	Fried pastry, shaped by funneling the batter into hot oil
Filling	Stuffing made from mashed potatoes, and more filling
Funeral pie	Raisin pie
Huddlestrow	A huge pancake that gets chopped up as it cooks
Montgomery pie	Lemon-molasses custard with a layer of cake on top
Rivel soup	A soup made with chicken and corn and tiny noodles
Schnitz und knepp	A meal of smoked ham, apples, and dumplings
Scrapple	Breakfast meat made of pork and cornmeal, then fried
Shoofly pie (dry)	Molasses and crumb coffee cake
Shoofly pie (wet)	Molasses and crumb pie
Streusel kuchen	Raised coffee cake

Jim's Steaks

400 South St., Philadelphia, PA	$
(215) 928-1911	LD

Jim's, since 1939, is a deco-tiled cheese steakery that actually offers a choice of cheeses on your sandwich. Cheese Whiz is standard; if you don't tell the counter people otherwise, your tender beef is globbed with it (which some aficionados contend is the only proper topping), but more refined palates can request provolone or American, laid on in precut slices that turn soft from the warmth of the beef and give the sandwich a relatively epicurean twist. The bread is excellent, the fried onions are appropriately slippery, and the optional hot peppers are breathtaking. Have a Dr. Brown's soda on the side, and you've got a cheap-eats meal to remember.

Little Red Schoolhouse

Rte. 116 and Race Horse Rd., Brushtown, PA	$
(717) 632-0454	B L

Good old-fashioned scrapple is harder and harder to find, but here is a charming little breakfast stop near Gettysburg where it is as delectable as you'll taste anywhere. If scrapple isn't your dish—the cornmeal and pork pudding is a bit too piggy for some—proprietor and cook Sharon Kerchner makes another Pennsylvania treat every morning—creamed chipped beef on toast (or, better yet, on home fried potatoes cooked in a well-seasoned iron skillet). In addition, the pancakes are superb and the coffee is tasty. These good meals are served in a former classroom decorated with antique cookware; daily specials are written in chalk on the old blackboard.

Mama's

426 Belmont Ave., Bala-Cynwyd, PA	$
(610) 664-4757	L D

In an unlikely suburban pizzeria with help that actually verges on being polite (heresy!), you find superb cheese steak sandwiches. Lengths of delicious fresh Italian bread are piled with shaved beef that is well spiced and luxuriously juicy and laced with plump ribbons of sweet sautéed onions, then draped with a layer of provolone cheese. For forty years now, Mama's has been making this Philly classic, not to be missed by anyone in search of cheap-eats greatness.

America's Fine Diners

A great diner is like great art: hard to define, but you know it when you see it. The classic examples feature gleaming stainless steel fixtures and a well-worn counter arrayed with thick crockery plates and coffee mugs; but even nontraditional diners have a sassy attitude all their own.

In a diner, no supercilious waiter is going to tell you his first name and arch an eyebrow if you order your chicken croquettes and volcano-shaped mashed potatoes with double gravy; instead, you'll likely deal with a good ol' gal in orthopedic shoes with a starched hankie pinned to her bosom and a spiel like some sort of culinary evangelist. She'll call you "Hon" and slap down your check when she brings your dish full of wiggling red Jell-O for dessert.

At its best, diner duisine is as sincere as Forrest Gump: pot roast, pork chops, and breakfasts featuring mountains of fried potatoes. The problem faced by hungry travelers is that not all diners live up to their reputation as the place savvy truckers go for excellent food. (Anyway, who anointed teamsters as *bec fins*?) Even some of the most beautiful ones, the art-deco roadside attractions with floors made of tiny octagon tiles and gracefully curved barrel roofs, sometimes dish out chow reminiscent more of bad school lunch than of Mom's home cooking.

Olivieri's Prince of Steaks

Reading Terminal Market, 12th and Arch Sts., Philadelphia,	$
PA (215) 925-4320; Reading Market general information	£
number (215) 922-2317	

Cheese steak connoisseurship is a complex passion. Is the beef tender? You don't want it gristly, but beef that is *too* fine or fancy works against the outlaw savor of this most impudent of street sandwiches. Is the bread fresh? (It must be.) Is the cheese plebeian? (Deluxe cheese would be ridiculous.) Most important, is the service brash? One place you can answer an unqualified yes to all these vital questions is Olivieri's, where the bustle and commotion of the Reading Terminal

There are gleaming diners nearly everywhere in the U.S., but most of them are in the Northeast, where they are manufactured. This honor roll is not simply a list of the beauties. In fact, many of our favorite diners are *not* silver stream-liners. But they are all places that have real diner soul and serve true diner meals.

☛ <u>Clarksville Diner</u>, Decorah, IA (p. 191)
☛ <u>Durango Diner</u>, Durango, CO (p. 264)
☛ <u>Family Diner</u>, White Haven, PA (p. 70)
☛ <u>Jigger's Diner</u>, East Greenwich, RI (p. 35)
☛ <u>Miss Wakefield Diner</u>, Sanbornville, NH (p. 29)
☛ <u>Norma's Café</u>, Farmer's Branch, TX (p. 299)
☛ <u>Orem's Diner</u>, Wilton, CT (p. 7)
☛ <u>O'Rourke's</u>, Middletown, CT (p. 8)
☛ <u>Silver Spur Café</u>, Sheridan, WY (p. 251)
☛ <u>Wasp's Snack Bar</u>, Woodstock, VT (p. 41)
☛ <u>Yankee Doodle</u>, New Haven, CT (p. 12)

Market provide just the right background for ingesting the regal sandwich that is Philadelphia's greatest contribution to American gastronomy.

Pat's King of Steaks

1237 E. Passyunk Ave., Philadelphia, PA (215) 468-1546	$
always open	

One of America's great sandwiches was invented at this ultraurban food stand in 1930: the Philly cheese steak, a mountain of shaved beef, sopped with gravy and laced with slippery onions, piled into a good Italian loaf and gobbed with molten Cheese Whiz. Nothing could be finer, especially at 3 am under harsh fluorescent lights, standing on a sidewalk (no tables here) where, according to a brass plaque, Sylvester Stallone once stood and ate.

Primanti Brothers	
46 W. 18th St., Pittsburgh, PA (412) 263-2142	**$**
always open	

Pittsburghers like mixed-up food. Steak salad is a favorite local meal: chopped beef nestled in lettuce and garnished with French fries; ham is deliriously "chipped-chopped" for sandwiches; and often times French fries, cole slaw, and tomatoes are heaped inside the bread right with the meat. The place that invented the latter configuration is Primanti's, an open-all-night joint in the produce district. A gigantic fry and slaw stuffed ham sandwich at about 2 am in the company of fruit haulers, swing-shift factory personnel, and glazed-eyed night owls, is a dining experience no other city on earth can match.

Shank & Evelyn's	
932 South 10th St., Philadelphia, PA (215) 629-1093	**$**
Tues–Sat	**฿£**

Great only-in-Philly neighborhood Italian food, with plenty of attitude, is what you'll get at the counter and tables of this family-run luncheonette. Homemade? Don't ask! Of course it's all homemade, and lovingly so: the meatballs, the veal scallopini, the eggplant parmigiana, the juicy chicken cutlet sandwiches on good bread topped with broccoli rabe, the pasta e fagioli soup. Breakfast is more ordinary bacon-and-egg fare, but the ebb and flow of characters at the counter and behind it is even more fun when the day is new and the coffee is strong.

Mid-South

ALL-AMERICAN

KENTUCKY

NORTH CAROLINA

TENNESSEE

VIRGINIA

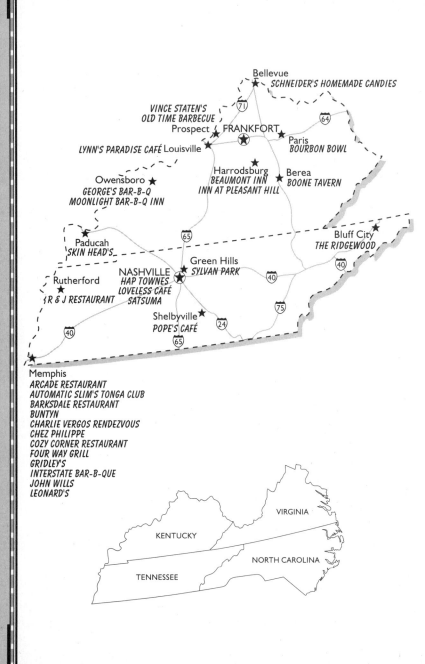

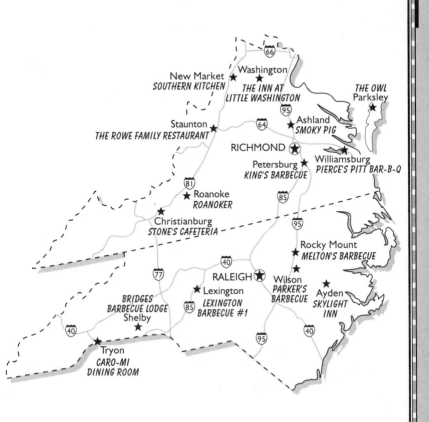

New Market
SOUTHERN KITCHEN

Washington
★
*THE INN AT
LITTLE WASHINGTON*

THE OWL
Parksley

Staunton
THE ROWE FAMILY RESTAURANT

Ashland
SMOKY PIG

RICHMOND ★

Petersburg ★
KING'S BARBECUE

Williamsburg
PIERCE'S PITT BAR-B-Q

Roanoke
ROANOKER

Christianburg
STONE'S CAFETERIA

Rocky Mount
MELTON'S BARBECUE

RALEIGH ★

Lexington
*LEXINGTON
BARBECUE #1*

Wilson
*PARKER'S
BARBECUE*

Ayden
*SKYLIGHT
INN*

*BRIDGES
BARBECUE LODGE*
Shelby

Tryon
*CARO-MI
DINING ROOM*

MID-SOUTH

KENTUCKY

☆ ☆ ☆

Beaumont Inn

638 Beaumont Inn Dr., Harrodsburg, KY (606) 734-3381	*$$*
(reservations suggested)	*LD*

Formerly a finishing school for young ladies in the sweet small town of Harrodsburg, the Beaumont Inn is now a refined plantation-style hostelry. The setting is serene, service is courtly, guest accommodations are spacious and tasteful, and in the dining room, the two-year-cured smoked country ham, served with biscuits and corn pudding, and sweet layer cake for dessert, is a Dixie paradigm.

Boone Tavern

Rte. 25, Berea, KY (606) 986-9358	*$$*
(dress code in the evening)	*BLD*

Dinner at the Boone Tavern wants to be gracious (men need jackets, which the house will supply if you come without one), but the enthusiasm and occasional uncertainty of the staff, who are mostly students from Appalachia working their way through Berea College, make the occasion a beguiling mixture of formality and fun. The evening meal begins with warm spoon bread, fluffy as a soufflé, then moves into an eclectic repertoire that features upscale mountain-home cooking: cured ham with sweet lemon sauce, chicken flakes Elsinore in a crisp potato nest, Kentucky turkey with fresh cranberry relish, and fried chicken so neatly cooked you actually want to eat it with a fork and knife.

Country Ham

Country ham is an acquired taste that, once acquired, nothing else will satisfy. Certainly not a blubbery pale pink canned ham, and not even a fine Italian prosciutto, although that can come close. Authentic country ham is a treat as precious as caviar or truffles, with a salty resonance so intense that it must be sliced thin; even then, its wallop is often muffled inside a buttermilk biscuit.

The salt smack veils a subtle, fetching flavor that titillates the tongue and awakes that special fascination that tastebuds have for flavors that teeter on the good side of rot. Like old, veined cheese or slow-risen sourdough, a slice of country ham is exciting, even a little wild. Its muscular personality is developed by a primitive curing process that cannot be quickened or modernized—at least six months of labor-intensive curing in a ham house, during which the ham is rubbed with salt, then allowed to "sweat," meaning lose moisture and develop its wonderful rank flavor. All this time, the ham man keeps track of the progress, plunging his pick deep inside each ham and sniffing what's there to make sure the meat is on its way to perfection.

Many hams are smoked after several months' hanging. Originally, smoke was a way of keeping flies away, but the taste of burning hickory adds an extra savor to the meat that some connoisseurs find irresistible.

The easiest way to indulge in country ham is in a restaurant, where the chef does all the hard work of scraping off the mold, soaking, sawing, and boiling that a whole one requires. Some good ham stops in the Mid-South include

- Beaumont Inn, Harrodsburg, KY (p. 80)
- Caro-Mi Dining Room, Tryon, NC (p. 86)
- Four Way Grill, Memphis, TN (p. 95)
- Loveless Café, Nashville, TN (p. 100)
- Pope's Café, Shelbyville, TN (p. 101)
- Roanoker, Roanoke, VA (p. 108)

Bourbon Bowl

Hwy. 68, south of Paris, KY	$
(606) 987-3161	D

If the red pin appears in your lane on Saturday night and you roll a strike, the game is free. The cuisine at this snack bar is as straightforward as the place itself, and exactly as it was nearly forty years ago when the Bourbon Bowl first opened. For a hot cheeseburger and a cold beer to the sound of crashing ten pins, there's not a nicer place on earth.

George's Bar-B-Q

1346 East Fourth St., Owensboro, KY	$
(502) 926-9276	BLD

George's pit-cooked mutton is one reason Owensboro can make a legitimate claim to its title as the "Bar-B-Q Capital of the World." In this humble place, where a country and western jukebox provides suitable background music, the long-smoked lamb, cut into shreds, is juicy and high-flavored, imbued with powerhouse sauce. The Q menu also includes pork shoulder or ribs, beef, ham, and chicken; but the one other dish you need to know about is burgoo. A western Kentucky specialty originally brought from Wales (via Virginia, where its modern progeny is now known as Brunswick stew), burgoo began as hunter's potluck containing the varmint du jour. George's burgoo is thick with shreds of smoky mutton, vegetables, and an explosive dose of spice. No varmints that we could see.

Inn at Pleasant Hill

3500 Lexington Rd., Harrodsburg, KY	$$
(606) 734-5411	BLD

The last of the Shakers died in 1923, and their Kentucky paradise lay idle until it was restored as a hotel and historical landmark in the 1960s. Guest rooms are furnished with reproduction furniture (plus phones, showers, and TVs), and they smell of the hewn wood of which they're made. It is impossible to describe the tranquillity that settles in the evening when you stroll the pathways among the solid brick buildings. Cattle low in nearby fields, an owl hoots overhead, a faint clatter is heard from the kitchen in the Trustees' House dining room, where cherrywood tables are set with candles in hurricane lamps.

Shakers ate well because they needed fuel for all the hard work they did (and also, one supposes, as a substitute pleasure for the sex they weren't allowed to have). Choose from such entrees as crisp fried chicken, aged country ham, and turkey with dressing made from Shaker sage. Relishes, hot corn sticks, and vegetables, including a luscious salsify casserole, are served in bowls that get passed around the table family-style. To end this meal, there is a fine chess pie or the classic Shaker specialty, lemon pie, which is an eye-opening little wedge of supreme sweetness and sour citrus tang. There is no liquor or wine served; the Shakers weren't tipplers, and anyway, Shakertown's county is dry.

Lynn's Paradise Café

984 Barret Ave., Louisville, KY (502) 583-3447	$
Tues–Sun, D Thur–Sat	BL

Once a grocery store, now a folksy café, Lynn's dishes up satisfying plates of meat loaf and mashed potatoes, fried chicken, and glorious black bean chili over rice, as well as a repertoire of first-class hamburgers. Breakfast is the great meal of the day, served until the end of lunch hour at 2 pm. You can eat perfectly respectable plates of eggs, grits, and biscuits or opt for more exotic fare, which usually includes such taste wonders as fruit-sauced tropical French toast, bourbon-ball

French toast, or banana split pancakes. Our best memory is of a sausage-pepper-egg scramble loaded with kielbasa, sided by delightful buttermilk biscuits and baked apple slices.

Moonlight Bar-b-q Inn	
2840 W. Parrish, Owensboro, KY	$
(502) 684-8143	£𝔇

The Moonlight is the best place to eat barbecued mutton, which is western Kentucky's favorite smoke house meat. It is strong-flavored stuff with more oomph than beef, certainly more than pork, but the long cooking process insinuates enough smoke to turn it wonderfully tender.

Mutton at the Moonlight is served at a vast buffet that also includes barbecued pork and beef, lots of southern-style vegetables, and the local melting-pot stew known as burgoo. Once your plate is piled high, you can choose among several degrees of hot sauce to further adorn the meat; but good as the sauces are, we like the basic stuff that the mutton comes with . . . all the better to savor its unique tang.

Schneider's Homemade Candies	
420 Fairfield Ave., Bellevue, KY	$
(606) 431-3545	£𝔇

If, like us, you consider it your duty to find (and eat) all of America's greatest caramel apples, you need to know about Schneider's. Crisp and fresh, gooey but edible without utensils, these mighty orbs-on-a-stick are apple epiphanies. Since 1939, the old-fashioned sweet shop on Route 8 has also been known for dainty cream-centered chocolates called opera creams (made only around Christmas) as well as ice ball ice cream, which is a scoop of homemade vanilla packed in ice, enveloped in syrup—a summertime favorite.

Skin Head's

1021 S. Twenty-First St., Paducah, KY	$
(502) 442-6471	BLD

Don't be alarmed by the name of this fine restaurant. It predates the era of talk-show neo-Nazis and refers to the bald noggin of the founder. "Remember now," the menu says, "short, fat, thin, or tall, 'Ole Skin Head' will try to feed y'all." We have been fans of Skin Head's hot grits and country ham with red-eye gravy since we first hit the road more than two decades ago. We love the big, puffy biscuits for breakfast and the skillet-fried catfish or brittle-crisp pork tenderloin sandwich at lunch. There isn't a more satisfying place to eat for miles around than at a rickety booth in this friendly "breakfast house of the South."

Vince Staten's Old Time Barbecue

9219 US 42, Prospect, KY	$
(502) 228-7427	LD

Vince Staten wrote the book on barbecue. Literally. *Real Barbecue,* which he co-authored with Greg Johnson several years ago, is a fine guide to smoke house meals from coast to coast. His expertise is reflected in his restaurant's menu, which includes seven different sauces inspired by American regional barbecue from "Texas Sweet" and "Tennessee Jack [Daniel's]" to "Legal Limit Hot Sauce" and one ultrahot one called "Death to Amateurs." The meat is far-ranging too: pulled pork, chicken, or beef, plus baby back ribs cooked Memphis-dry style (rubbed with spice). On the side there are saucy barbecue beans, corn on the cob, baked potato, or a dish called "I fought the slaw and the slaw won."

It isn't exactly an unspoiled, in-the-rough barbecue eating experience, but the sense of play and the extra amenities are welcome. We especially like the fact that Vince has a dessert menu (a rarity in most monomaniacal barbecue joints). The banana pudding is a Mid-South classic, and there is a similar one made with Oreo cookies. And, because this truly is a southern eat shack, there is moon pie.

NORTH CAROLINA

Bridges Barbecue Lodge

Hwy. 74 Bypass, Shelby, NC	$
(704) 482-8567	£D

Bridges has the stripped-down, meditative atmosphere of the South's finest pork parlors. When we entered, we saw a sure sign of smoke house excellence: five police officers at a table toward the back. Cops are an infallible guide to roadside food in all parts of the country; plates piled high with pork, these lawmen conversed in hushed tones, as if it would be sacrilegious to be raucous in this decent eat-place.

There is no formal menu, just the slip of paper used by the waitress to take orders. You can get a sandwich, a tray, or a plate. A tray is barbecue and barbecue slaw; a plate also holds French fries, lettuce, tomato, and pickle. Both are accompanied by a basket of hush puppies, and whether you select sandwich, tray, or plate, you will have to decide if you want your meat chopped or sliced. It is a big decision: chopped meat is hacked into moist hash with some shreds of chewy crust, held together by a smidgen of tomato-based sauce with a strong vinegar tang. Sliced barbecue comes as big, soft flaps, mostly white, as tender as pork can be, just barely laced with the fragrance of the smoke pit.

Caro-Mi Dining Room

1433 Hwy. 176 N., Tryon, NC (704) 859-5200	$$
Wed–Sun	D

As you wet your whistle from the relish tray, proprietor Charles Stafford explains the menu. He almost sings when he talks about his steaks, boasting that they are aged four weeks. The shrimps are big ones, he gloats, boiled and peeled with loving care. Rainbow trout is another house specialty, pan sautéed in butter to a parchment crisp. "Ours is real country ham," Stafford beams. "It is cured with salt—just enough—and brown sugar." If more than one person at the table orders ham, it is served family-style, stacked on a platter. It comes with grits and red-eye gravy, pork-speckled green beans, and sweet, slow-cooked apples.

The best part of a meal at Caro-Mi just may be the afterglow. When you are done with dessert (congenial things such as butterscotch or chocolate sundae or strawberry shortcake made atop a biscuit), step outside to the wide front porch where a dozen rocking chairs are marshaled in a row. Have a seat. Rock a spell. Listen to the river flow and the twilight crickets chirp. Maybe it isn't heaven, but this little spot in

Elvis Presley's Favorite Pound Cake

Canelle McComb, who was Elvis's friend from the time he was a lad in Tupelo, Mississippi, used to bake two loaves of this cake every Christmas and bring them to Graceland. On a good day, Elvis could eat one all by himself. He shared the other with his entourage.

3 cups sugar
1/2 pound butter, softened
7 eggs, room temperature
3 cups cake flour, sifted twice (do not use "self-rising" flour)
1 cup heavy cream (not whipped)
2 teaspoons vanilla extract

Thoroughly butter and flour a 10-inch tube pan.
Cream together the sugar and butter.
Add eggs one at a time, beating extremely well after each addition. Mix in half the flour, then the whipping cream, then the other half of the flour. Beat 5 full minutes. Add vanilla.
Pour batter into the prepared pan. Set in *cold* oven and turn heat to 350°. Bake 1 hour to 90 minutes, until a sharp knife inserted in cake comes out clean. Cool in the pan 5 minutes. Remove the cake from the pan and cool thoroughly. Wrapped well in aluminum foil, this cake keeps several days.

the western hills of North Carolina will do just fine until it is time to try the macaroni salad at the Pearly Gates buffet up yonder.

Lexington Barbecue #1	
10 Hwy. 29–70 S, Lexington, NC (910) 249-9814	**$**
Mon–Sat	**£ 𝔇**

L exington is a major barbecue town, with well over a dozen places serving hickory-smoked pork bathed in a vinegar-tomato sauce that teeters delectably between sweet and hot. Lexington #1, formerly known as Honey Monk's, is the daddy of 'em all. Its barbecue is hacked into a fine, tender hash peppered with crisp pieces from the outside of the roast, served in buns with fine cole slaw or as half of a platter along with crunchy hush puppies. The platters are easy to eat in your car: the sauced pig meat and hush pups are packed into a small cardboard boat, sort of like a trough.

Melton's Barbecue	
631 Ridge St., Rocky Mount, NC	**$**
(919) 446-8513	**£ 𝔇**

M elton's is a lazy-looking place on a shady street overlooking a muddy river. Its specialty is North Carolina–style barbecue, which means elegant, ambrosial pork. A Melton's "pig pickin'" begins with a palate-teaser of tart mustard slaw, then moves directly to heaps of meat that is amazing for its textural variety: moist, motley shreds, velvet-soft chunks, and succulent "outside" nuggets crusted with basting juice. The pork arrives with hush puppies, Brunswick stew, and potatoes, but it is unsauced—all the better to savor its porcine subtleties. Those who want to gild it concoct their own sauce from an assortment of Tabasco, pickled peppers, vinegar, and hot condiments set at every place. Eating at an unclothed table in this wood-paneled dining room helps you understand why native North Carolinians get overwhelmed with emotion on the subject of barbecue, and why Melton's is a culinary legend.

Parker's Barbecue

US 301, Wilson, NC	$
(919) 237-0972	**£ℑ**

A barbecue barn, an eating institution, a tarheel pork parlor to be reckoned with, Parker's is one grand roadside attraction. It is loud, noisy, and crowded, and the meals it serves are huge and porky. Barbecue feasts are its claim to fame: chopped meat piled high, boiled potatoes, corn dodgers, and cole slaw, all served individually or in family-style bowls, accompanied by iced tea. The pork is pale and exquisite, with a thin vinegar sauce nothing like the opaque ketchupy emulsions used on pig meat west of Lexington. It is said that this style sauce goes back to a time when cooks shunned tomatoes as poisonous. Whether or not that's true, Parker's barbecue is just the way people in this part of North Carolina have liked it for centuries.

Skylight Inn

South Lee St., Ayden, NC	$
(919) 746-4113	**£ℑ**

Coarse-shredded pork that has been tenderized and perfumed by wood smoke is served with just a soupçon of hot sauce, on a bun or on a cardboard tray with cole slaw and corn bread. Pete Jones's renowned barbecue is a simple meal about as close to perfection as pork gets, an archetypal taste of the downhome style of pig-pickin' unique to coastal North Carolina.

TENNESSEE

✩ ✩ ✩

540 South Main, Memphis, TN	$
(901) 526-5757	BLD

Take the trolley to the end of the line and travel to Memphis fifty years ago. Actually, this big old town lunchroom goes back further, to 1919, but its interior decor and its menu suggest mid-century America. Well-worn boomerang-pattern Formica adorns the long counter. In the second dining room, panoramic black-and-white pictures show a long-ago bustling downtown Memphis, and a vintage sign advertises a "steak plate dinner," with drink, for forty cents.

The kitchen is a cache of southern probity, offering a rotating array of such plate lunch stalwarts as meat loaf and gravy, baked chicken with wild rice, pork chops, and (always) roast beef au jus. With each entree, you choose two vegetables from a daily array of a dozen; or you can do as we often do, which is make a lunch of three or four vegetables without meat. It's not that the meat is bad—we love the fried chicken every Thursday and Monday's meat loaf—but the vegetables are sensational. Yams are deep, dark orange, bathed in syrup; mashed potatoes are stout, smooth, and laced with butter; macaroni and cheese is served with plenty of patches of chewy cheese among the softer stuff; and turnip greens are limp, leafy, and pungent. And there are sticks of corn bread with a delectable golden crunch of a crust and a faintly sour milk tang inside.

A humble restaurant, an everyday kind of place, but such unaffected food is a national treasure.

Automatic Slim's Tonga Club

83 S. Second, Memphis, TN (901) 525-7948	*$$*
(reservations suggested)	*LD*

Where hip Memphis dines and drinks. Named for a Beale Street bluesman and a teen hangout popular in the rockabilly era, this tongue-in-cheeky joint (cacti and coyotes! zebra-skin upholstery!) is not so silly when it comes to food. Fusing Caribbean and southwestern tastes with the soul of the South, it creates such festive meals as shrimp sheathed in a coconut mango crust, crisp whole red snapper with jalapeño relish, and Jamaican jerk duck with sun-dried cranberries. Slim's also happens to be one of the few places in town where a vegetarian can eat well, and the Tonga martini (vodka with a fruit infusion) is as easy to imbibe as lemonade.

Barksdale Restaurant

237 S. Cooper, Memphis, TN (901) 722-2193	*$*
but only until 6 pm	*BLD*

Most Memphians think of this wood-paneled corner café for lunch—square meals such as pork chops (every Monday), country-fried steak (Wednesday and Thursday), and catfish (Friday) accompanied by a trio of well-cooked vegetables and followed by lemon icebox pie, banana pudding, or peach cobbler. You can't go wrong.

Barksdale breakfast is a treasure, too: aromatic country ham that is resilient but easy to slice, served with red-eye gravy to spoon on grits or dunk your biscuit in. Peppery milk gravy is also available, and it is superb.

The wall is lined with signed pictures of Barksdale fans who have 8 × 10 glossies to send, including musicians, local celebrities, and a few Elvis impersonators. Each inscribed the photo with a sentiment. One handsome face we didn't recognize wrote, *Thanks for the gravy fix!*

Buntyn

3070 Southern, Memphis, TN (901) 458-8776	$
Mon–Fri only	£ D

When we walked in Buntyn's door at 11 am, the staff stood circled around a table in the front room, their heads lowered and hands joined as young Bill Wiggins led them in a prayer, asking God to help them bring joy into customers' lives. These people *believe* in what they do; and we guarantee that if you like good southern food, they will make a believer out of you.

Who couldn't love a waitress who begins a meal by telling her table what's available in words that sound to us like plate-lunch haiku:

> We've got corned beef and cabbage
> Gizzards and rice.
> The okra's boiled
> And corn's on the cob.

Home cooking better than Mom's is served on unbreakable partitioned plates. Shattering crisp fried chicken; crusty fried steak; soulful meat loaf in tomato sauce—such entrees are blue-plate paradigms. We would kill for that fried chicken, but it is their vegetables and side dishes that win our eternal loyalty. There is a list of well over a dozen to choose from every day, from pungent turnip greens and purple hull peas to macaroni and cheese, buttered squash, and dripping-sweet candied yams. Lime cream salad is a baroque jaw-dropper: sweet, creamy, pistachio-colored Jell-O packed with nuts and chunks of pineapple. Every meal comes with triangles of moist corn bread and/or the world's best hot-from-the-oven dinner rolls.

P.S.: Buntyn desserts are exquisite. Coconut meringue pie, rising a jiggly six inches above the plate, and lemon icebox pie on a bed of crumbs are always on the menu. There is a different fruit cobbler every day, and Wednesday is banana pudding day.

Meat-and-Three

Cafés throughout mid-Tennessee serve a midday meal known as meat-and-three. Customers choose one meat and three vegetables from the day's list, and the meal is generally served on a heavy unbreakable plate with raised partitions to keep the collard green juices from running into the yam casserole. Meat-and-three is always accompanied by biscuits or corn bread and a tall glass of tea, and generally followed by pie, pudding, or cobbler.

In our experience, the quality of the meat may vary, but the vegetables are almost always spectacularly southern, which means well-cooked, hog-jowl flavored, vigorously seasoned, cheese-enriched, bread crumb-gilded, and margarine-sopped. That is why many customers opt for meat-and-three without the meat, meaning an all-vegetable plate of three or four selections.

Charlie Vergos Rendezvous

52 S. Second St., Memphis, TN	$$
(enter through General Washburn Alley)	D
(901) 523-2746	

This vast underground cavern of a beer hall with red-checked tablecloths and walls loaded with vintage Memphiana is a legend of American porklore. It is a good-times place ruled over by a staff of charmingly brusque waiters, mobbed with barbecue pilgrims and tourists. Midafternoon, when the kitchen gets in gear, the Rendezvous broadcasts the scent of sizzling, smoky meat throughout a significant part of downtown, even into the lobby of the Peabody Hotel across the street. The kitchen's main attraction is ribs, which are prepared with a "dry rub" rather than a wet sauce; thus their succulence is sealed inside a dizzyingly spiced coat. Pork shoulder and pork loin are less aggressively seasoned than the ribs, which will leave you parched till morning, and the pork shoulder sandwich is a classic.

Note: The Rendezvous ships ribs, sauce, and seasoning. Call 1-800-827-RIBS.

Chez Philippe

in the Peabody Hotel, 149 Union, Memphis, TN	$$$
(901) 529-4188	D

Much as we enjoy them, we haven't included many hotel restaurants in this book, directing our attention toward more adventurous dining experiences. But it would be a shame to eat one's way around Memphis without a taste of the swankest possible variations of mid-southern cooking, as created by chef Jose Gutierrez of the Peabody's Chez Philippe. Put on your bib and tucker, polish up your credit card, and prepare to enjoy a grand, genuinely interesting, and finally delicious meal created by fusing Memphis tradition with modern culinary technique: hush puppies stuffed with shrimp Provençale, smoked pork tenderloin with fried green tomatoes and grits pilaf, smoked sweet potatoes to accompany venison loin à la Choctaw, and marinated shrimp accompanied by sugarcane and wondrous persimmon ketchup. All of this is served with grace and high style in a posh room in a truly grand hotel.

Cozy Corner Restaurant

745 N. Parkway, Memphis, TN	$
(901) 527-9158	L D

Fluorescent lights, wood paneling, a large order area, and a few tables in a small dining room: all are signs of barbecue excellence, further suggested by the aroma of hickory burning in the pit oven, and utterly confirmed when you ease your teeth into a chunk of pitmaster Raymond Robinson's sublime pork shoulder. Sprinkled with plenty of pepper as it cooks, the meat develops a wicked blackened crust, which is not only savory itself but also performs the function of sealing in juices. Piled into a sandwich with a bit of cole slaw (that is the Memphis way), it is one of the most delicious things a person can eat—sloppy, drippy, lip-tingling hot, and downright sexy. Such supreme succulence is what makes Memphis the pork capital of America, and there is no better place to wallow in that fact than the Cozy Corner.

Ribs are sensational, too, big and meaty, and Mr. Robinson

makes a specialty of barbecued Cornish hens and turkeys. The former are elegant little fowls with crisp mahogany skin and meat that pulls off the bone in soft, savory shreds. On the side comes good barbecued beans or profoundly soulful barbecued spaghetti—slim, droopy noodles bathed in smoky sauce.

Dining at the Cozy Corner, or just ordering food here to take out, is a delightful experience. Mrs. Robinson, the chef's mother, frequently holds court on a couch near the order counter where she greets customers and carries on conversations with them and the restaurant staff, which she boasts is three generations of Robinsons. When we order a barbecued baloney sandwich (a thick oinky disk of meat, bathed in ultrahot sauce), she exclaims, "That is my son's favorite!" then asks a man behind the counter, "Richard, what is your favorite?"

"Rib tips," he replies.

"Mm-hm," she agrees. "I love them, too." She points to a row of effulgent aloe vera plants growing in former spice buckets along the window. "You see those plants," she says to a stranger. "They have been here for years. Look how healthy they are. They thrive on smoke from the barbecue."

Four Way Grill

| 998 Mississippi, Memphis, TN | $ |
| (901) 775-2351 | BLD |

Most people who eat here are African-Americans; they come for dripping-good, crunch-crusted fried chicken and such other expertly prepared soul food as buffalo fish with buttered rice and okra or baked chicken and dressing with turnip greens and yams, followed by supersweet peach cobbler.

Four Way is a neighborhood café, where regulars feel so at home they watch TV while they eat. The tube is set up on the counter, and one recent morning when we came for breakfast, folks at several tables were engrossed in the Audie Murphy movie *Sierra* as they ate pork chops or country ham. On one wall a portrait of three famous ministers of the Church of God in Christ is headlined AMERICAN IMMORTALS . . . MAKERS OF HISTORY . . . BUILDERS OF INTERRACIAL GOOD WILL. And the fact is, good will prevails in this little eat shop, which used to have a sign on another wall forbidding profanity.

Although fried chicken is a signature dish, we like breakfast at the Four Way best, mostly because the kitchen makes the most wonderful red-eye gravy with country ham. The ham itself is good and smelly, at a point of maximum savor, and rugged enough to require a sharp knife. Impolite food, for sure, but how fully it rewards a good chew. The gravy, presented in a little bowl, is nothing but rendered fat from this ham—amber, speckled with bits of meat and spice, and just a little thicker than water. It is the most delectable liquid on earth—pure, piggy fat, as rich as liquid bacon. Spooned onto rice or as a dip for biscuits, it is the pinnacle of culinary luxury—even if it is served in a modest Memphis café with an old Audie Murphy movie playing on the counter television.

Gridley's	
6065 Macon, Memphis, TN (901) 388-7003	**$$**
there are other Gridley's in Memphis, but the	**£D**
"satellite" stores have a limited menu	

Gridley's ritual barbecue meal always begins with bread—buttery little loaves that resemble the prefab ones served by some slothful restaurants but are in fact freshly baked and hot from the oven, and barbecue's ideal companion. Use them to mop a plate, cushion shreds of pork, and salve a tongue on fire from too much hot sauce.

You probably want to save all your appetite for pork, which is what Gridley's does best, but we must tell you that the seafood gumbo is a sensation—loaded with crabmeat, chunks of shrimp, and vegetables, served over rice, and deliriously spiced.

Slow cooked over coals, the pork is moist and savory, available as shoulder meat that is chopped (nearly pulverized) or pulled (variegated shreds and hunks), or on the rib. It is mild, delicate-flavored meat . . . until you pour on some of Gridley's roaring-hot barbecue sauce, which will make your lips and tongue glow.

Barbecue salad is a regional oddity and yet another way to honor pork. A bed of cool lettuce is covered with large and small chunks of pulled pork shoulder that is lukewarm. On the side you get a cup of thick blue cheese dressing. And you can get barbecued pizza, too, topped with tomato sauce and shreds of pulled pork: what's not to like about that?

Also recommended: bar-b-q shrimp, which are served peel 'em and eat 'em–style with a buttery dipping sauce. And most wonderful of all, Mrs. Gridley's lemon icebox pie. Made with fresh lemons, it is extremely tart but also extremely sweet. Precisely what a tongue craves after a bout with barbecue of such grand character.

Hap Townes

493 Humphrey St., Nashville, TN	$
(615) 242-7035	£

Hap Townes has been Nashville's plate lunch mecca for more than half a century, serving what locals call meat-and-three: pick one meat and three vegetables from a daily list of about a dozen choices. The vegetables include silk-textured butter beans shimmering in their juices, peppery puffs of hominy, sheaves of limp steamed cabbage with a jolt of fatback flavor, tomatoes stewed with shreds of toasted bread and sugar until the whole melange becomes a zesty relish, apples cooked with cinnamon so they transform into translucent caramel candy, mashed potatoes seasoned and swirled into a lumpy mound, and toothsome stewed raisins. There is always corn bread—a griddle-cooked tan oval cake with a fetching sour tang of buttermilk; and the choice of meats includes country fried steak smothered in gravy, roast beef smothered in gravy, and chicken 'n' dumplings served in a bowl of thick, sunny gravy.

Service is buffet-style. When you enter the tiny restaurant you walk up to a short counter connected to the open kitchen. Make your choice, and a member of the staff dips your plate. In Tennessee, to "dip a plate" is to pile it high with food straight from the pan and kettle. Find a table and commence eating; if you want seconds, return to the counter and get more. When finished, stand up and tell the person at the cash register what you ate and pay accordingly.

Things That Are Barbecued in Memphis

Memphis, Tennessee, is America's pork capital, with boundless variations on the duo of smoky pig meat and sweet sauce.

<u>Wet ribs</u> Glazed with enough spicy red sauce to require many napkins and moist towelettes

<u>Dry ribs</u> Rubbed with seasoning that forms a dry crust enveloping succulent meat

<u>Pig sandwich</u> Pork pulled off the smoked shoulder, drenched with tangy sauce and embellished with cole slaw in a broad bun

<u>Barbecue pizza</u> Hacked, shredded, sauced pork atop cheese and crust

<u>Barbecue spaghetti</u> Limp noodles in zesty sauce (meatless), served as a side dish like barbecued beans, often with barbecue cole slaw (cabbage salad with sauce)

<u>Barbecue salad</u> Similar to a chef's salad, but with chunks of pork instead of ham and turkey on the lettuce, topped with cool barbecue sauce or salad dressing or both

<u>Barbecue shrimp</u> Usually served "u-peel-'em" style, sopped with a buttery version of the house barbecue sauce—an unholy, irresistible mess to eat

<u>Hot links</u> Thick, porcine sausages glazed with sauce

<u>Turkeys and Cornish hens</u> Fabulous specialties of the Cozy Corner (p. 94)

Interstate Bar-B-Que

2265 S. Third St., Memphis, TN	$
(901) 775-2304	**LD**

Inside and out, Interstate is perfumed by smoke from slow-sizzling barbecue. A modest-looking pork house serving ribs, shoulder meat, sausages, and bologna with all the proper fixin's, including addictive bar-b-q spaghetti (soft noodles in breathtaking sauce), it is a jewel in the crown of Memphis pits. Eat at a table in the simple dining room where a "Wall of Fame" boasts critics' accolades and 8 × 10s from celebrity fans; or enter next door and get it to go, by the sandwich, plate, or whole slab of ribs.

When you lift a rib, meat slides off the bone. It is chewy with a deep savor haloed by the perfume of wood smoke. Chopped pork shoulder has a few crusty outside shreds and tatters among the pillowy pile of interior meat; slices are less gooped with sauce, and not as messy, but not as succulent, either. A large chopped pork sandwich is the most Memphian dish on the menu, made as per local custom with a layer of cool cole slaw atop the well-sauced meat—a total mess that disintegrates as you eat it.

John Wills

5101 Sanderlin, Memphis, TN	$
(901) 761-5101	**LD**

John Wills's pork shoulder is tender as cream. It is cut into chunks and served as part of a plate with saucy barbecued beans, an eye-opening mustard slaw, and bread; or you can get a sandwich spread with slaw and sauce. We also like the ribs, sausage, barbecue spaghetti, and barbecued bologna that is more succulent than any other pit-cooked food except perhaps the snoots of St. Louis.

Warning: John Wills is suspiciously civilized. There is actual decor on the wood-paneled walls (portraits of pigs) and silverware at every place (wrapped in paper napkins). Despite such niceness, however, Mr. Wills purveys some mean barbecue.

Leonard's

5465 Fox Plaza Dr., Memphis, TN	$
(901) 360-1963	£D

In 1922, pitmaster Leonard Heuberger invented the pig sandwich, which has since become a standard configuration in Memphis and beyond—pulled pork on a bun, drenched with tangy sauce and embellished with cole slaw. It was advertised with a wonderful sign that showed a pig in top hat and tails, captioned MR. BROWN GOES TO TOWN. "Mr. Brown" was the connoisseur's code for the dark, chewy, succulent meat from the outside of the pork roast, of which the sandwich had plenty. Mr. Heuberger and his smoke shack are gone, but the modern Leonard's still serves a superb pig sandwich and also sports the dapper neon pig.

Loveless Café

Hwy. 100, Nashville, TN	$
(615) 646-9700	BLD

On the highway heading west out of Nashville, the Loveless Café is a country-western diamond in the rough. For years it has been a favorite haunt among Grand Ol' Opry performers (it's not unusual to see a celebrity's tour bus at the back of the lot), but fame hasn't spoiled the Loveless one bit. It still serves its brittle-crusted fried chicken on red-checked tablecloths, and hot buttermilk biscuits are served with homemade blackberry and peach preserves. Even more than fried chicken and biscuits, ham is the pride of the Loveless kitchen. It is slow-cured country ham, fried on a griddle until its rim of fat turns translucent amber and the coral pink meat gets speckled sandy brown. It comes with a bowl of red-eye gravy for dipping, cream gravy, sorghum molasses, honey, and bowls of preserves. It all adds up to one of America's great breakfasts, any time of day.

Pope's Café

on the Square, Shelbyville, TN	$
(615) 684-7933	BLD

Pope's Cafe is a plate lunch parlor with a vegetable roster that customarily includes macaroni with stewed tomatoes, pinto beans, crowder peas, crisp disks of deep-fried squash, turnip greens soaking in their pot likker, mashed or steamed potatoes, and sliced fresh tomatoes. Desserts are delectably southern, too, including chocolate, coconut, and lemon meringue pie; Charlie Pride pie (named after a famous local horse who was named after the country singer); and a simple but irresistible chess pie. The most compelling reason to eat at Pope's is country ham—rank, complex, and very literally mouth-watering.

A charming place on the town square of the Walking Horse Capital of the World, Pope's offers a choice of sitting at tables with individual jukeboxes or at a long, sociable counter where waitresses Wanda and Janie will take good care of you.

R & J Restaurant

Hwy. 45, Rutherford, TN (901) 665-6999	$
(closed Sun)	LD

Pork ribs, cooked over smoldering charcoal and hickory chips and bathed with secret recipe sauce, are R & J's main claim to fame, although we would never kick the tender chopped pork shoulder off our plate. In fact, anything smokemaster John Wayne James cooks in his open pit—including a strange, luscious prime rib—is a sure winner of a meal, complemented by superior cole slaw and crisp hush puppies.

Ribs are available only on Thursday, Friday, and Saturday, when they sometimes sell out as 10 pm approaches. Even if you are not planning on a visit to Rutherford, if you call a few days in advance, R & J will overnight-express ribs or barbecued pork shoulder to your home.

The Ridgewood

900 Elizabethton Hwy., Bluff City, TN (423) 538-7543	$
(closed Mon)	£D

At the insistence of a reporter who needed a headline, we once declared the Ridgewood to be the best barbecue in America. We weren't lying, but it did seem a little crazy to choose just one restaurant out of the several dozen supreme BBQs from Chicago's South Side to the Texas Hill Country and from Kentucky's mutton parlors to the Basque smoke wagons of the Rockies' western slopes.

Still, we do adore dining at the Ridgewood; if it isn't the single best barbecue, it surely is in the uppermost echelon of America's pork palaces. The meat itself is sensationally tasty—tender, sweet pork sliced thick and piled high, then doused with a suave red sauce that is tangy but not painfully hot. It is heaped into a bun or on a plate with superb, meaty barbecue beans and fine French fries on the side. Adding to the pleasure of the food is the well-worn ambiance of this fifty-year-old country restaurant with its double-wide aisles to accommodate a staff of double-wide waitresses who can be perfectly polite, but who have been known to cut off the heads of any customer who dares question the time-honored Ridgewood codes of service (you'll likely wait in line; no extra sauce is provided with meals).

If you are a pilgrim in search of smoke house greatness, the Ridgewood is a religious experience.

Satsuma

417 Union St., Nashville, TN	$
(615) 256-0760	£

Long ago, when we wrote a retro cookbook called *Square Meals,* the Satsuma was an inspiration. Serving ladies lunch since 1918, this gentle dining room knows all there is to know about such honest food as turkey à la king, freshly made chicken salad, and healthful turnip greens with hog jowl and corn sticks to mop up the gravy. Write your own order on the little pad provided every table, and don't forget a few servings of dessert, in which Satsuma is especially proficient. Lemon

Mid-South Splurges

Expensive, fancy, and/or fashionable regional restaurants that are worth it.

- ☛ Beaumont Inn, Harrodsburg, KY (p. 80)
- ☛ Boone Tavern, Berea, KY (p. 80)
- ☛ Caro-Mi Dining Room, Tryon, NC (p. 86)
- ☛ Automatic Slim's Tonga Club, Memphis, TN (p. 91)
- ☛ Chez Philippe, Memphis, TN (p. 94)
- ☛ The Inn at Little Washington, Washington, VA (p. 104)

cake and chocolate meringue pie are our personal favorites, accompanied by a serving of the kitchen's immemorial sherry ice cream.

At the front of the main floor dining room one can buy baked goods and several cookbooks of Satsuma's recipes. We've had a great time making good things from them, but there is no way to take home the time-honored traditions of efficiency, courtesy, and southern charm that make this restaurant such a special place to eat.

Sylvan Park

2201 Bandywood Dr., Green Hills (Nashville), TN	$
(615) 292-6449	£𝒟
also at a few other locations around Nashville	

Sylvan Park serves honest southern lunch at low prices in civilized surroundings. One day's menu offers sixteen different vegetables including a great drift of flavorful turnip greens, luscious mashed turnips, luxurious macaroni and cheese, dainty niblets of corn in cream sauce, syrupy candied yams, pork-infused baby lima beans, and congealed (gelatinized) fruit salad. The meats include roast turkey and dressing, sugar-cured baked ham, and breaded pork cutlets. Every meat-and-three platter is served with a choice of hot, pale biscuits with creamy insides or weighty chunks of sour milk corn bread so buttery rich that it will make your fingers glisten when you pick one up. "Aren't they good?" asks our waitress when we request a second basket of these superb breadstuffs to mop the gravy off our plates. For dessert, there is hot cobbler or your choice of chocolate, pecan, or lemon icebox pie.

VIRGINIA

☆ ☆ ☆

The Inn at Little Washington	
Middle and Main, Washington, VA (540) 675-3800	*$$$*
Wed–Sun (reservations essential)	*D*

A magic hostelry in the Virginia countryside just seventy-five miles (but light-years) away from the capital, the Inn at Little Washington is a national treasure. For a secluded night of romance and/or a memorable gourmet dinner, it should be in every sybarite's little black book. The menu, which changes according to the availability of local produce and seafood, features creative new American dishes that range from rabbit sausage braised in Virginia Riesling or American foie gras to rhubarb pizza served with ginger ice cream for dessert. It is possible to eat simple and beautifully prepared steaks and chops, but the kitchen is best known for more elaborate dishes, such as duck breast with currants in port wine sauce or sweetbreads with three-mustard sauce.

Call weeks ahead for a reservation. Overnight guests enjoy afternoon tea as well as breakfast.

King's Barbeque

3221 W. Washington Rd., Petersburg, VA	$
(804) 732-5861	BLD

King's is a king-size restaurant that has been in the barbecue business for half a century. It serves both beef and pork, and the carvers at the end of the long counter will either slice or chop your choice for platters or sandwiches. This barbecue spot has actual tables and silverware and even some food items *not* cooked over hickory wood, such as fried chicken, ham steak, wonderful biscuits that go with everything, and even dessert in the form of hot apple pie. There are banquet rooms for big parties and comfortable tables and chairs. Such amenities make King's a place unsuited to the barbecue purist who wants nothing but smoky meat in a bare-bones setting; but if you're in the area and you have a hankering for good slow-cooked pork with all the trimmings, we highly recommend it.

The Owl

Rte. 13, N. of Accomac in Parksley, VA	$
(804) 665-5191	BLD

This modest roadside dining room, adjacent to a small motel, has been in business since the mid-1930s, and the homespun decor seems to have changed little over the decades. Roadside food connoisseurs have marked the Owl in their book of wonders for its crusty pan-fried chicken, Chincoteague oysters sheathed in brittle breading, crab au gratin, and cold-weather oyster stew. On the side of these tidewater comfort-food classics come such superb dishes as fried sweet potatoes (an autumn specialty), spoon bread cut into little quivery squares, and crisp squash fritters. Naturally, good biscuits are also served. The desserts are memorable: chocolate rum pie on a melting-light pale white meringue crust, and moist orange sweet potato pie, which is the tongue-soothing way to top off a meal of the Owl's vigorous country ham and gravy.

Barbecue's Map

There is no way to chart every different style of American barbecue (although such a quest would be a nice life's project), but it is important to have a general idea of what gets barbecued where so you don't commit the embarrassing *faux pas* of eating beef barbecue in Chattanooga or asking for a pig sandwich in El Paso.

That's the fundamental disparity: pork versus beef. Pork is king throughout the Mid-South and Deep South. Even if beef happens to be on the menu there, it should be ignored. Look for signs that show happy dancing pigs or "bink" spelled out in neon in the window. Bubba's of Eureka Springs, Arkansas, announced by a lovely sign in the shape of a pig, is a good example (p. 121).

Basic southern variations on the theme are found in

- ☛ North Carolina, where smoked pork is mixed with a spicy vinegar sauce (no tomato in it at all), as at Melton's Barbecue (p. 88)
- ☛ South Carolina, where many of the best sauces are mustard-based, as at Maurice's Piggy Park (p. 160)
- ☛ Memphis, where pork is hacked into "pig sandwiches" with cole slaw and where ribs are cooked either wet or dry. (Charlie Vergos Rendezvous, p. 93, and the Cozy Corner, p. 94, are two exemplary Memphis restaurants.)
- ☛ Georgia, where barbecue is frequently accompanied by Brunswick stew, a hearty gallimaufry of vegetables and pork shreds in gravy. Melear's (p. 134) is a classic.

In Texas and most of the West, beef is what's best—brisket, usually, but also succulent sausage links. There might be mounted cows' heads on walls,

Pierce's Pitt Bar-B-Q

447 Rochambeau Dr., Williamsburg, VA	$
(804) 565-2955	*BLD*

Pierce's is one of the great pits of the East, and the last place you'll find good barbecue heading north out of pork country. It isn't

John Wayne portraits, and cowboy-theme decor, but the greatest Southwestern barbecues are austere and without any frills to distract you from the meat. Louie Muller's of Tyler, Texas (p. 297) is the purest such place.

Oklahoma is a great beef state, but local smokehounds also favor barbecued bologna: thick slabs much spicier than the presliced supermarket variety. See Leo's Barbecue (p. 285).

Santa Maria—style barbecue in California is cooked directly over flames (of live oak wood), not indirectly over smoke. Although you'll find chicken, sausages, even filets mignon cooked this way, the traditional cut of choice is a beef tri-tip. (Good Santa Maria barbecue is available from street-corner vendors on weekends in many small towns in California cattle country. The Far Western Tavern in Guadalupe and the Hitching Post in Casmalia are two of the best restaurants that serve it, pp. 320 and 322.)

Western Kentucky is strange. It is mutton country, where mature lamb is slow-cooked over hickory wood and served as part of a ritual meal that includes barbecue-flavored beans, potato salad, onion slices, and white or tan bread suitable for mopping. Barbecued mutton also often finds its way into the Kentucky stew known as burgoo. The Moonlight Bar-b-q Inn has been a premier mutton house for decades (p. 84).

Many midwestern cities have great barbecue cooked by men and women who learned their trade in the South and serve superb pork (ribs in particular) with a sweet glaze. St. Louis has the added attraction of being the home of snoots—crisp-friend pig snouts bathed in sauce, as served at C&K (p. 206). Being more western, Kansas City smoke houses offer good beef brisket *as well* as good pork, and even mutton. Arthur Bryant's is the essential K.C. smoke house (p. 206).

much to look at—a cinderblock fast-food outlet in bright orange and yellow with a smoke house out back—but the sandwiches are ravishing, available in jumbo or regular sizes with French fries, hush puppies, and slaw on the side. The meat, hacked into irregularly sized chunks and shreds, comes bathed in Pierce's sensational sauce, which is tomato based with a vinegar tang that will tease your tongue all the way up past the Mason-Dixon line.

Roanoker

2522 Colonial Ave., Roanoke, VA	$
(540) 344-7746	**BLD**

The Roanoker lost its *intime* café charms when it moved and spruced up several years ago, transforming itself into a sanitary middle-class lunchroom, but breakfast of country ham with red-eye gravy and biscuits is still terrific, as are most of the large repertoire of southern-style side dishes that accompany lunch and dinner: crunchy corn sticks, candied yams, peppery boiled cabbage, congealed salads (aka Jell-O), and always a selection of high-seasoned greens and beans. One fine lunch we enjoyed not too long ago featured a heap of crisp-cooked chicken livers sided by "Swiss mix" (broccoli and cauliflower), dressing and gravy, and hot apple pie for dessert.

Rowe Family Restaurant

Rte. 250, Staunton, VA	$
(540) 886-1833	**BLD**

An essential fried-chicken-'n'-fixin's stop off Interstate 81 (at exit 57). The much-abused term "home cooking" means something in this big but friendly roadside restaurant, where the biscuits are warm, the pan-fried chicken is crisp (and takes an honest forty-five minutes to prepare), and the banana pudding is as nice as baby food. All the pies are extraordinarily good, especially apple and mince in the autumn, the latter topped with rum sauce.

Smokey Pig

212 S. Washington Hwy., Ashland, VA	$
(804) 798-4590	£ D

A strange barbecue parlor, located in a building that was once a general store, the Smokey Pig bills itself as "elegantly informal." We assume the *elegant* part of the equation refers to the fact that the kitchen goes beyond barbecue and offers crab cakes (mighty tasty), quiche, chicken salad sandwiches, and, on one occasion, a cup of gazpacho soup that was quite good. Daily specials include such other non-smoked meals as meat loaf (Tuesday) and pot roast (Wednesday), accompanied by choices from a broad vegetable repertoire and cocktails or wine from a list of four items: chablis, rose, Burgundy, and blush. Despite such elegance, the great thing to eat at the Smokey Pig is, simply, smokey pig: delicious slow-cooked pork, chopped or sliced, served in a sandwich or as a dinner with slaw, potatoes, and hush puppies.

Southern Kitchen

US 11, New Market, VA	$
(540) 740-3514	B £ D

The Southern Kitchen is a fine town café where the clientele is a mix of locals and Shenandoah Valley tourists. The counter or pale green booths are good places to eat a quick country-ham breakfast; in the more demure adjacent dining room, families come for crisp fried chicken, local trout, and all-American hamburgers. The most distinctive menu item, and a true Virginia treat, is peanut soup, a smooth bisque with a faint onion zest that perfectly balances the opulence of the goober base.

Stone's Cafeteria

Roanoke Rd., Christiansburg, VA	$
(540) 382-8970	BLD

Since 1956, Stone's has been the upright restaurant east of town, its orange Naugahyde booths occupied by families who come for classic southern-style suppers such as baked chicken casserole and tender-crusted fried chicken. The ladies who dish out the food in the cafeteria line know the likes and dislikes of their regulars and keep up a steady patter with customers pushing their trays along. If you are a stranger, they are most solicitous about your preferences: "Extra gravy for those tenderloin tips? . . . yams on the side of that pork chop? . . . or would you prefer mashed potatoes? . . . or squash with bacon?" Such queries send us into cafeteria ecstasy, for all the food is fresh and homey. Topped off with a Stone's dessert such as coconut cream pie or layered strawberry pie, these are honest meals to remember.

Deep South

ALL-AMERICAN

ALABAMA

ARKANSAS

FLORIDA

GEORGIA

LOUISIANA

MISSISSIPPI

SOUTH CAROLINA

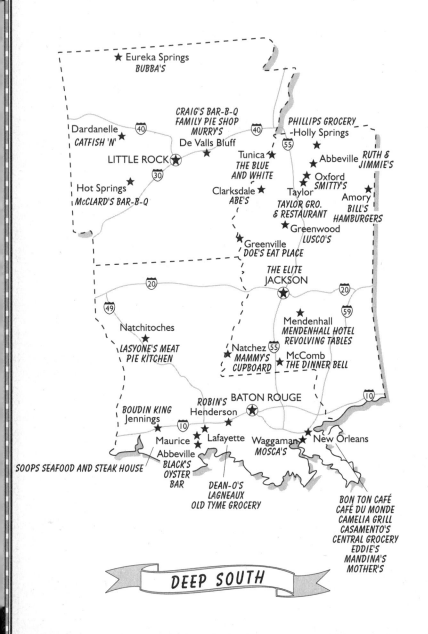

★ Eureka Springs
BUBBA'S

CRAIG'S BAR-B-Q
FAMILY PIE SHOP
MURRY'S
De Valls Bluff

Dardanelle
CATFISH 'N'

40

40

55

PHILLIPS GROCERY
-Holly Springs

Tunica
THE BLUE
AND WHITE

Abbeville *RUTH &*
JIMMIE'S

LITTLE ROCK ★

30

Oxford
SMITTY'S

Hot Springs
McCLARD'S BAR-B-Q

Clarksdale
ABE'S

Taylor
TAYLOR GRO.
& RESTAURANT

Amory
BILL'S
HAMBURGERS

Greenwood
LUSCO'S

Greenville
DOE'S EAT PLACE

20

THE ELITE
JACKSON

20

59

49

Natchitoches

LASYONE'S MEAT
PIE KITCHEN

Mendenhall
MENDENHALL HOTEL
REVOLVING TABLES

Natchez
MAMMY'S
CUPBOARD

55

McComb
THE DINNER BELL

ROBIN'S

BATON ROUGE

10

BOUDIN KING Henderson
Jennings

10

Maurice

Lafayette

Waggaman
MOSCA'S

New Orleans

Abbeville
BLACK'S
OYSTER
BAR

DEAN-O'S
LAGNEAUX
OLD TYME GROCERY

SOOPS SEAFOOD AND STEAK HOUSE

BON TON CAFÉ
CAFÉ DU MONDE
CAMELIA GRILL
CASAMENTO'S
CENTRAL GROCERY
EDDIE'S
MANDINA'S
MOTHER'S

DEEP SOUTH

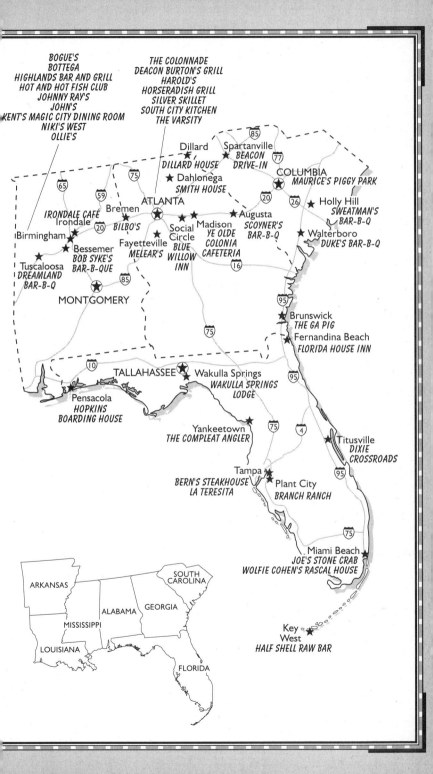

BOGUE'S
BOTTEGA
HIGHLANDS BAR AND GRILL
HOT AND HOT FISH CLUB
JOHNNY RAY'S
JOHN'S
KENT'S MAGIC CITY DINING ROOM
NIKI'S WEST
OLLIE'S

THE COLONNADE
DEACON BURTON'S GRILL
HAROLD'S
HORSERADISH GRILL
SILVER SKILLET
SOUTH CITY KITCHEN
THE VARSITY

Dillard
DILLARD HOUSE

Spartanville
BEACON DRIVE-IN

COLUMBIA
MAURICE'S PIGGY PARK

Dahlonega
SMITH HOUSE

ATLANTA

Holly Hill
SWEATMAN'S BAR-B-Q

IRONDALE CAFE
Bremen
Irondale
BILBO'S

Augusta
SCOYNER'S BAR-B-Q

Social
Circle

Madison
YE OLDE COLONIA CAFETERIA

Walterboro
DUKE'S BAR-B-Q

Birmingham

Fayetteville
MELEAR'S

BLUE WILLOW INN

Bessemer
BOB SYKE'S BAR-B-QUE

Tuscaloosa
DREAMLAND BAR-B-Q

MONTGOMERY

Brunswick
THE GA PIG

Fernandina Beach
FLORIDA HOUSE INN

TALLAHASSEE

Wakulla Springs
WAKULLA SPRINGS LODGE

Pensacola
HOPKINS BOARDING HOUSE

Yankeetown
THE COMPLEAT ANGLER

Titusville
DIXIE CROSSROADS

Tampa
*BERN'S STEAKHOUSE
LA TERESITA*

Plant City
BRANCH RANCH

Miami Beach
*JOE'S STONE CRAB
WOLFIE COHEN'S RASCAL HOUSE*

Key
West
HALF SHELL RAW BAR

ARKANSAS

SOUTH
CAROLINA

ALABAMA

GEORGIA

MISSISSIPPI

LOUISIANA

FLORIDA

ALABAMA

Bob Sykes Bar-B-Que

1724 9th Ave., Bessemer, AL	$
(205) 426-1400	LD

Three of the biggest rocking chairs ever made are positioned opposite the order counter at Bob Sykes, making it easy for even the widest-assed customers to wait in comfort while the order they've given is assembled. Tote your own food to the table (veterans ask for a pitcher of extra sauce for dipping bread and sopping meat), then prepare to smack your lips over one of the choicest Alabama smoke house meals. Finely chopped pork and especially succulent shredded beef are our favorite things to eat, although Sykes's ribs are plenty good, too. French fries are deliciously spuddy, beans are powerfully sweet, and meringue-topped lemon pie is a local legend.

Sykes is just a few blocks from exit 112 off I-20 and has a drive-through window if you are in a hurry and need barbecue fast.

Bogue's

3028 Clairmont Ave., Birmingham, AL	$
(205) 254-9780	BLD

For those who enjoy a neighborhood café with attitude, Bogue's is irresistible. Its well-cooled, double-wide dining room with pea green plaster walls and slick-textured Naugahyde booths has been a three-meal-a-day haunt for Birminghamians since mid-century. It is especially popular among all-night revelers who arrive when it opens, at 6 am, for kill-or-cure plates of high-powered country ham with biscuits, grits, and peppery cream gravy. Lunch specials include such Dixie standards as country-fried steak, catfish, and Gulf Coast stuffed devil crabs. On the side come legions of vegetables: collard greens, snap peas, sautéed squash, rice and gravy, etc., etc.

Honestly, it is not the food that keeps the clientele so loyal; it is the staff. Even if you are a first-timer, the waitress is likely to call you "Hon," pour your coffee and leave the pot so you have instant access to more, and engage in Ciceronian hash-house repartee. "Aw, take a pill and hush up!" our gal instructs a nearby customer who complains too much about the weather.

"Make me," he says.

She whisks the coffeepot from his table and holds it hostage until he apologizes for his bad attitude.

Veterans recall the days Mr. Bogue ran the place, when his advertising slogan was "It's vogue to eat at Bogue." In a reverse-chic sort of way, it still is.

Bottega

2240 Highland Ave. S., Birmingham, AL (205) 939-1000	$$$
(the adjoining café, open from 11 am, has prices in the $$ range)	D

Bottega is the second Birmingham restaurant of Frank Stitt, whose Highlands Bar and Grill (p. 116) earned him a reputation as one of the country's top chefs. The location itself is remarkable: a handsome stone villa originally built as a fine clothing store in the 1920s, its main dining room paneled in figured walnut that once walled fitting booths and fixtures. Just inside the front door, you feast your eyes on a vista of the evening's focaccias, fresh-picked (that morning) tomatoes, and herbed olives. The airy, high-ceilinged room is bustling with sybaritic Birminghamians who are eating, drinking, and living the good life.

The food, a modern Mediterranean repertoire with strong emphasis on locally grown produce, is world-class. From an antipasto of creamy, garlicky Parmesan soufflé in sherry-wine sauce, to entrees of braised osso buco with sweet onions or crawfish risotto with fresh herbs, to dazzling dessert sorbets made from sweet melons, the daily changing menu is a festival for adventurous palates.

(Next door to the restaurant, Bottega Café serves less elaborate and less expensive Mediterranean-accented food in a more casual setting from lunch hour through dinner. The Café has become one of the city's major see-and-be-seen places, with revelers spilling onto the patio and sidewalk by dusk.)

Dreamland Bar-B-Q

5535 15th Ave. E., Tuscaloosa, AL (205) 758-8135;	$
also in Birmingham at 1427 14th Ave., S. (205) 933-2133	£Ð

Ribs, juicy and crusted with sauce, draw crowds to this old smoke house, which dates back to the 1950s. Service is do-it-yourself, and decor in the utilitarian dining room includes pictures of celebrity clientele, vintage license plates, and stacks of hickory and oak wood all around the pit. White bread, pickle slices, and potato chips are all that is needed to make a pig-perfect meal that will set your tongue aglow for hours. (Dreamland sauce is packaged to go, a precious Alabama souvenir.)

Highlands Bar and Grill

2011 Eleventh Ave., S., Birmingham, AL (205) 939-1400	$$$
(reservations advised)	Ð

Highlands Bar and Grill is truly and deeply Alabaman. Ingredients are as indigenous as eggs from free-range chickens on a nearby farm and tomatoes from the proprietor's garden, and you'll find such well-known southernisms as grits and Gulf Coast crab claws on the menu. But there is much more to this delicious kitchen than regional loyalty. Chef Frank Stitt III, an Alabama boy, transcends parochial recipes and makes everything his own, sometimes in the most audacious ways: grilled dayboat swordfish (fresh!) is sauced with a pungent gravy made from porcini mushrooms and salty little tiles of apple-smoked bacon. Did we say fish with pork sauce? Believe us, it works. Grits are baked with wild mushrooms, country ham, and fresh thyme. Spit-roasted duck is accompanied by lacy sweet potato French fries.

We could enumerate many good things we have eaten, but the menu changes, so when you dine at Highlands Bar and Grill, you will have a menu all your own. It is a supremely comfortable restaurant, polite but not stuffy, with a convivial dining room, an even more lively bar, and a joyous marble oyster bar (watch Rod Clark, Alabama's best shucker, at work). The staff is suave and knowledgeable, and fellow diners all seem to have a jolly time tossing raw oysters down the hatch, sipping fresh-squeezed watermelon margaritas, and savoring the extraordinary meals that follow. An evening here is a memorable splurge in a great American restaurant.

Hot and Hot Fish Club

2180 11th Court, S., Birmingham, AL	$$$
(205) 933-5474	D

In a semisubterranean, semicircular space that used to be a raffish tavern, chef Christopher Hastings has established a premier restaurant of high spirits and creative food. There are handsomely crafted tables and chairs arrayed across the old octagon-tile floor, but socially gregarious and culinarily curious customers sit along the curving counter, where a row of high-backed stools provides a view of the open kitchen in which modern artisans prepare such delights as sweet corn and tomato salad with field peas, the world's tastiest fried okra (fresh from the garden, cooked whole), and downhome barbecued beef short ribs with succotash and hot biscuits. It is a delight to sit and watch the show, exchange gastronomic views with neighbors, and sip Hot and Hot martinis, which are made by muddling Ketyl One vodka with hot peppers.

Named for the nineteenth-century South Carolina epicurean club to which the chef's great-great-grandfather belonged, the Hot and Hot Fish Club serves various meats and poultry (vanilla-cured pork rack, grilled sirloin, roasted quail), but it makes a specialty of seafood, including *fresh* grilled anchovies (soft, warm, and tender) for a romaine salad and gorgeous whole snapper roasted in the brick oven. One of our favorite taste memories is of a glistening pink grilled fillet of salmon, presented on a low platform of little spud pilings described on the menu as "fresh dug potatoes."

Irondale Café

At the train station in downtown Irondale, AL	**$**
(205) 956-5258	**£ D**

The Irondale Café is the Whistle Stop Café made famous in Fannie Flagg's book and the movie made from it, *Fried Green Tomatoes.* In business since the 1930s, and now something of a tourist attraction, it is still as easygoing as a plate of field peas and turnip greens (always on the Sunday menu). Service is cafeteria style, and the menu is different each day of the week. To accompany such stalwart entrees as meat loaf, fried chicken, and country steak, there are about a dozen vegetables from which to choose, *always* including fried green tomatoes. We especially recommend the deliciously starchy crowder peas, on the menu Monday through Thursday, and the supersweet, Marshmallow Fluff–topped sweet potato soufflé Sunday and Wednesday.

Johnny Ray's

316 Valley Ave., Birmingham, AL	**$**
(205) 945-7437	**£ D**

A small Alabama chain with one branch in Crestview, Florida, Johnnie Ray's is considered by many connoisseurs to be the best place around for barbecue and pie. The Q includes beef, blonde chicken (white meat) and brunette chicken (dark meat), chopped or sliced pork, and big spare ribs crusted with hot-spiced red sauce so tongue-tingling it can seem effervescent. Although pig purists insist on eating nothing but ribs or Johnny Ray's pulverized chopped pork, there are a couple of iconoclastic combo sandwiches we like a lot—double-decker pork and beef, and a pork-beef-chicken combo with baked beans, cole slaw, and French fries on the side.

Now, about those pies: they are pure Dixie, powerfully sweet, piled high with gobs of whipped cream. The lemon pie is cool and just faintly tart on a yummy Graham cracker crust; coconut is thicker, on a crumbly crust; chocolate pie, made with good ol' Hershey's syrup, is a chocolate dessert from an age of innocence, not sinfully sweet, but angelically so.

John's

112 21st St., Birmingham, AL	$$
(205) 322-6014	£D

A rather regal downtown luncheonette with deluxe foil wallpaper and silverware wrapped in white linen, John's is a bastion of proper southern food with a Greek accent. Alabama's coastal setting and the proprietor's Aegean heritage make seafood the star of the menu. Since 1944, Birminghamians have enjoyed dark, smoky gumbo accompanied by crisp corn sticks, charcoal-broiled snapper in a lemony oregenate sauce, and Gulf crabmeat served plain in a cocktail or marinated for the delicious "West Indies salad" unique to the Gulf Coast. Fish frowners can feast on tender pot roast with natural gravy, ham steak with red-eye gravy, or high-seasoned, crisp-skinned Greek chicken with luxuriously cooked southern-style vegetables on the side. One curious not-to-be-missed specialty is John's cole slaw, which arrives at the table as nothing but finely shredded raw cabbage in a bowl. There is a squeeze bottle on the table containing secret-recipe slaw dressing, which each customer squeezes on to taste. It is beguiling

Boardinghouse Meals

The Deep South still has a handful of old-fashioned hostelries that serve food family-style at big communal tables. The cuisine is tradition incarnate: fried chicken is the customary entree, always surrounded by phalanxes of well-cooked, powerfully seasoned, and sinfully enriched vegetables. It's great fun to break bread with strangers and, as the motto of the Mendenhall Hotel implores, EAT 'TIL IT OUCHES.

- Florida House Inn, Fernandina Beach, FL (p. 126)
- Hopkins Boarding House, Pensacola, FL (p. 127)
- Dillard House, Dillard, GA (p. 132)
- Smith House, Dahlonega, GA (p. 136)
- The Dinner Bell, McComb, MS (p. 150)
- Mendenhall Hotel Revolving Tables, Mendenhall, MS (p. 153)

opaque orange stuff, vaguely like sweet Russian dressing but with sharp, spicy undertones.

Niki's West

233 Finley Ave., W., Birmingham, AL	$
(205) 252-5751	BLD

A weird, wonderful, out-of-the-way dining treasure, Niki's West is located across the road from the Birmingham Food Terminal, a complex of buildings where produce is bought and sold. Although the streets outside rumble with trucks, the cavernous interior of Niki's is cool and secluded, decorated in a Mediterranean seafood motif. Service is cafeteria-style; select from an astonishing array of approximately four dozen vegetables, all direct from the market and cooked southern-style, meaning candied, stewed, and enriched. We adore such indulgences as broccoli-rice-cheese casserole and sweet stewed tomatoes, but simple in-season choices, such as sliced tomatoes, watermelon, and cantaloupe, are farm-fresh and wonderful, too.

Entrees include such cafeteria standbys as fried pork chops and country steak; but there are always a few Greek-accented items available, such as baked chicken, roast lamb, and kabobs, which we highly recommend. Also notable is seafood, which sparkles: broiled mackerel almondine, baked fish Creole, fried shrimp and flounder.

Dessert pies are unremarkable, although a nice little dish of creamy banana pudding—here considered a vegetable!—is an appropriately sybaritic conclusion for a Niki's banquet.

Ollie's

515 University Blvd., Birmingham, AL	$
(205) 324-9485	LD

Entering Ollie's is appetizing, not only for the smell of smoke and sizzling pork but for the display up front—bottled sauce and Bible literature are for sale. That's a combination that almost always signals smoke house greatness. And the food served on Ollie's thick, unbreakable plates confirms it: this is pork-lover's Q, cut into big chunky slices of both tender inside and crusty outside meat (unless you specify you want more of one or the other) and served sauceless. The pale, flavorful meat, insinuated with the taste of smoke, is elegant stuff. Sauce, available on the side, is a thin, tangy dressing with a vinegar bite that complements the pork but doesn't overwhelm it.

Ollie's menu is simple: pork or chicken, chili in the winter, and a short list of sandwiches. For dessert, you can pick up an Eskimo Pie or Nutty Buddy ice cream cone from a freezer near the cash register.

ARKANSAS

☆ ☆ ☆

Bubba's	
Hwy. 62 W, Eureka Springs, AR	**$$**
(501) 253-7706	**£𝔇**

Baby back ribs—the tenderest of pig parts you can barbecue—are a Bubba's delight, cooked long and slow in an earthen-floored pit and basted with sweet sauce. But these tender little bones are available only after 5 pm; earlier in the day, you'll have to settle for excellent pork shoulder, packed into sandwiches with cole slaw or as part of a fine dinner with barbecued beans and slaw. Also notable is the "Bubba link," a smoky hot sausage blanketed with spicy chili and cheddar cheese, served on a sturdy (but not sturdy enough) French roll.

For a barbecue house, Bubba's is quite civilized. There is a written menu, and there are actually nonbarbecued items on the menu to eat, including hamburgers, nachos, and grilled cheese sandwiches.

Catfish 'N'

Dardanelle Dam Rd., Dardanelle, AR	$
(501) 229-3321	D

Catfish 'N' is an eating barn above the Arkansas River where the catfish is succulent, encased in a golden crust, and accompanied by fine, onion-sweet hush puppies. Cole slaw and French fries are also part of the help-yourself, all-you-can-eat deal, as are a good assortment of pickles, onions, hot sauces, peppers, and lemon wedges. The big feed here, an Arkansas custom, is immensely popular among locals as well as travelers along I-40, so beware of long lines and a wait at mealtime.

Craig's Bar-B-Q

Rte. 70, De Valls Bluff, AR	$
(501) 998-2616	LD

Circle De Valls Bluff, along I-40, on your map of Arkansas. Get off and stop at Craig's for superb Ozark barbecue: pork, slow-cooked to sublime tenderness, sauced mild, medium, hot, or extra hot (and how!), served on a bun with cole slaw, accompanied by silky sweet beans. Craig's is a one-room joint with a handful of tables inside and a lot of take-out business from Q connoisseurs who prefer to dine in the front seats of their pickup trucks.

Family Pie Shop

Rte. 70, De Valls Bluff, AR (501) 998-2279	$
Tues–Sat, BL Sun	BLD

Not a restaurant, the Family Pie Shop is nevertheless a place all hungry travelers need to know about. For more than fifteen years now, Mary Thomas has been attracting locals and travelers to her backyard bakery by selling fantastic pies of every sort: pecan pie to die for, sweet potato pie that sets the standard, fluffy-topped meringues, and small, folded over fried pies filled with spiced apples or peaches. The latter are individually sized, and Mrs. Thomas recently took to making miniature (two-portion) versions of some of her favorites for passers-by who don't have enough appetite to polish off eight slices before they get to Little Rock.

McClard's Bar-B-Q

505 Albert Pike, Hot Springs, AR (501) 623-9665 or	$
624-9586	£ᴅ
Tues–Sat	

Best in the state since '28" is the truthful motto of McClard's, where exquisitely tender, hickory-cooked beef, pork, and pork ribs are served with stupendously good hot sauce and accompanied by chili-spiked barbecued beans, hand-cut French fries, and exemplary milk shakes or beer. For barbecue believers in search of smoke house enlightenment, McClard's is a holy place.

Murry's

Cypress St., De Valls Bluff, AR (501) 998-2247	$
Thur–Sat	ᴅ

Catfish, deep fried, accompanied by steamy corn cakes, French fries, and cole slaw: that's the consummate country-style meal in these parts, nowhere better than at Murry's. Formerly housed in a collection of house trailers and serving Arkansans since the 1950s, Mr. Murry's spruced-up restaurant also deep-fries shrimp and oysters, and steak is on the menu as well. But it's those crisp-fried Arkansas mud puppies—sweet and moist and satisfying like no other fish—that draw the crowds (and there *are* crowds every precious night Murry's is open).

FLORIDA

☆ ☆ ☆

Bern's Steak House

1208 S. Howard St., Tampa, FL	*$$$*
(813) 251-2421	*D*

There isn't a restaurant in the nation more conspicuously opulent than Bern's Steak House. To the tune of a strolling accordionist in plush dining rooms where Louis XIV would have felt at home, you eat what many enthusiastic carnivores consider the best steak in America. It's dry-aged on the premises, available in every known cut and whatever size you like, selected from a menu titled "Art in Steaks," and accompanied by the best of everything else that money can buy and human ingenuity can bring to the dining table.

Bern Laxer grows his own organic vegetables, offers the largest wine list in the world, roasts his coffee beans, and blends his tea from flowering tips and tops only. To conclude the ultimate in sybaritic meals, customers leave their dinner tables and repair to rooms devoted to nothing but eating dessert and drinking dessert wine and coffee.

Branch Ranch

Branch-Forbes exit off I-4 in Plant City, FL	*$$*
(813) 752-1957	*LD*
Tues–Sun	

Farm feasts, served to hungry hordes: that's the Branch Ranch experience, a gourmand's ritual ever since Mary Branch began inviting friends to dinner at her home in the 1950s. The private home has given way to a vast barn of a restaurant; but the family-style meal never changes. Choose your entree—chicken, ham (baked or country-style) or steak—and it comes with a feast that includes pickled beets and bread-and-butter pickles, hot buttermilk biscuits with marmalade and strawberry jam, candied yams, scalloped eggplant, pole beans, baked yellow squash, and dumpling-topped chicken pot pie. Dessert is apple or peach cobbler or coconut cake.

You will wait for a table at busy mealtimes, and the ambiance can be as hectic as a college mess hall. But don't let the commotion dissuade you. A Branch Ranch meal is true and pure country cooking.

The Compleat Angler

at Izaak Walton Lodge, off 63rd St. in Yankeetown, FL	$$
(352) 447-2311	D

"A room for $34 a night where Babe Ruth used to take his mistresses, manatees swimming nearby, and pan-fried grouper in the dining room—what more could a traveler want?" So wrote enthusiastic tipster David Pease when he returned from a trip to "Florida's Nature Coast" and a stay at the Izaac Walton Lodge. The Compleat Angler is the Lodge's dining room, its name derived from the title of naturist Walton's 1653 essay that contended fishing was more civilized than hunting. It is a civilized place (flowers on the table, espresso with dessert) with an inspiring view of the Withlacoochee River and a menu that includes such big-date fare as chateaubriand and rack of lamb. But the best reason to visit is the seafood: oysters or mustard shrimp to start, then grouper or red snapper, both available simply cooked or dolled up with crabmeat. A deluxe meal, and a true taste of Florida.

(The Little Angler, a less deluxe dining room in the Lodge, is open for lunch.)

Dixie Crossroads

1475 Garden St., Titusville, FL	$$
(407) 268-5000	LD

Rock shrimp are the specialty of the house. Order them by the pound, or in the all-you-can-eat offer, and they arrive grouped in crowded rows, splayed open and in the shell like an army of tiny split rock lobster tails. A cocktail fork is provided to pull the meat out of its hard translucent shell. It comes away easily in one whole, hefty piece. A buttery dunk is provided, but it seems like gilt for the lily, for there is hardly any seafood more inherently buttery than these glistening creatures.

Also on the menu are tiny, briny local scallops hardly bigger than pencil erasers; catfish with a frail, nut-brown crust; and mullet, broiled or smoked. Meals are preceded by can't-stop-eating-'em corn fritters with crunchy red-gold crusts, dusted with powdered sugar.

Just across the river from the John F. Kennedy Space Center, the Crossroads is a popular, sprawling eatery, especially crowded around shuttle launch times, when the clientele includes not only tourists but friends and family of astronauts.

Florida House Inn

22 S. Third St., Fernandina Beach, FL (904) 261-3300	$
(Sun brunch only, Mon lunch only)	LD

The oldest hotel in Florida, now a quaint bed and breakfast with four-poster beds and a romantic fireplace in most rooms, also serves groaning-board meals to the public. At tables-for-twelve, guests and suppertime visitors help themselves, family-style, to bowls full of collard greens, stewed okra with tomatoes, seasoned rice, green beans, corn bread, fried chicken, and pork chops with gravy (and seafood jambalaya on Friday night). Desserts include banana pudding, chocolate-frosted yellow cake, and apple cobbler. The beverage, naturally, is iced tea, available sweetened or plain. As in any traditional boardinghouse, guests are expected to bus their own plates after they've had enough to eat.

Half Shell Raw Bar

1 Lands End Village, Key West, FL	$$
(305) 294-7496	LD

onch chowder is a fascinating brew, made from the mollusk by which south Floridians like to label their own distinctly hedonistic ocean culture. There are few better places to taste it than the Half Shell, a breezy joint at the shrimp docks in Key West. There is a blackboard menu that ranges from good hamburgers and deep-fried shark nuggets to deluxe crab-stuffed local lobsters, fine, fresh fish as well as clams and oysters on the half shell. We love the crusty conch fritters as well as the smooth, savory chowder. With an afternoon's worth of beers on the Half Shell porch, such fare is the basis of great vacation eating.

Hopkins Boarding House

900 N. Spring St., Pensacola, FL (904) 438-3979	$
Tues–Sat, BL Sun	BLD

ating at the Hopkins Boarding House always feels like a holiday. Share a table, pass the platters, eat until you have to let out your belt a notch, then eat some more. The food is deeply, deliciously southern, with plenty of fresh vegetables, plain and fancy; biscuits and breadstuffs; plus fried chicken and some other meat as a second choice. Hot cobblers arrive for dessert and, on occasion, there is fine banana pudding to sample.

Located in the old part of Pensacola, Hopkins is a grand landmark of happy eating with a fan club of customers who come from coast to coast.

Joe's Stone Crab

227 Biscayne St., Miami Beach, FL (305) 673-0365	$$$
(stone crabs are available only Oct 15 to May 15)	£Đ

You have not tasted Miami Beach until you have eaten a platter of stone crabs at Joe's. Plump and juicy, not cold but not too warm, easy to extract from their coral-pink claws, dipped in Joe's creamy mustard sauce, these beautiful hunks of food are vastly expensive—Damon Runyon once said, "they sell by the karat"—but no other shellfish meat is quite as sweet. There are good side dishes, including creamed spinach and cottage fried sweet potatoes, and a full menu of local lobsters, shrimp, and oysters. But it's stone crabs on which the reputation of this old place was built.

A grand, rambling landmark with formally attired staff, Joe's itself is a memorable experience. A timeless south Florida eating establishment still in the family of Joe Weiss, who opened for business back in 1913, it is mobbed by Miami Beach natives as well as tourists.

La Teresita

3248 W. Columbus Dr., Tampa, FL	$
(813) 879-4909	BℒĐ

Customers sit at the serpentine counter (there are no booths or tables) and eat what are known hereabouts as "Cuban sandwiches"—roast pork heaped into lengths of elegant toasted and buttered bread. With the mighty sandwiches, they gulp down coffee thick as syrup and strong as TNT. At breakfast, the same good bread is warm and buttered with cups of café con leche, and at lunch, the bread accompanies such Caribbean standbys as black beans and rice, carne asada, and roast chicken. Throughout the day, you'll see groups of happy gents gathering in the street after dining at La Teresita. Here they fire up big made-in-Tampa cigars and look like kings who have just enjoyed a royal feast.

Wakulla Springs Lodge

1 Springs Dr., Wakulla Springs, FL	$$
(904) 224-5950	BLD

Surrounded by a thick pine and oak forest, Wakulla Springs Lodge is a Spanish-style retreat for nature lovers, with the added attraction of good southern food served three times a day: fried chicken, country ham, and such Gulf Coast specialties as Apalachicola oysters, deviled crab, and broiled or fried shrimp. Whatever else you order, don't miss the navy bean soup, a legend for decades. To tell the truth, our favorite meal is breakfast, bright and early, when the birds outside the great arched windows of the dining room are busy on their morning errands and provide a spectacular backdrop to a table piled high with sizzled ham steak, hot grits, biscuits, and gravy.

The nearby Springs are a true wonder of the world, crystal clear and undisturbed by visitors. Back in the mid-1950s, the primeval setting was used to film location footage for *Creature from the Black Lagoon.*

Wolfie Cohen's Rascal House

17190 Collins Ave., Miami Beach, FL	$
(305) 947-4581	BLD

With pink tile walls, aqua upholstery, and white-uniformed waitresses with big hankies pinned to their chests, Wolfie's is a Miami Beach delicatessen rhapsody. The leitmotif is schmaltz (chicken fat), spread on corned beef sandwiches if the meat isn't fatty enough for you, blended into luscious chopped liver, and infusing crusty potato pancakes. Puckery pickles start the meal—half-sours, green tomatoes—and the bread includes chewy mini–onion rolls and tough-crusted rye and pumpernickel. You can drink a glass of cool flamingo-pink borscht, available with or without a boiled potato, choose from a long list of sandwiches and smoked fish platters, then conclude with berry-topped cheesecake or mile-high lemon meringue pie. It isn't a light meal, but if classic Jewish deli food is what you hanker for, it gets no better than this.

At busy meal times, prepare to wait in a mazelike system of lines, depending on how many are in your party. The people-watching is good, usually including Miami Beach yentas, Cubans, Haitians, and homesick New Yorkers in search of a pastrami fix.

GEORGIA

★ ★ ★

Hwy. 78 W, Bremen, GA (404) 537-4180	$
Tues–Sat	£𝔇

Just a few minutes from exit 3 off I-20 near the Alabama border, Bilbo's is a restaurant that hungry travelers need to know about. There are two entrances: one to the dining room, a modest wood-paneled space with leatherette booths, the other to the take-out window. The menu includes steaks and chicken, but aside from hickory-smoked prime rib (a weekend-only special), what's interesting is pork barbecue. It is quite delicious, chopped fine and mixed with a sweet, tangy sauce and served on a bun or on a plate with cole slaw, French fries, and Brunswick stew. The stew, a traditional companion to smoked meat meals in these parts, is a thick pork gravy, laced with meat and vegetables, and positively addictive once you start mopping it with bread or spooning it up from the bowl with crackers crumbled on top.

Blue Willow Inn

294 N. Cherokee Rd., Social Circle, GA	$$
(404) 464-0599	£ⅅ

Come to Social Circle, Georgia, one of the loveliest towns in all the South, find this pillared antebellum mansion, and eat to your heart's delight. The prices are fixed, from $8.95 for a weekday lunch to $14.95 for the Friday night seafood and southern food buffet, and the choices are staggering. "We have two rules here," the waitress warns us at the beginning of a meal. "Rule one is that no one goes home hungry. Rule two is that everybody has to have at least two desserts."

With a minimum of four meats and more than a dozen vegetables on display at the buffet tables, not to mention the umpteen pies, cakes, cookies, brownies, and cobbler, you either aim for a tiny bite of everything you like or you make hard choices: pass up opulent macaroni and cheese in favor of skillet squash; ignore corn bread dressing so you have room on the plate for a heap of fried green tomatoes. If you fancy baked and smothered pork chops, then you likely won't have a chance to savor streak o' lean—thick strips of bacony pork that vary in texture from wickedly crusty to meltaway-lush, blanketed with smooth white gravy. Customers are welcome to return to the buffet for second, third, fourth, and fifth helpings, but the problem is that some dishes (like the fried chicken) are so dang delicious that you want to pile your plate with them again and again, recklessly sacrificing variety for monomaniacal satisfaction.

The Colonnade

1879 Cheshire Bridge Rd., Atlanta, GA	$$
(404) 874-5642	£ⅅ

Trust the Colonnade's waitstaff of good ol' girls to take good care of you. In this polite place, a bastion of southern food since the 1920s, waitresses speed broad trays of food to tables full of families who have been customers for generations. The specialties, which never change, include excellent fried chicken and crusty catfish, served with plenty of soulful southern-style vegetables (great okra!) and genteel side dishes that include tomato aspic, lovely corn muffins, and yeast rolls.

Deacon Burton's Grill

1029 Edgewood Ave., Atlanta, GA (404) 523-1929	$
Mon–Fri	BLD

Deacon Burton, who founded this soul-food institution in 1930, passed away in 1992, but his son Lenn and daughter-in-law Beverly sustain his legacy. In this case, tradition demands they serve Atlanta's finest fried chicken accompanied by collard greens and corn bread and followed by banana pudding. Decor is minimal, service is cafeteria-style, and prices are feloniously low. Nevertheless, eat here enough times and, sooner or later, you will meet everyone who is anyone in Atlanta.

Dillard House

Hwy. 441, Dillard, GA	$
(706) 746-5349	LD

Bring a mighty big appetite to Dillard House. You'll need it to plow through the extravagant feast that has inscribed this boisterous eating hall onto America's good food registry. Tables may be shared by strangers during peak summer hours, but that doesn't inhibit anybody from having a wildly good time tucking into country ham and fried chicken, yams, biscuits, and peach cobbler, all served family-style in communal bowls that are replenished by the kitchen until all diners have had their fill. Aside from lavish food, Dillard House is a favorite travelers' destination for its location. The north Georgia landscape that includes awe-inspiring waterfalls, enchanting backwoods cabins, hiking trails, and picturesque highways served as scenery in several good ol' boy movies starring Burt Reynolds, whose signed 8 × 10 hangs on the dining room wall.

The GA Pig

exit 6 off I-95, Brunswick, GA	$
(912) 264-6664	LD

Pork is slow-cooked over hickory wood, basted with sweet sauce, then hacked into juicy chunks that are mixed with another soupçon of sauce. The resulting food is an attraction all hungry travelers along I-95 in Georgia need to know about. It is served on platter or sandwich with delectable barbecue beans on the side. If you are in a hurry, you can get it to gobble in your car, or there are picnic tables, inside and out, that make this pine-shaded rustic shack a pleasant place to linger.

Harold's

171 McDonough Blvd. SE, Atlanta, GA	$
(404) 627-9268	LD

Pork, smoked and sliced to mouth-watering succulence, with Brunswick stew and cracklin' corn bread on the side—it is the definitive Georgia smoke house meal, nowhere tastier than at Harold's, a pit on the wrong side of town (that's the Federal Pen just down the street; Harold's windows have bars on them, too). Good manners prevail in this humble dining room where walls are decorated with religious slogans and no alcohol is served. Established in 1947 by Harold Hembree, now operated by his widow and children, it's a retreat where good food transcends a bad neighborhood.

Horseradish Grill

4320 Powers Ferry Rd., Atlanta, GA	*$$$*
(404) 255-7277	*D*

Chef David Berry has made his handsome, wood-floored restaurant north of downtown into a manifesto on behalf of New Southern Cooking. What that means is that familiar regional foods are prepared in novel ways that reawaken the palate to their splendors while also adhering to a virtuous nutritional consciousness. Fried chicken, lightly crusted with a buttermilk batter made of potato flour, is as luscious as any, but magically greaseless and easy to devour. Trout from waters in the Georgia hills is delicately grilled with herbs that bring out its deep flavor; daily vegetable plates include sparklingly healthy-seeming piles of greens, gingered beets, and high-flavored black-eyed peas. For dessert, the translucent gold lemon chess pie, while not in any way revolutionary, is a dear old friend.

Melear's

GA 85, Fayetteville, GA	*$*
(770) 461-7180	*BLD*

The Melear family has been known for its barbecue skills since grandpa John Melear started selling pork south of Atlanta in the 1920s. Today's roadside restaurant, with its old wood tables and deeply saturated smoke smell, is a north Georgia pork shrine. Cooked over hickory and oak, the meat is mild and sweet. It is hacked up and served in sandwiches or as part of a platter with the side dish known as Brunswick stew, itself a zesty gallimaufry of sauce, meat, and vegetables. You can also try the meat in an item listed on the menu as a "bowl of pork," which is nothing but meat and sauce, a meal fit for monomaniacs.

Note: Melear's iced tea is a sweet southern paradigm, served in huge tumblers that are refilled on the house. Eat enough of this spicy meat and Brunswick stew, and you'll need it.

Sconyer's Bar-B-Q

2511 Windsor Spring Rd., Augusta, GA (706) 790-5411	$
Thur–Sat	£D

Sconyer's is huge, impersonal, and way too busy. But its chopped pork sopped with tangy sauce and its racks of meaty ribs are piggy perfection, at once lean and dizzyingly succulent. On the side of whatever you order, you want hash (or you can make a meal of it), a Deep South treat made of all the barbecued meats—ham, chicken, and beef—chopped up with tomatoes, onions, potatoes, and plenty of good sauce.

Silver Skillet

200 14th St., Atlanta, GA	$
(404) 874-1388	BLD

We highly recommend you go to the bathroom at the Silver Skillet. The route leads through the kitchen, which is hot as Hades but provides an incredibly appetizing tour of fine food being created by masters in humble surroundings: onion rings pulled from hot oil, country ham drizzled with powerhouse red-eye gravy, great slabs of meat loaf plated alongside sweet yams and butter-tender cabbage and tangy fried green tomatoes.

The dining room itself, where glass windows slant rakishly outward at the angle of 1950s tailfins, is a blast from the past; green-and-orange Naugahyde-upholstered booths frame boomerang-pattern Formica tables. A sign on the wall advises, USE A LITTLE SUGAR AND STIR LIKE HELL. WE DON'T MIND THE NOISE. Each table is strewn with pencils. As you peruse the written menu and the long list of daily vegetables and specials posted above the counter, a waitress delivers you a couple of checks on which you write your own order.

Breakfast is especially worthwhile. The skillet-cooked ham is the real thing, strong and salty; biscuits are oven-hot; grits and gravy are pure country. And the people-watching is swell; high and low, rich and poor, the famous, the notorious, and the unknown all make themselves right at home in these old booths.

Smith House

202 S. Chestatee St., Dahlonega, GA	$$
(706) 864-3566	£D

Country cooking, served family-style—for a half-century, the Smith House has been luring appetites with its pay-one-price, eat-till-you-drop meals. Fried chicken is always the main attraction, with ham or catfish as alternatives, surrounded by a glorious assortment of such vegetables as candied sweet potatoes, brandied chestnut soufflé, fried okra, and turnip greens and accompanied by a battery of biscuits, rolls, and corn bread. It is a high-spirited feast, with strangers becoming friends as they pass the butter beans and exchange tales of wondrous meals they have eaten in their travels.

South City Kitchen

1144 Crescent Ave., Atlanta, GA	$$$
(404) 873-7358	D

Deluxe southern food put chef Scott Walker's midtown restaurant on the map just months after it opened a short while ago. Situated in a sturdy wood-frame home that has been thoroughly renovated and decorated in high style, the South City Kitchen is a place to eat extremely sophisticated meals in which traditional ingredients get the royal treatment; turnip greens are flavored with a sun-dried tomato vinaigrette, finely shredded sweet/salty French fried yams accompany duck breast with braised cabbage, barbecued swordfish comes on a pallet of stone ground grits, catfish is served with amazingly delicious hoppin' john.

In the early days of South City Kitchen desserts were an afterthought, but on a recent visit we were bowled over by the chocolate pecan pie, and the smooth, luxurious crème caramel was a foodstuff fit for gods.

The Varsity

61 North Ave., Atlanta, GA (404) 881-1706;	$
also on Broad at Milledge in Athens (404) 548-6325	BLD

An Atlanta institution since 1928, the Varsity is a huge drive-in with seats inside for some 800 customers, plus curb service. It is famous for not just fast food but *lightning-fast* food, garnished with plenty of hash-slinger sass. "What'll ya have?" countermen bellow, calling out to the vast kitchen orders for "Yankee steaks" (hamburgers with yellow mustard), "strings" (French fries), and "FOs" (frosted orange drinks). The aplomb of the staff is of mythic proportions. Senator Phil Gramm recently recalled that when he was at college in Atlanta, the *Journal-Constitution* had a party for its paperboys. The organizer stepped up and ordered *six thousand* steaks, to go. The counterman, without missing a beat, shot back, "Watcha drinkin'?"

Hot dogs are the house specialty, little pink tube steaks served in steamy-soft buns, begging to be dolled up with condiments. The prime adornment is chili, a finely pulverized brew that perfectly complements either dog or burger. Chili dogs are customarily served with stripes of yellow mustard across their tops, accompanied by cardboard boats full of crusty onion rings and/or excellent French fries.

By the way, this is health food, at least according to Varsity founder Frank Gordy, who once proclaimed, "A couple of chili dogs a day keep you young."

Ye Olde Colonial Cafeteria

On the Square, Madison, GA	$
(706) 342-2211	BLD

We cannot say what, exactly, is Colonial about Ye Olde Colonial Cafeteria, which is located in a former bank building in a town full of antebellum mansions, but we can tell you this for sure: it is a great place to eat true southern cooking, served southern-style in a short cafeteria line. The fried chicken is cooked to crisp succulence, and the shredded pork barbecue is moist and saucy. These tasty entrees are served alongside classic Dixie vegetables that include rutabaga casserole, candied yams, and collard greens drenched in pot likker. Corn sticks have a fetching crunch, apple cobbler is irresistible, tables are equipped with pitchers full of presweetened iced tea. Ye Olde Colonial, the nice place in town, is a great eating opportunity for anyone on the road between Atlanta and Augusta.

LOUISIANA

Black's Oyster Bar	
311 Pere Merget St., Abbeville, LA (318) 893-4266	$
Aug through Apr	£𝔇

Live Longer! Love Longer!" is the promise of Black's menu to all who eat enough oysters. If you do relish oysters, fresh from the Gulf and on the half shell, this is the place to eat them by the dozen, with an assortment of hot sauces to add spice and oyster crackers to cleanse the palate.

If twenty or thirty oysters only pique your appetite, follow them with some delicious fried oysters or fried shrimp, both available on a platter or, the best deal of all, combined and stuffed into a po' boy sandwich with mayo and/or mustard as a garnish. Once you've had this sandwich, you will long to return to Cajun country during oyster season.

Bon Ton Café	
401 Magazine, New Orleans, LA	$$
(504) 524-3386	£𝔇

Elegant but not snooty, pricey but worthwhile, a vintage city restaurant that is equally good to old-timers and tourists, the Bon Ton

Café is the best place we know for a pleasant, classic Creole meal. In starched white outfits, the suave staff will serve you such local delicacies as oyster pan roast, crawfish étouffée in crawfish season (shrimp étouffée in the summer), and not-to-be-missed redfish Bon Ton, served with a delicious crabmeat-laced sauce. There is only one dessert you need to know about: bread pudding with whiskey sauce. There are many food-savvy New Orleaneans who say this thick block of cake is the best bread pudding in town, and in this bread-pudding-crazed city, that is saying plenty.

Crawdad Variations

In Cajun country, the crawfish is king. The lobstery fresh-water crustacean is generally at its biggest and best in the spring. The simplest way to enjoy it is boiled. Twist the tail from the head, crack the top of the tail, squeeze, and out pops one sweet, succulent mouthful of meat. Then scoop the "butter" (actually crawfish fat) from the head. Four or five pounds make a nice meal.

But of course restless Cajun country cooks aren't satisfied with merely boiling and seasoning anything, so many restaurants in the area offer these ways with the delicacy known to its friends as the mudbug:

Cajun popcorn	Deep fried crawfish tails
Crawfish bisque	Buttery soup filled with crawfish heads
Crawfish boulettes	Crawfish meatballs
Crawfish gumbo	Thick stew, often including okra
Crawfish étouffée	Tails stirred into a peppery sauce, served over rice
Crawfish pie	Baked with garlic and vegetables in a thin crust

Creole Menu Crib Sheet

~◦◦◦~

First, you should know that the difference between Cajun and Creole is itself a little blurred, the former originally referring to swamp-country folk culture, the latter to the more cosmopolitan ways of city folks. Culinarily, the two are now too mixed up to separate neatly. These are terms from both traditions you need to know to eat well in New Orleans or out in the bayous.

Andouille	Spicy smoked pork sausage, usually grilled
Biegnet	A light, holeless donut customarily served with café au lait
Boudin	Country sausage, traditionally made blanc or rouge (with or without blood)
Court bouillon	A dense, spicy tomato sauce, customarily served on redfish
Dirty rice	White rice cooked with giblets and gravy
Étouffée	Simply, "smothered," but crawfish or shrimp étouffée are not simple!
Grillades and grits	Seasoned steak or beef or veal with gravy and grits on the side
Gumbo	A pot-au-feu built upon long-cooked roux (butter and flour)
Jambalaya	A gallimaufry with almost anything, but usually ham and rice
Muffuletta	A circular Italian-flavored cold-cut sandwich with chopped olives
Pain perdu	French toast, made with French bread
Po' boy	A long loaf of French bread jam-packed with ingredients
Praline	Creamy candy made with pecans
Remoulade	Piquant mayonnaise used for dressing chilled shellfish

Boudin King

906 W. Division St., Jennings, LA	$
(318) 824-6593	LD

The powerfully spiced pork sausage known as boudin is a hallmark of the Cajun kitchen, and it's the food on which Ellis Cormier's drive-in restaurant has built its reputation since Monsieur Cormier, the Boudin King of swamp country fairs and food festivals, opened for business in 1975. His boudin is sold in large links, mild or spicy, for eating here or to take home. But beware, even the mild boudin packs a punch, so spicy it's sinus-draining. Either kind is porky, powerful food, best enjoyed in the company of other good things served up by his kitchen. They include smoky gumbo, crisp-fried catfish and fried crawfish, as well as freshly made hog's head cheese. Although the restaurant looks like any modern franchise, it is one of a kind, and one of the reasons it is such a pleasure to eat one's way through Louisiana.

Café du Monde

800 Decatur St., New Orleans, LA (504) 587-0840	$
always open	

No traveling eater is allowed to visit New Orleans without breakfast at Café du Monde, the open-air, open-all-night café where the café au lait is bracing, the beignets (little holeless rectangular donuts sprinkled with sugar) are sweet, and the people-watching is spectacular. Fellow customers early in the morning range from fresh-scrubbed little-old-ladies off the Dubuque Scenic Tours bus to drag queens and French Quarter kooks finishing a long, hard night.

Camelia Grill

626 S. Carrollton Ave., New Orleans, LA	$
(504) 866-9573	BLD

heese and chili omelets, pecan waffles, chocolate milk shakes—what a joy it is to watch the food being prepared as you sit at the counter of this distinguished diner, where the waiters are dressed formally but the meals are cheap and delicious. An only-in-New Orleans eating experience.

Casamento's

4330 Magazine, New Orleans, LA (504) 895-9761	$$
(closed June–Sept)	LD

asamento's is a ship-shape little oyster bar that serves a distinctive sandwich called an oyster loaf, which is like a po' boy but bigger. Sweet, freshly fried oysters are piled into an entire loaf of white bread that is cut lengthwise and scooped out to make a big fried-fish pocket. There is no easy way to eat it, but that's of no concern, for the contrast between the cushiony bread and crisp, briny oysters induces a kind of ravenous ecstasy that makes you want to tear at the food and feel its textures on your fingertips even before you savor them on your tongue.

The oyster loaf is the signature dish all newcomers must have, but regular customers patronize the vintage neighborhood spot for other delicacies, such as raw oysters by the dozen, fried shrimp, the Italian Creole pot roast known as daube, as well as good old-fashioned spaghetti.

Deep South Splurges

Expensive, fancy, and/or fashionable regional restaurants that are worth it.

- ☛ Bottega, Birmingham, AL (p. 115)
- ☛ Highlands Bar and Grill, Birmingham, AL (p. 116)
- ☛ Hot and Hot Fish Club, Birmingham, AL (p. 117)
- ☛ Bern's Steak House, Tampa, FL (p. 124)
- ☛ Joe's Stone Crab, Miami Beach, FL (p. 128)
- ☛ Horseradish Grill, Atlanta, GA (p. 134)
- ☛ South City Kitchen, Atlanta, GA (p. 136)
- ☛ Bon Ton Café, New Orleans, LA (p. 138)
- ☛ Robin's, Henderson, LA (p. 148)
- ☛ Doe's Eat Place, Greenville, MS (p. 151)
- ☛ Lusco's, Greenwood, MS (p. 152)

Central Grocery

923 Decatur St., New Orleans, LA	$
(504) 523-1620	BLD

Central Grocery lays claim to inventing the muffaletta, a New Orleans sandwich on a circular loaf of chewy bread that is sliced horizontally, like a yeasty flying saucer. The cold cuts loaded on the bottom half include salami, ham, and provolone, topped with a spicy melange of chopped green and black olives fragrant with anchovies and garlic; the bread is generously sprinkled with olive oil; and the whole package is wrapped in paper so you can carry it away. There are no tables or chairs in the old grocery store, where the air is perfumed by cheese and sausage; most customers take their sandwich, with a bottle of root beer, to a bench in Jackson Square at the French Market. The muffaletta, cut in quarters by the deli man, is a mighty handful, one of the Crescent City's culinary wonders.

Dean-O's

305 Bertrand Dr., Lafayette, LA	$
(318) 233-5446	£D

Trust us. When you see Dean-O's, you will want to drive right past. It looks about as interesting as a Domino's franchise. In fact, you can order some pretty ordinary pizza in this plasticine place. But if you did, you would then miss the truly sensational pizzas they make that are topped with small, succulent marinated crawfish tails (in season after Mardi Gras), shrimp, or big pieces of fresh Gulf crabmeat.

Eddie's

2119 Law St., New Orleans, LA	$$
(504) 945-2207	£D

Eddie's is a gumbo shop, and then some. On a forbidding side street near Elysian Fields, it is an insider's haunt that all serious fans of New Orleans soul food need to seek out. The diverse and mouth-watering menu includes luscious fried chicken with powerhouse greens on the side, stuffed pork chops with oyster stuffing more oystery than the law allows, red beans and rice with a garlic wallop, and cold-cut po' boys on fine French bread, as well as a classic oyster loaf loaded with crunchy nuggets of sweet seafood. The gumbo is a Creole paradigm— dark and smoky, loaded with shrimp, oysters, chicken, ham, hot sausage, beef, and pork—so brilliantly spiced it will make you dizzy.

Lagneaux

445 Ridge Rd., Lafayette, LA	$
(318) 984-1415	D

There is a sit-down menu, but who can resist a buffet that features such satisfying swamp country meals as crawfish-stuffed peppers and jambalayas of Gulf seafood, plus crunch-crusted fried chicken and a large selection of well-cooked vegetables on the side, with biscuits or lengths of good bread to mop it all off the plate? At low single-digit prices, these high-spiced everyday feasts are exactly what make an eating trip through Creole country so extraordinary.

Lasyone's Meat Pie Kitchen

622 Second St., Natchitoches, LA	$
(318) 352-3353	BL

Once sold from corner carts all over town, the lusty bayou specialty known as a Cane River meat pie had nearly vanished from Natchitoches when James Lasyone opened up a meat pie kitchen in 1967. His little restaurant on the picturesque cobblestone streets of Natchitoches (where *Steel Magnolias* was filmed) is now a good-eats landmark, and meat pies are back.

Mr. Lasyone's is a beaut, a golden-crusted pastry pocket about the size of a taco, crunchy near the crimp, soft near its mounded center. Inside the flaky sheaf is a heap of seasoned ground beef, moist enough to make gravy irrelevant. Spicy but not fire-hot, complex and succulent, Lasyone's meat pie is an honest piece of food that satisfies in an old-fashioned way. You can get one for breakfast, accompanied by eggs and hash browns; most steady customers come midday to get a pair of them for lunch, with soulful "dirty rice" on the side, darkened with gizzards and topped with zesty gravy. After meat pie, our personal weakness is a dessert Mr. Lasyone invented some years back called Cane River cream pie, which is similar to Boston cream pie but dark and spicy and made from gingerbread.

Mandina's

3800 Canal St., New Orleans, LA	$$
(504) 482-9179	£D

Not a tourist attraction, but nonetheless mobbed at mealtime (with loyal locals), Mandina's is the sine qua non of any genuine New Orleans eating tour. Nothing fancy, not too expensive, and a bit down-at-the-heels, it is a neighborhood restaurant where the French bread is impeccably fresh, the marinated crab claws are plump and succulent, the seafood po' boys are loaded with crisp oysters and/or shrimp, and the bread pudding with whiskey sauce is heavenly. Like so many of the definitive New Orleans restaurants, Mandina's Creole cuisine has a strong Italian accent. Even the Jambalaya has a soulful Mediterranean twist to its spices, and you can't go wrong ordering spaghetti and meatballs or Italian sausage. Whatever else you taste, begin with turtle au sherry soup.

Middendorf's

US 51 N, Pass Manchac, LA	$$
(504) 386-6666	£D

Oh, how our culinary dreams dance with great, heaping plates of Middendorf's thin-sliced fried catfish! Crisp, sweet, exquisitely seasoned, and impossible to stop eating, catfish has made this Tangipoa Parish restaurant into a favorite destination for big eaters since Louis and Josie Middendorf opened for business in 1934. There are fine thick catfish fillets on the menu, too, juicier than their thin counterparts (but without the irresistibly sinful deep-fried crunch), and there is a whole menu of local seafood, including oysters, crab, crawfish, shrimp, good gumbo, and po' boy sandwiches. As a concession to the fat-obsessed customer, broiled catfish has recently been added to the menu. However, to come to this big, happy barn of a restaurant and not eat something fried would be as dumb as going to a Kansas City steak house for the vegetarian platter.

Mosca's	
4137 US 90, Waggaman, LA	$$
(504) 436-9942	D

You will think you are lost on the way to Mosca's, situated in a god-forsaken swamp far outside of town. Even when you find it, you will wonder, Can this ramshackle way station with the blaring jukebox really be the most famous Creole roadhouse in America? Once oil and butter from the spaghetti bordelaise begin dripping down your chin and you inhale the fragrant bouquet of chicken à la grandee or herbed Italian oyster casserole, you will know you have found a culinary epiphany. Rude as it is, roadside food gets no better, or more garlicky, or heartier, than this. Go to Mosca's with friends: the bigger the group, the more different wonders you can sample; and besides, everything is served family-style.

Mother's	
401 Poydras, New Orleans, LA (504) 523-9656	$
(closed Sun and Mon)	BL

This only-in-New Orleans proletarian cafeteria has been dishing out biscuit breakfast and hot lunch since 1938, and it remains one of the great Creole eating experiences, regardless of its low-low prices. Red beans and rice, with hefty lengths of sausage, is a definitive rib-sticker, with good corn bread on the side; baked ham, piled into fleecy French bread along with little bits of cracklin' from the outside of the roast, may be the tastiest ham on earth. It is the star attraction in a messy but magnificent po' boy called a Ferdi, where it is combined with roast beef, cole slaw, assorted condiments, and an item known as debris, which is gravy-sopped little shreds and succulent morsels from the roast beef. The debris is so good that you can get a po' boy with nothing but.

Less renowned, but one of the city's culinary wonders, is Mother's breakfast, which includes a crawfish étouffée omelet and an omelet made with green onions and nuggets of crusty sweet ham from the outside of a roast, both served, of course, with oven-warm biscuits and grits.

Old Tyme Grocery

218 W. St. Mary Blvd., Lafayette, LA	$
(318) 235-8165	£D

Old Tyme Grocery is not a sit-down restaurant, but it is an essential stop on the po' boy trail. At the meat counter, yard-long loaves of fresh, fluffy-centered bread are stuffed with whatever ingredients you specify. Connoisseur's choice: crusty fried shrimp, about eight hundred of 'em in a single sandwich. While the man makes your sandwich, you can admire such local favorites in the cold case as hog's head cheese and dark, scary-looking sausages.

Robin's

Hwy. 352, Henderson, LA	$$
(318) 228-7594	£D

Crawfish heaven! Lionel Robin's restaurant makes all sorts of wonderful Cajun food, but in the spring at the height of crawfish season, that's all you want to know. Get 'em stewed, fried, boiled, étoufféed, brewed in gumbo, and creamed for bisque. Or have garlicky crawfish pie, in which the butter-rich creatures are accompanied by a handful of vegetables in a paper-thin crust.

Robin's is worth a trip even when it isn't crawfish season. Okra gumbo made with shrimp and even the nonseafood sausage gumbo are outstanding meals. Henderson is a dot on the map, miles from everywhere, but if you want to eat well in southern Louisiana, a visit to Robin's is urgent.

Soops Seafood and Steak House

Maurice, LA	$
(318) 893-2462	£Ⓓ

Soop Hebert, who started the "Specialty Meats" shop next door, also opened the Cajun eatery that bears his name. Now run by Soop's daughters, it is one of the gumbo beacons of Cajun country. Thick with sausage and vibrant with spice, Soop's brew is intoxicating just to sniff; eating it—slowly, as rapture builds and tastebuds weep for joy— is a not-to-be-missed culinary experience. Soop's menu is a bonanza of local flavors: crabmeat, crawfish, stuffed rabbit, quail, and alligator, with homemade cherry pie for dessert.

MISSISSIPPI

Abe's

616 State St., Clarksdale, MS	$
(601) 624-9211	£Ⓓ

A winsome pig plays the violin in a mural on the wall of Abe's little dining room, where the smoke-cooked pork is lean, sweet, and tender. It is served sliced, sizzled on the grill, along with sauce-spritzed slaw and beans. Add your own sauce to the meat; you get a choice of mild or lip-searing hot. Barbecue has been Abe's fame since the 1920s; connoisseurs of regional fare will also want to savor tamales, served with or without chili on top, but not available during the sultry summer months.

Bill's Hamburgers

Main St., Amory, MS (601) 256-2085	$
Mon–Sat (opens at 7 am, but no breakfast food is served)	BL

Dine on a bar stool with a view of burgers being cooked. The menu at Bill's is simplicity itself: a single or double burger, with or without onions and cheese (but no lettuce or tomatoes are available), with French fries on the side. The fine, old-fashioned burgers—like the kind every drugstore lunch counter once served—are presented wrapped in wax paper. That's the way it is at this culinary relic from seven o'clock every morning (hamburgers for breakfast!), and that's the way it's been, since 1929.

The Blue and White

Hwy. 61, Tunica, MS	$
(601) 363-1371	BLD

Breakfast at the Blue and White truck stop is a Route 61 rite of passage. Since the 1930s, this broad-shouldered roadside restaurant has become a landmark for drivers, farmers, and wanderers who come for huge morning meals of eggs and grits with ham and red-eye gravy, accompanied by bottomless cups of coffee. It is all dished out by a staff of take-no-prisoners waitresses who can fill you in on good local gossip from a hundred-mile radius.

The Dinner Bell

229 Fifth Ave., McComb, MS (601) 684-4883	$
Tues–Sun; D Fri and Sat only	£

The Dinner Bell is one of the South's great big feeds. Serve yourself from lazy Susans in the center of the round tables shared by strangers. Vegetables are always outstanding and include such local delights as butter beans, field peas, fried okra, and sweet potato casserole. Chicken and dumplings, ham, and fried chicken are some of the entrees from which to choose, and there is always a good assortment of oven-warm biscuits and corn breads. The fun and the challenge of a communal meal like this is to grab what you want when the lazy Susan spins by. You want to be quick (although platters are replenished throughout the dinner hour), and a boardinghouse reach is perfectly appropriate.

Doe's Eat Place

502 Nelson, Greenville, MS (601) 334-3315;	**$$$**
also at 1551 Hwy. 1 S (601) 332-2171;	**D**
and there is a branch in Little Rock, AR at 1023 W. Markham St. (501) 376-1195	

Many people believe that the original Doe's Eat Place of Greenville serves the best steaks in America. It is impressive to see the raw ones paraded out from the cooler for customers' inspection, and even more thrilling when they arrive at the table awhile later, sputtering hot and seeping savory juice onto the plate.

Everything else Doe's serves is terrific, too: French fries are sizzled to tan perfection in a deep iron skillet, spicy hot tamales could be a meal unto themselves, and fresh salads are mixed with lemon juice and olive oil dressing at kitchen tables that share space with dining tables.

The real fun of this place is its extreme informality. Located on a side street in a broken-down building that used to be a grocery store, just getting to it is an adventure. Once inside, eating a meal is like supper at Grandma's. Customers sit in mismatched chairs at assorted tables in a back room kitchen and in other miscellaneous rooms where the proprietors used to live.

The Elite

141 E. Capitol, Jackson, MS	$
(601) 352-5606	BLD

Where the elite (and everyone else) in downtown Jackson meet, this 1940s-era three-meals-a-day café is a pleasure for anyone who appreciates quick, home-cooked plates of food at low prices. The dinner rolls are superb and the breakfast biscuits are steamy-hot; the southern vegetables—greens, yams, squash, etc.—are classics; entrees range from a stupendously good enchilada plate to catfish or pork chops and a veal cutlet as crisp and succulent as a good chicken-fried steak.

Lusco's

722 Carrolton Ave., Greenwood, MS	$$$
(601) 453-5365	D

The walls of a big, wood-floored vestibule are painted institutional green and festooned with small game trophies. In one corner are some waiting-room chairs and a couch arranged around a television set and an old kiosk with a pay phone inside. In the back, private dining carrels are arranged off dim hallways, so although you can hear other customers, you see no one but your dining companions across a field of luxurious white cotton cloth and thick folded napkins. To summon help, each booth is equipped with a buzzer.

The strangeness of the setting has no doubt enhanced Lusco's reputation in the Delta where eccentricity is treasured, but the main reason for its renown is deluxe food. Founders Mama and Papa Lusco were Italian by way of Louisiana, so the flavors of the kitchen they established are as much Creole as they are southern or Italian. Gumbo, crab, and shrimp are always on the menu, and oysters are a specialty in season, on the half-shell or baked with bacon. Because so many regular patrons have always been big spenders from well-to-do cotton families, the menu is best known among them for its high-end items. Lusco's T-bone steaks are some of the finest anywhere; sumptuous cuts are brought raw to the table for your approval, then broiled to pillowy succulence. Pompano has for many years been a house trademark, broiled and served whole, bathed in a magical sauce made of butter, lemon, and secret spices.

Mammy's Cupboard	
555 Hwy. 61 S, Natchez, MS (601) 445-8957	$
Tues–Sat	£

Mammy's Cupboard, a restaurant shaped like a woman (you dine under her skirt), has gone through many changes since it was built over fifty years ago. Originally, Mammy was an African-American maid with a black face, and crisp fried chicken was the specialty of the house. Now the cuisine is more ladylike Dixie tearoom fare, with cold vegetables to start the meal, good soup, sandwiches on homemade bread, and one hot lunch special every day—roast pork loin with rice and chicken pot pie with broccoli corn bread are the ones we enjoyed. The restaurant itself has been politically corrected and the face of the woman under whom you eat is European-American.

Mendenhall Hotel Revolving Tables	
Old Hwy. 49, Mendenhall, MS	$$
(601) 847-3113	£D

At the center of each large round table in the Mendenhall Hotel's dining rooms is a big lazy Susan piled with food. Spin it and take what you like from a vast assortment of beautifully prepared Dixie dishes that range from biscuits and cracklin' corn bread to hot peach cobbler for dessert. Entrees include fried chicken, pork chops, and barbecued beef, and there are always way too many vegetable casseroles to ever get a chance to sample all of them—candied yams, buttered squash, creamed spinach, etc. It is a feast to remember, all the more fun for the high spirits that prevail among hungry strangers sharing the fun in a dining room where a needlepoint sampler on the wall advises, EAT 'TIL IT OUCHES.

Phillips Grocery

541-A East Van Dorn Ave., Holly Springs, MS	$
(601) 252-4671	£𝔇

A two-story wood-frame house by the railroad tracks, Phillips has built its reputation on hamburgers since the 1940s. Many customers buy them to go, but there are seats, too: a short counter with stools, a handful of wooden school desks, and a few odd tables where regulars finish off their meals with a short stack of marshmallowy Moon Pies from the grocery shelf.

Hamburgers are available in various sizes and are wrapped in yellow wax paper inside a bag for easy toting. When you peel back the wrapping, particularly on a half-pound Super-Deluxe, you behold a vision of beauty-in-a-bun. Cooked on a hot grill, it is a thick patty with a luscious crunch to its nearly blackened skin. Inside, the meat is moist enough to ooze juice when you gently squeeze the soft bun wrapped around it. The flavor is fresh, beefy, and sumptuous, an American classic on a par with the esteemed hamburgers of Cassell's in Los Angeles, Louis Lunch in New Haven, and Kincaid's Market in Fort Worth.

Ruth & Jimmie's

Business Rte. 7, Abbeville, MS	$
(601) 234-4312	£

A sign outside this little shop sums it up pretty well: RUTH & JIMMIE'S SPORTING GOODS AND CAFÉ, HUNTING AND FISHING SUPPLIES, LIVE BAITS AND LICENSES. Up front, shelves are stocked with bullets and orange safety vests, outboard motor oil and Think-Safe flotation devices. The live bait is usually kept outside, in buckets near the gas pumps.

At the back of the one-room market are an open kitchen, a few booths, and a counter. From any seat, the view is of plate-lunch heaven: crisp fried chicken is plucked from bubbling oil; stockpots boil with turnip greens; macaroni and cheese is scooped from its pan, tender and extravagantly rich; apples are simmered until they are soft and sugary; bite-size nuggets of fried okra emerge from the kettle with a lacy web of crust. There are slaws and salads and pickled beets, sweet corn and limp-cooked cabbage, and mashed potatoes whipped up right before lunch begins.

Smitty's	
208 S. Lamar, Oxford, MS	$
(601) 234-9111	BLD

Oxford's good old town café, patronized by Ole Miss students and townies alike, Smitty's is a fine place to go for biscuits and grits in the morning, served with country ham and red-eye or creamy sawmill gravy. Lunch classics include sandy-crusted whole catfish, fried steak smothered with gravy, and a heap of greens with hog jowl and corn bread. The beverage of choice, naturally, is iced tea.

Taylor Gro. & Restaurant	
Taylor, MS	$
(601) 236-1716	D

In this ramshackle joint in the crossroads town of Taylor, the walls are covered with years of Ole Miss graffiti, and on football weekends the place is a madhouse. Taylor's specialty is catfish supper with all the trimmings, including French fries, hush puppies, and cole slaw. The fish is sandy-crusted and served whole (although fillets are available); its meat is heavy and sweet—a definitive Mississippi meal.

SOUTH CAROLINA

Alice's Fine Foods

468–470 King St., Charleston, SC	$
(803) 873-9366	*LD*

An airy, multiroom cafeteria with a television at one end and a freezer with sixteen flavors of ice cream at the other, Alice's is where Charlestonians go to eat low country soul food. Fried shrimp and oysters are served by the dozen, sheathed in melting-crisp crust; deviled crab is plump and spicy; and okra is served in a spicy soup with beans and tomatoes. Side dishes include: collard greens dotted with hunks of salty ham, macaroni thick with cheese, rice laced with chicken and giblets. Desserts include plain and perfect layer cakes.

The Bakers Café

214 King St., Charleston, SC	$
(803) 577-2694	*BL*

Here are beautiful poached eggs in all configurations. Have 'em southern style on corn bread with country ham, "a la hash" atop a crisp cake of corned beef hash with dark Madiera sauce, with artichokes or bacon and cheese or crabmeat. Plates are handsomely garnished, and portions are demure enough that you might also want one of Bakers' delicious glazed Danish pastries or rugged raspberry scones on the side. This is a quiet, civilized little café, suitable for morning meditation over breakfast coffee, and a nice place for lunch, when the egg menu is supplemented by sandwiches and light entrees.

Southernisms

Southern menus contain many wonderful things to eat that non-Southerners might not recognize. Here are a few basics to help you choose wisely and eat well south of the Mason-Dixon line:

Boiled peanuts	A roadside-stand treat, best eaten warm from the kettle
Chess pie	Simple sugar pie, so named perhaps because it's "jes' pie."
Congealed salad	Jell-O
Country captain	Hunter's stew, usually made with curry powder, in Georgia
Frogmore stew	Shrimp, sausage, and corn stew, native to the Carolina coast
Greens	Collard, turnip, or mustard; long cooked with pork till tender
Grits	Hot, creamy corn cereal, especially good with ham and gravy
Hush puppies	Deep-fried cornmeal balls, almost always served with catfish
Perloo	A South Carolina jambalaya, also spelled pilau and pilaf
Pine bark stew	A spicy fish stew indigenous to the Carolinas and Georgia
Pot likker	The porcine soup retrieved when greens are cooked with pork
Red rice	Seasoned rice usually made with peppers, onion, and tomato
Red-eye gravy	Ham drippings, usually mixed with black coffee or water
Sawmill gravy	Thick, creamy white gravy, frequently used to top biscuits
Spoon bread	Cornmeal soufflé

Beacon Drive-In

225 Reidsville Rd., Spartanburg, SC (864) 585-9387	$
Mon–Sat	**BLD**

The Beacon is a huge drive-in with speedy car service. But the connoisseur's way to dine is inside, where you experience the rudest, and most exhilarating, cafeteria service in America. If you are slow choosing between a chili cheeseburger and a pork-a-plenty platter, you'll be yelled at, and likely pushed aside by others who have come into this madhouse knowing exactly what they want. "Move!" counterman J. C. Strobel hollers. "Come on, come on down," he shouts to those who have placed their order and aren't quick enough getting to the cash register. It all happens so fast that novices are left in a daze. But if you survive, you will walk away with a tray of excellent pork barbecue (inside or outside meat can be specified, depending whether you like it creamy soft or crunchy), sided by hash, slaw, and onion rings, or any one of several dozen hamburger variations. The iced tea, served in titanic tumblers, is Beacon barbecue's perfect companion. It is served sweetened to the max. In fact, a counterman here once bragged to us that the Beacon uses two tons of sugar every week, just for tea. Yum!

Duke's Bar-B-Q

725 Robertson Blvd., Walterboro, SC (803) 549-1446	$
Thur, Fri, Sat only	**LD**

Duke's is Pork Paradise, South Carolina–style. A clean, plain eatplace with picnic table seating and weekend-only hours, it descends from the pig-pickin' fetes that people in these parts have enjoyed for centuries. Service is cafeteria-style. Help yourself to tender, succulent hacked pork with a choice of three sauces, spoon some hash over your rice (hash is a visceral stew made from pork parts), take some bread and pickles and all the sweet iced tea you want. (There is also fried chicken available, and it looks good, but pork wins our vote every time.) Although simple and cheap, this is a grand regional meal to remember.

Note: there is a second Duke's on Hwy. 17 S in Ridgeland (that's exit 22 off I-95). The phone there is 726-3882. Open on weekends only.

Field Guide to South Carolina Barbecue

Every region of the country has its own unique way with barbecue, but no place is as diverse as South Carolina, where at least four distinct variations of sauce are served (the meat is invariably pork):

- Northwest South Carolina: tomato-based, with a whisper of sweet relish.
- Northeast South Carolina: vinegar-based marinade, no tomato whatever.
- Central South Carolina: mustard-flavored. To the north, sauces are a mixture of ketchup and mustard, but the closer to the center of the state you get, the more mustard there is. Columbia's best sauces have no tomato or ketchup in them at all.
- Southern South Carolina: vinegar-based sauces, but often flavored with a dash of mustard.

Edisto Motel Café

Hwy. 17, Jacksonboro, SC (803) 893-2270	$
Thur–Sat	𝔇

Absolutely perfect frying," is how Edisto Motel Café food was described to us by John Martin Taylor, proprietor of Hoppin' John's culinary bookstore in Charleston and author of several evocative books on local foodways, including *Fearless Frying*, which happens to be dedicated to the Edisto. A small cinderblock dining room by the side of the highway with a perpetual line of customers waiting to get in, this inconspicuous place serves deep-fried seafood platters the likes of which you'll find nowhere else on earth: dozens of snapping-fresh, crisp-veiled shrimp per order, savory oysters sheathed in a brittle crust, flounder, scallops, or deviled crabs. The finely chopped cole slaw is delicious, the beer is cold, and the service is fast and friendly. No low country meal could be simpler, or more delicious.

Jestine's Kitchen

251 Meeting St., Charleston, SC (803) 722-7224	$
Tues–Sun	£ 𝔇

S outhern food with lots of soul" is the motto of Jestine's, a tidy storefront with a mouth-watering menu of blue-plate specials and a dozen vegetables every day. Named by owner Dana Berlin for Jestine Matthews, the 112-year-old African-American woman who raised her (and developed many of the kitchen's recipes), Jestine's is a place to feast on classic low country food such as crab cakes on Saturdays, shrimp and grits on Sundays, and okra gumbo every day. Even the simplest foods have a soulful twist: macaroni and cheese is chewy and luscious, mashed potatoes are laced with savory gravy, red rice glows with a kaleidoscope of spice. A sound system that plays old-time jazz quietly in the background completes the pleasant scene.

Maurice's Piggy Park

1600 Charleston Hwy., Columbia, SC	$
(803) 796-0220	£ 𝔇

A cclaimed by traveling trenchermen for its hickory-cooked pork, and known for its huge flag flapping over the parking lot and lightning-fast curb service, the Piggy Park is one tasty chunk of Americana. Pull into one of the tin-covered car slots, peruse the illuminated menu, and call your order in using the intercom provided. Less than three minutes later—guaranteed!—out speeds a carhop, dressed in a crisp uniform of red, white, and blue, carrying your tray of barbecue. Piggie Park Q is tantalizing stuff, infused not only with the taste of smoke but with a dose of Bessinger's eye-opening, cider-sweet, mustard-flavored sauce. On the menu, the sauce is referred to as a "million-dollar heirloom recipe."

Middleton Place

Hwy. 61 (Ashley River Rd.), Charleston, SC (803) 556-6020	$
daily, D Fri and Sat	£

Not quite an ordinary public dining room (you pay $12 per person to pass through the front gate), Middleton Place Restaurant is part of a grand effort to interpret the low country's cultural heritage on the grounds of the vast old Middleton Plantation. When it opened as a tearoom run by the Junior League in 1928, its specialties were okra soup and sandwiches. In recent years, recipes were developed by chef Edna Lewis, whose expertise in southern foodways resulted in a lunch

Drive-By Snacking

Roadside stands tend to be ephemeral—open one year, gone the next—so we don't list many in this book. Nevertheless, they can be a delicious way to eat your way across the U.S.A. We aren't talking about drive-ins or snack bars, and certainly not about such city street food as soft pretzels in Philadelphia, pizza slices in New York, or red hots in Chicago, all of which are more "walking around" fare intended for pedestrian dining. Drive-by snacks are for gobbling while you drive or, in the case of messier ones, while briefly parked by the side of the road. These are some of the regional drive-by snacks to watch for as you travel:

Washed Black Cherries	Northern Michigan, late summer
Boiled Peanuts	Mid-South
Chile-Roasted Pecans	New Mexico
Roasted Chile Sandwiches	New Mexico, during the autumn chile harvest
Cheese Curds	Northern Minnesota and Michigan's Upper Penisula
Jerky	The Southwest, Oklahoma in particular
Salmon Jerky	Washington State
Whoopie Pie	Maine

menu that is a knock-out sampler of low country favorites. Start with creamy she-crab soup, move on to ham biscuits or shrimp gumbo with hoppin' john and sweet corn pudding, and top things off with a gooey-chewy piece of Huguenot torte. On the side, drink iced tea, which, curiously, comes unsweetened. "You have to sweeten it yourself!" griped a southern gentleman sitting next to us, stirring sugar into his glass. "And they call this a plantation!"

Pinckney Café

Motley Lane and Pinckney St., Charleston, SC	$
(803) 577-0961	£𝔇
Tues–Sat	

Patronized by artistic Charlestonians, savvy tourists, and many of the city's creative young chefs, the laid-back Pinckney Café is a little jewel in the rough. Place your order at the kitchen and take a seat, indoors or on the piazza. Soon you will be spooning into scrumptious Cajun gumbo thick with seafood, or forking up a copious black bean burrito or such daily specials as San Diego–style fish tacos, vegetarian pizza, or a pasta du jour. Specialty coffees include a dreamy cappuccino float, the beer list is long and distinguished, and do not consider your life complete until you taste the bread pudding. It is one of the great desserts in this universe or any other.

Summerton Diner

exit 108 off I-95, Summerton, SC	$
(803) 485-6835	𝔅£𝔇

A beacon of hearty food along I-95: enjoy bacon and eggs and grits or hotcakes and sausage for breakfast; or better yet, come for lunch. Our favorite lunch specials are fried chicken with mashed potatoes and gravy (or rice and gravy) and a rich casserole of sausage, potatoes, and cheese. There is always a good choice of vegetables, including sweet yam sticks, collard greens, squash casserole, and an apple salad to re-member. For dessert, you want pie, preferably coconut cream.

Sweatman's Bar-B-Q	
SC Rte. 453, Holly Hill, SC (no phone)	**$**
Fri and Sat only	**£D**

Bub Sweatman's place is consummate pig-pickin' served in an old country farmhouse shaded by pecan trees. Meat is cooked the old-fashioned way, in an open pit out back, and it is set out on the buffet unsauced so that purists can savor its succulence *au naturel.* If you do want sauce, try the South Carolina stuff, with its mustard base. Along-side the choice chunks of pork, you can also choose ribs, pork hash over rice, and even strips of fried pigskin. Pay one price and pile your plate high, find a seat at an oilcloth-covered table in one of Bub's lovely rustic dining rooms, then tuck into a feast that Carolinians have en-joyed for a couple of centuries.

Note the weekend-only hours.

The Wreck of the Richard & Charlene	
106 Haddrell Point, Mount Pleasant, SC	**$$**
(803) 884-0052	**£D**

There is no sign, not even an address, outside the ramshackle bait locker tucked between the Wando Seafood Company and Mag-wood & Sons Seafood on Shem Creek, and you enter through a hall-way decorated with stacked-up beer cartons. But at mealtimes, the Wreck (named for a ship hit by Hurricane Hugo) is mobbed. Dis-criminating locals skip the tourist-oriented eateries on the docks nearby and find a paper-topped table on the breezy porch to feast on *fresh* fried oysters, shrimp, and flounder, boiled shrimp and stone crab claws by the pound, with beer (served in the bottle) to wash it down.

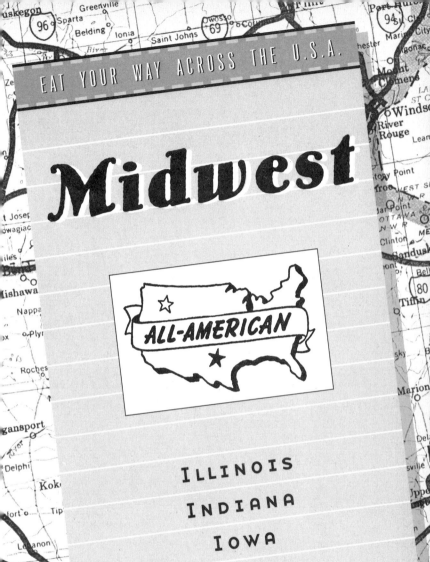

Midwest

ALL-AMERICAN

ILLINOIS

INDIANA

IOWA

MICHIGAN

MINNESOTA

MISSOURI

OHIO

WISCONSIN

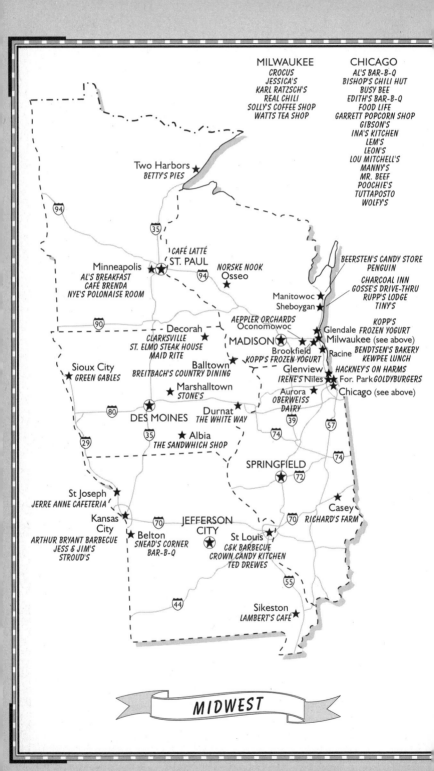

MILWAUKEE
CROCUS
JESSICA'S
KARL RATZSCH'S
REAL CHILI
SOLLY'S COFFEE SHOP
WATTS TEA SHOP

CHICAGO
AL'S BAR-B-Q
BISHOP'S CHILI HUT
BUSY BEE
EDITH'S BAR-B-Q
FOOD LIFE
GARRETT POPCORN SHOP
GIBSON'S
INA'S KITCHEN
LEM'S
LEON'S
LOU MITCHELL'S
MANNY'S
MR. BEEF
POOCHIE'S
TUTTAPOSTO
WOLFY'S

Two Harbors ★
BETTY'S PIES

CAFÉ LATTÉ
ST. PAUL
Minneapolis ★
AL'S BREAKFAST
CAFÉ BRENDA
NYE'S POLONAISE ROOM

NORSKE NOOK
Osseo ★

Manitowoc ★
Sheboygan ★

BEERSTEN'S CANDY STORE
PENGUIN
CHARCOAL INN
GOSSE'S DRIVE-THRU
RUPP'S LODGE
TINY'S

AEPPLER ORCHARDS
Oconomowoc ★

Decorah ─ ★
CLARKSVILLE
ST. ELMO STEAK HOUSE
MAID RITE

MADISON ★
Brookfield ★
KOPP'S FROZEN YOGURT

Glendale *KOPP'S*
Milwaukee *FROZEN YOGURT* (see above)
Racine ★ *BENDTSEN'S BAKERY*
KEWPEE LUNCH

Sioux City ★
GREEN GABLES

Balltown ★
BREITBACH'S COUNTRY DINING

Glenview ★ *HACKNEY'S ON HARMS*
IRENE'S Niles ★ For. Park *GOLDYBURGERS*
Chicago (see above)

Marshalltown ★
STONE'S

Aurora ★
OBERWEISS
DAIRY

DES MOINES ★
Durnat ★
THE WHITE WAY

Albia ★
THE SANDWICH SHOP

SPRINGFIELD ★

St Joseph ★
JERRE ANNE CAFETERIA

Kansas ★
City
ARTHUR BRYANT BARBECUE
JESS & JIM'S
STROUD'S

Belton ★
SNEAD'S CORNER
BAR-B-Q

JEFFERSON
CITY

St Louis ★
C&K BARBECUE
CROWN CANDY KITCHEN
TED DREWES

Casey ★
RICHARD'S FARM

Sikeston ★
LAMBERT'S CAFÉ

MIDWEST

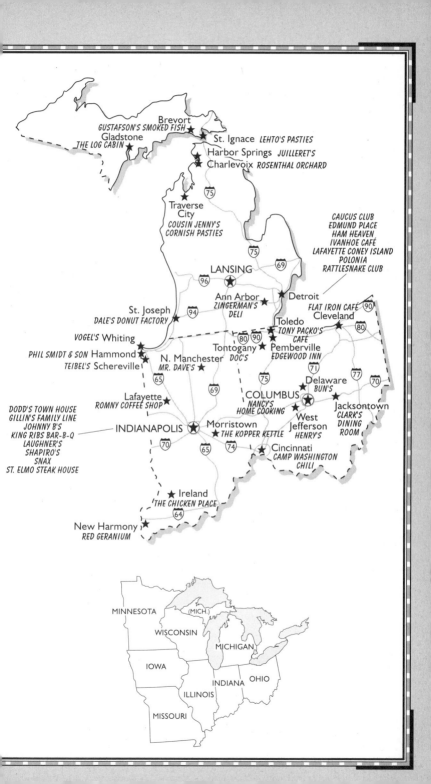

Brevort
GUSTAFSON'S SMOKED FISH ★
Gladstone
THE LOG CABIN ★
St. Ignace *LEHTO'S PASTIES*
Harbor Springs *JUILLERET'S*
Charlevoix *ROSENTHAL ORCHARD*

Traverse
City
*COUSIN JENNY'S
CORNISH PASTIES*

75

75

69

*CAUCUS CLUB
EDMUND PLACE
HAM HEAVEN
IVANHOE CAFÉ
LAFAYETTE CONEY ISLAND
POLONIA
RATTLESNAKE CLUB*

LANSING ★

96

Ann Arbor ★ Detroit
*ZINGERMAN'S
DELI*

St. Joseph
DALE'S DONUT FACTORY ★

94

FLAT IRON CAFÉ 90
Toledo Cleveland
*TONY PACKO'S
CAFE*

80

80

VOGEL'S Whiting ★
PHIL SMIDT & SON Hammond ★
TEIBEL'S Schereville ★

N. Manchester ★
MR. DAVE'S

Tontogany ★ Pemberville
DOC'S *EDGEWOOD INN*

75

71

77 70

Lafayette
ROMNY COFFEE SHOP ★

65

69

COLUMBUS ★
*NANCY'S
HOME COOKING*

Delaware
BUN'S

Jacksontown
*CLARK'S
DINING
ROOM*

*DODD'S TOWN HOUSE
GILLIN'S FAMILY LINE
JOHNNY B'S
KING RIBS BAR-B-Q
LAUGHNER'S
SHAPIRO'S
SNAX
ST. ELMO STEAK HOUSE*

INDIANAPOLIS ★

70

Morristown
★ *THE KOPPER KETTLE*

65

74

West
Jefferson
HENRY'S

Cincinnati ★
*CAMP WASHINGTON
CHILI*

★ Ireland
THE CHICKEN PLACE

64

New Harmony ★
RED GERANIUM

MINNESOTA

(MICH.)

WISCONSIN

MICHIGAN

IOWA

INDIANA OHIO

ILLINOIS

MISSOURI

ILLINOIS

Al's Bar-B-Q

1079 W. Taylor St., Chicago, IL	$
(312) 733-8896	£Đ

I n Chicago's old Little Italy, Al's is a small shop with a tremendous reputation for Italian beef sandwiches and taut charcoal-grilled sausages. In nice weather, you'll find us picnicking on Al's superb sandwiches and good French fries off the trunk of our car, along with legions of cops, beef hounds, and local wise guys. Afterward we stroll across the street to the Italian ice shop for the perfect dessert.

Bishop's Chili Hut

1958 W. 18th St., Chicago, IL	$
(312) 829-6345	ß£Đ

C hicago is not widely known for chili, but Bishop's Chili Hut has been a shrine for chiliheads since Helen Bishop sold her first bowl of beef here seventy years ago. As her heirs now tell the story, Chicago was rich with chili parlors in the 1920s, and Mrs. Bishop, who worked at the illustrious Ollie's nearby, decided to cut out on her own. Her recipe, still used today, makes a spicy bowl of fine-ground meat with beans, served with pepper sauce for heat and oyster crackers for relief. With noodles, this deliciously plebeian concoction is known as chili mac—the connoisseur's choice, especially flavorsome with a side order of a big Thuringer sausage in a bun and a tall beer (or good draft root beer) to slake inevitable thirst.

There are now four Bishop's around town; this one is the original. It is quite a sight on big sports weekends to see take-out customers carrying the stuff home by the five-gallon tub.

Busy Bee

1546 N. Damen Ave., Chicago, IL	$
(312) 772-4433	BLD

The clientele at the well-worn counter of this tin-ceiling Polish café is hipsters and grannies, aldermen and town nuts, local beauty queens and workers in overalls, cops on the beat and culinary pilgrims in search of great meat loaf. It is a gathering place with an inspired old-neighborhood feel, chaotic and always interesting (and slightly less hectic in the adjacent Old Wicker Park dining room).

Many customers come for the low-priced Polish food—pierogi glistening with butter, packed with sweet cheese or onion-laced potatoes; stuffed cabbage; hunter's stew—but the meat loaf cannot be ignored. A thick block of rugged-textured loaf comes smothered in gravy, accompanied by a big scoop of chunky mashed potatoes. Put a point on it with a Busy Bee Stinger (brandy, Krupnik, and crème de menthe).

Edith's Bar-B-Q

1863 N. Clybourn Ave., Chicago, IL	$
(312) 327-5160	LD

The wall of Edith's soul-food rib shack in Chicago may be the only place on earth that is decorated with portraits of both actor John Wayne and former Mayor Harold Washington—strange bedfellows, indeed, and proof that barbecue is edible democracy. People from all walks of life come to Edith's, some to dine here at one of three oilcloth-covered tables or the short counter, many more to take the ribs home or on a picnic. They are lavish ribs, big, meaty bats imbued with a spicy top-secret sauce with southern flair. Be sure to ask for extra sauce if you are getting ribs to go. You will want to dunk everything in it. Buy 'em by the slab, small or large end, tips, or sandwich.

Food Life

835 N. Michigan Ave., Chicago, IL	$
(312) 335-3663	£D

Food Life is to mall food courts what Disney World is to roadside attractions: a spectacle beyond belief. Located in posh Water Tower Place, it is a whole 'nother culinary universe, where all appetites are satisfied. Armed with plastic debit cards inspired by the punch cards used at vintage delicatessen counters, grazers in this vast culinary theme park select what they want from twelve terminals, each with a different theme: burritos and fajitas, seafood, pastas, etc.

The choices are mesmerizing. There is no assembly-line franchised food here; everything is fresh and appealing, and you can eat wholesome fare everywhere you turn. Stuff a potato with al dente steamed broccoli or low-fat yogurt, enjoy luxurious but egg-free Caesar salad dressing, or plow into a casserole of grains and roasted vegetables. There are many rich things to eat (baby back ribs, hefty burgers, flourless chocolate cake), but vegetarians, dieters, and anyone in search of a fast, fit meal will have a field day.

Garrett Popcorn Shop

670 N. Michigan Ave., Chicago, IL (312) 944-4730;	$
also at 2 W. Jackson Blvd., 360-1108,	£D
and 676 N. St. Clair, 944-4730	

The warm caramel smell is overwhelming at the Garrett Popcorn Shop on Michigan Avenue. It is a tiny store (one of three Garretts in Chicago), but it bustles with popcorn-eaters calling out orders by the ounce or pound, all day and long into the night.

"Mix!" is the connoisseur's cry—a bag of equal thirds of caramel corn, cheese corn, and buttered popcorn. The cheese corn is thick and rich; the butter corn makes fingers glisten. Caramel corn is simply the world's best, crunchy but not so brittle it has lost the puffy lightness of popped corn. Each kernel is veiled with a buttery sweet coat of dark amber that teeters on tasting burnt and makes taste buds cry for more, more, more.

Gibson's

1028 N. Rush St., Chicago, IL	$$$
(312) 266-8999	D

Expensive but not particularly elegant, and not even very old (it's where Mr. Kelly's nightclub used to be), Gibson's is a definitive American steak house. It is a place to splurge (calories as well as cash), where portions are huge and quality is unsurpassed.

Of course, you start with cocktails—the Gibson is lovely, served in a giant martini glass. Savor the fresh raisin-pumpernickel, rye, and sourdough in the bread basket; plow into a manly salad; then, as is Chicago custom, see what's to eat . . . literally. Cuts of steak are brought raw to the table for inspection. Among the beautifully marbled sirloins, fillets, and rib-eyes is a monstrous lobster tail, going for seventy-three dollars à la carte, or ninety-five dollars if you want it as half of a surf 'n' turf plate. The beef is impeccable—aged, juicy, full of

Hot Dog Hall of Fame

This roster of America's wonderful wieners does not include Wisconsin brats, Cajun sausages, Texas hot links, Spanish chorizo of the West, or Portuguese linguica of the Northeast. It is limited strictly to cheap, pink tube steaks dished out in long buns, with or without chili, in eat-places of which your mother would likely disapprove.

- Camp Washington Chili, Cincinnati, OH (p. 211)
- Katz's Deli, New York, NY (p. 62)
- Lafayette Coney Island, Detroit, MI (p. 198)
- Nick Tahou, Rochester, NY (p. 64)
- Pink's Chili Dogs, Los Angeles, CA (p. 327)
- Poochie's, Chicago, IL (p. 178)
- Ted's Jumbo Red Hots, Tonawanda, NY (p. 68)
- The Varsity, Atlanta, GA (p. 137)
- Wolfy's, Chicago, IL (p. 180)

flavor—and well complemented by Gibson's cream-soft baked potatoes or an order of crisp-skinned onion rings.

Desserts are ridiculously big, especially one called "banana dream," which is in the shape of a slice of cake but so tall that you wonder if the Gibsons you drank have thrown perspective askew. It is a foot tall, four layers of yellow cake with bananas and icing, packed with about a half-pound of chopped nuts, atop a pool of chocolate sauce, with vanilla ice cream on the side. *Nota bene:* The cake is impressive not only for its size. Like everything else in this extravagant restaurant, it is made of the finest ingredients, and it is delicious.

Goldyburgers

7316 Circle Ave., Forest Park, IL	$
(708) 366-0750	**D**

"Never a bad one" is the motto of this comfortable vintage-1926 Chicagoland sports bar, referring to the many and wondrous hamburgers that put it on the good-eats map. Of the half-dozen varieties available, we recommend the Royal Bleuburger, a half-pound broiled sirloin patty topped with melted blue cheese and crisp bacon; and the Big Daddy, three quarters of a pound of beef with adornments of your choice. Fried potatoes and vegetables are available on the side.

Hackney's on Harms

1241 Harms Rd., Glenview, IL	$
(708) 724-5577	**£D**

This pleasant suburban restaurant with an outdoor patio under tall silver poplars is one of a small local chain that built its reputation on hamburgers. *Huge* hamburgers: one-half pound of rosy beef, encased in dark crust, arrives at your table with dark rye bread, the implication being you could eat it like a sandwich. But it is way too big to pick up in your hands, and the juicy red meat tends to fall apart (unless you have it cooked well done and thereby mummified). So you

Chicago Pizza

Deep dish. The medium-thick crust supports boatloads of ingredients because it has a wall around the edge to shore everything in. The wall requires the pizza be cooked in a pan (rather than on a flat sheet), hence its name "pan pizza."

Soufflé pizza. Pan pizza heaped with an airy layer of cheese in which ingredients are suspended.

Stuffed pizza. A magnification of the pan pizza idea, with a sauce-frosted crust on top.

Thin crust. A little-appreciated talent of Chicago pizzaioli. Many top places in town offer good thin crust—foldable, like a New York slice—as well as *superthin* crust you can almost see through, so elegant it tends to break rather than bend.

dig in to the mighty mound with knife and fork. A Hackneyburger comes with French fries, cole slaw, and sliced raw onion, but those in the know pay extra for fried onion rings—a glorious stack of them with a devilish crunch.

Hamburgers are Hackney's glory, but we must also tip our hats to dandy daily specials that have been on the menu at least since we became regular customers back in the 1960s: bratwurst on Monday, hot turkey sandwiches with mashed potatoes on Tuesday, meat loaf on Wednesday, corned beef and cabbage on Thursday, and a crunchy fish fry on Friday, when the choice includes midwestern favorites lake perch and walleye pike.

Ina's Kitchen

448 E. Ontario, Chicago, IL	$
(312) 337-6700	BL

Being breakfast-hounds, we love Chicago: Lou Mitchell's for double-yolk eggs and sassy service, Walker Brothers for 10,000 calorie baked pancakes, and Ina's for healthy vegetable hash.

Ina's pancakes are swell, tangy sour cream or tawny oatmeal, but we cannot resist that strange, savory hash. Chunks of potato (sweet and white), corn niblets, onions, and Brussels sprouts, all cooked soft and buttery, make a unique, but totally delectable morning meal.

Irene's

6873 N. Milwaukee Ave., Niles, IL	$$
(847) 647-8147	LD

Irene's is a family restaurant across from a big cemetery. Its business card says that funeral lunches are a specialty, but you don't have to be bereaved to enjoy this treasure house of old-world meals, where all the neighborhood comes to eat. It is a snug sort of place, dark and quiet, with deluxe chandeliers and a thick rug. A majority of the clientele, as well as the staff, seem more comfortable speaking Polish than English.

Start with soup, accompanied by good rye bread. The red borscht has a healthy vegetable savor, and the czarnina soup is dark brown and mysterious, strangely sweet but not cloying, served with little pasta shells on top.

Blintzes are superb, served three to an order, buttery tender crepes with a filling that is slightly sour, slightly sweet. Pierogi are the works of a dumpling master; and potato pancakes are just coarse enough to savor the little bits of potato of which they are made. There are many glorious things to eat at Irene's, including pork cutlets sautéed in garlic butter, pork shank with sauerkraut, and simple (but unimprovable) boiled beef with horseradish gravy, but the dish we return for every time is roast duck, which is dripping rich and crisp-skinned, succulence incarnate.

Lem's

5914 S. State St., Chicago, IL	$$
(312) 684-5007	D

Smoky ribs with a crust that envelops strips of indescribably tender pork, Lem's bones are beyond good. Sauce is available, regular or ultrahot, but these perfect hunks of food scarcely require it. Come during daylight hours and plan to dine in your car or at a picnic table somewhere: seating is scarce or nonexistent, and there is no getting around the fact that the neighborhood is marginal. But a meal at Lem's is worth a little worry, for it is a genuine culinary landmark, serving the best ribs in Chicago since 1952.

Leon's

1640 E. 79th St., Chicago, IL (312) 731-1454	$$
also at 1158 W. 59th St. 778-7828	LD
and 8249 S. Cottage Grove 488-4556	

Slabs and half-slabs of glistening dark barbecued ribs are piled into cardboard boats with a mess of French fries glazed with sauce and a couple of tiles of white bread that will meld with the sauce and disintegrate before you can eat two ribs. That lustrous sauce, in its hot version, is one of the world's best, an artful balance of pepper's fire, sweet molasses, and an arsenal of spice. There are good hot links on the menu and whole chickens and wings, but it's ribs that have made Leon's a South Side pork-pilgrim mecca for decades.

The store on Cottage Grove has seats; the other outlets are strictly take-out. Although they are hospitable places, they are in neighborhoods we prefer to visit by light of day.

Lou Mitchell's

565 W. Jackson, Chicago, IL	$
(312) 939-3111	B L

Gorgeous three-egg omelets, made with double-yolk eggs and served in the pan, are reason enough to visit Lou Mitchell's coffee shop, but everything else on the menu is A-1, too, including fresh-squeezed juice, homemade marmalade, and burnished hash brown potatoes. The eggs come with thick-cut toast so substantial that we watched the biceps bulge on the ripped female body builder next to us each time she hoisted a piece. (Seating is army-style, at shared tables.) The same eggy "Greek bread" is used to make French toast, and there are malted-milk waffles, rolled pancakes with cooked fruit, and a large assortment of baked-here muffins, pecan rolls, and Danish pastries. Simply, this is breakfasters' paradise. As you wait in line—and you *will* wait—you can admire the display of roasted and unroasted coffee beans and tanks full of "pure filtered water" that are the source of Lou Mitchell's claim to the best cup in town.

Manny's

1141 S. Jefferson St., Chicago, IL	$
(312) 939-2855	B L D

You are never really alone at Manny's cafeteria at the edge of the Chicago Loop, even if you don't come with your business associates, attorney, parole officer, alderman, or image consultant. In this old-fashioned urban delicatessen, seating is perforce communal, and regulars hobnob loudly with one another even if they are four tables apart.

Wherever you sit in the double-wide dining room, you will smell corned beef: briny brick red, sliced thin as prosciutto, radiating mouth-watering pickly aroma as flaps of it are piled between slabs of seeded, sour-crusted rye bread. On the side of a Manny's corned beef sandwich, you want a potato pancake or two. They are hard-crusted but moist and tender inside, served hot on the side of sandwiches or with sour cream or apple sauce as a meal unto themselves. Other regular items in Manny's resplendent cafeteria line include chicken pot pie (Wednesday), oxtail stew (Thursday), meat-filled knishes, chicken soup with matzoh balls or little kreplach (meaty dumplings), and such lunch counter standards as beef stew, liver and onions, meat loaf, and stuffed cabbage.

Mr. Beef

666 N. Orleans, Chicago, IL	$
(312) 337-8500	BL

Good Italian beef sandwiches are sold throughout the city; Mr. Beef's are extraordinary—thin-sliced yet profoundly beefy, well-spiced and sopped with gravy, more tender than words can say, heaped into a bakery-fresh roll. Order it wet (the counterman soaks the roll in the gravy), sweet (with roasted sweet peppers), or hot (with hellish relish known as giardiniera); or get a combo, which adds a length of superb Italian sausage with a strong fennel kick. Until you have luxuriated in this sandwich, you cannot say you have eaten well in Chicago.

Oberweiss Dairy

945 Lake St., Aurora, IL	$
(708) 897-6600	LD

Oberweiss is a genuine dairy where they pack milk from local farms in glass bottles and make ice cream fresh every day. You can watch the process through a glass wall from a table in the front room soda parlor, where the menu is limited to sundaes, malts, and sodas made with the full repertoire of soda fountain toppings. Best dish: a turtle candy sundae, built upon a mound of silk-smooth vanilla ice cream that is gilded with warm caramel sauce, lush hot fudge, and a heap of roasted-crisp pecans.

Poochie's	
3832 Dempster, Chicago, IL	$
(312) 673-0100	£ D

Stand at the counter or perch on a stool in this rectangular storefront eatery. Choose from a menu limited to red hots, hamburgers, and Italian beef, accompanied by a motley order of delicious French fries with crunchy skins and creamy insides (or, better yet, cheddar fries, gobbed with melted cheese). The red hots are garlicky Vienna all-beef beauties, boiled or charred over coals until they develop an appealing tan. They are cushioned in utterly fresh, steamy soft poppy seed buns and are available, as per local custom, with any or all of a rainbow of condiments including mustard, ketchup, relish, raw onions, grilled onions, fresh tomatoes, pickles, celery salt, and fire-hot little peppers. Such humble elements transcend themselves and are a great meal unique to Chicago.

Richard's Farm	
Off Rte. 49 in Casey, IL	$$
(217) 932-5300	£ D

Eat in a barn at Richard's Farm. Don't worry, though, you don't share the dining room with livestock. This venerable 1930s hip-roof building, with its feedway down the center and butter churns for decor, is actually quite polite, with a truly farmy salad bar and a sophisticated hardwood grill in the kitchen. The specialty of the house is a mighty one-pound pork chop, broiled in a tangy red sauce (available also in half-pound size), and the fried chicken is crisp and moist. Desserts include warm peach cobbler, berry pies all summer long, and persimmon pudding on occasion in the fall.

Chicago Street
Food Fundamentals

No other American city has such an abundance of cheap-eats outlets where excellence is presupposed. We are not talking about "restaurants," not even pizza parlors or barbecue shacks. We mean little storefront dives, most without tables or chairs (maybe, at most, a counter to lean on while you dine), almost all of them marked by yellow and red signs provided by their meat supplier. In these inglorious outlets you can count on snapping-good, garlicky red hots (Chicago's term for hot dogs), spicy Italian beef sandwiches, and fragrant Greek gyros. Here are a few ordering tips.

Red hots. Plump all-beef dogs on fresh poppy-seed buns are the beginning. Condiments put this beauteous package over the top. Order yours "dragged through the garden" and the wienermeister will apply a dizzying assemblage of mustard, onions, piccalilli, sliced tomato and cucumber, lettuce, celery salt, and tiny hot "sport peppers."

Polish sausage. Similar to red hots, served in the same cornucopic configurations, but generally bigger and spicier and porkier and cooked until blistery black.

Italian beef. Thin-sliced beef sopped with gravy, piled into a fresh, crusty roll. The condiment of choice is giardiniera: hot peppers and diced vegetables in a powerhouse marinade.

Italian sausage. Sweet and succulent, sold at fine Italian beef stands, generally cooked over charcoal until crusty on the outside. Devil-may-care connoisseurs combine Italian beef and sausage in one sandwich.

Gyros. Although not unique to Chicago, these breathtaking sandwiches reach a deliciously evil apotheosis here. Lamb and beef are ground up and reconstituted into a frighteningly large circular roast that rotates in front of a vertical broiler and is cut into long slices that are heaped into pita bread with raw onions, tomatoes, and a creamy yogurt sauce. The scent and taste of this most odoriferous of all street foods will stay with you for hours.

Tuttaposto

| 646 North Franklin, Chicago, IL | **$$$** |
| (312) 943-6262 | **D** |

This trend-setting restaurant has an urbane ambiance and a worldly menu that ranges from Tunisian chicken wings to seared salmon with horseradish potatoes. The menu advises that "Garlic is the ketchup of intellectuals" and you will sniff it even before you walk in the door—caramelized cloves strewn across vegetable pizzas toted from the open kitchen through the dining room. Garlic also infuses neevik, a salubrious appetizer of sautéed spinach with lemon and garbanzo beans. Capellini dal pescatore—shrimp, clams, mussels, calamari, scallops, a lobster tail, and chunks of salmon atop fine noodles—is garlicky, too, but what's really bewitching about it is the peppery heat of the tomato broth.

Couscous is a featured attraction. It is accented with lemon to accompany wood-roasted quail and is the foundation of a splendid "couscous royale" of squab, tahini chicken, skewered lamb, and merguez sausage. There is even couscous for dessert—a tower made of honeyed couscous and adorned with fresh fruit and fruit sauces. That is, if you can pass up such temptations as checkerboard bread pudding and the chocolate praline pyramid. Eating healthy was never so sweet.

Wolfy's

| 2734 W. Peterson Ave., Chicago, IL | **$** |
| (312) 743-0207 | **LD** |

Wolfy's all-beef red hots, cushioned in Rosen's poppy-seeded buns, are among Chicago's elite, served singly or in pairs, topped with chili or cheese or dragged through the garden, which means smothered under yellow mustard, piccalilli, pickle spears, tomato slices, raw or fried onions, and a scattering of incendiary little pepper pods. It is impossible to eat such a piece of food with any decorum. It falls apart, drips, and oozes; but like all great Chicago doggeries, Wolfy's is equipped for such hazards: there are napkins galore, and all fixtures are easy-wipe plastic.

If regular red hots with crisp fries on the side aren't nutritionally wicked enough, try Wolfy's beef and pork Polish sausages—giant tube steaks with crackling crisp skins that spurt juice when bitten.

INDIANA

The Chicken Place

State Rd. 56, Ireland, IN (812) 482-7600	$$
(reservations Mon–Thur only)	D

The chicken in this pleasant little place is fried to a golden crisp and served with German-fried potatoes. If you don't make a reservation, or if it's a weekend night, you will wait in line outside for a precious seat where conversation, not surprisingly, tends to revolve around which restaurants serve the best chicken dinners, an Indiana passion.

Dodd's Town House

5694 N. Meridian St., Indianapolis, IN	$$
(317) 257-1872	LD

Dodd's is a homey restaurant that serves regal beef. Steaks are skillet-fried to crust-enveloped succulence, accompanied by fine baked potatoes, long-cooked green beans, and a wedge of iceberg lettuce with sweet garlic dressing. There are other good things on the menu, including crisp fried chicken (served family-style to parties of six or more) with fixin's that include mashed potatoes and gravy, green beans and corn and a little dish of ice cream. The only problem with the latter is that ice cream is definitely *not* what you want for dessert. At Dodd's, you want pie. Chocolate cream pie any time of year, blueberry in the autumn, buttermilk in the spring. With meat and potatoes, pie for dessert, Dodd's is heartland Americana to a T.

Gillin's Family Line	
2639 E. Michigan St., Indianapolis, IN	**$**
(317) 637-1147	**LD**

One of two dining rooms in this storefront shop has been partitioned into a "lounge" with a six-stool bar and a TV loud enough to serenade everybody. One day the tube was tuned to a *Jenny Jones* show on which hillbillies were yelling at one another. Until we realized there was a television in the lounge, we thought customers in the other dining room were having an argument. Gillin's is a taste of gen-u-wine Americana in the rough.

Get your food along a short buffet line, where the daily choices include such of-the-people meals as ham and beans with corn bread and baked chicken with dressing. These are real blue-plate specials, not gussied up, which means your sweet and sour pork chops will require sawing with a knife, and scalloped potatoes with ham—orange as a school bus—will stick to your ribs all day. The real culinary lure is state fair–level pie. What ecstasy it is to ease a fork into coconut macaroon filling perched atop a hand-formed crust! Gillin's also sells whole pies and cobblers to go; give a day's notice and they'll make whatever kind you want.

Johnny B's	
373 S. Illinois St., Indianapolis, IN	**$**
(317) 756-7254	**LD**

Johnny B's is a sports bar with exemplary fan food—massive nachos grande, piquant deep-fried jalapeño peppers, fried flowered onions, and one regional specialty crucial to any honest eating tour of the central Midwest, listed on the menu as "The" tenderloin.

Johnny B's tenderloin is a full eight inches across, so broad that it becomes a logistical issue as to whether your fingers are long enough to actually pick up the sandwich by its bun. The curvaceous cutlet has a hard sandy crust, and within this golden envelope is a ribbon of sweet, melt-in-the-mouth pork. It is a pleasure to crunch through it surrounded by the tavern's personality-plus decor, which includes mementos of favorite local teams and an impressive display of commemorative whiskey decanters in the shapes of Elvis, John Wayne, and the Pope.

King Ribs Bar-B-Q

4130 N. Keystone, Indianapolis, IN (317) 543-0841;	$
other locations in Indianapolis are 5610 Georgetown Rd.	£Ð
291-2695, 2660 Lafayette Rd. 488-0223, 7336 Pendleton Pike	
547-5464, 3599 S. East St. 781-8890	

Fourteen big drums are arrayed to smoke meat in the large front lot of this soul-food enterprise that looks like it used to be a drive-in lube shop. There is no dining room; there are no tables or chairs. All business is drive-through, walk-up, or home delivery. The house motto is "Fit for a King."

Ribs are super tender; their meat pulls away from the bone in heavy, succulent strips, barely glazed with sauce. The flavor is pure—long-cooked pork with a faint tingle of the smoke that cooked it. Side dishes include macaroni and cheese that is as thick as pudding, intensely cheesy, with noodles so soft they are almost indistinguishable from the cheese; and baked beans, fine-cut slaw, and white bread for mopping. For dessert, choose chess pie or sweet potato pie.

The Kopper Kettle

135 W. Main St., Morristown, IN	$$
(317) 763-6767	LD

The Kopper Kettle is rapturously retro-feminine, like a set in a 1950s "women's weepie" flick. Pink voile curtains shimmer at the windows, candelabra grace the larger tables, and among the antiques and bric-a-brac in this venerable family restaurant are tasteful *objets d'art* with the female form as subject; a bas-relief nude resides above the fireplace, a statuette shows Aphrodite running so fast that her toga blows away from her shapely body. Waitresses echo the artistic images, dressed in outfits that might be called Early American Milkmaid, with mobcaps and thigh-length skirts and thick petticoats.

People come from miles away to eat succulent skillet-fried chicken accompanied by mashed potatoes and porky green beans cooked until all their fight is gone.

Laughner's

Washington St. E. at I-465, Indianapolis, IN (317) 356-3388;	$$
for other locations call (317) 783-2907	LD

The Laughner family pioneered the self-service restaurant back in the 1880s, and today their six spacious Indianapolis cafeterias serve heavenly square meals to thousands of loyal customers daily. The chicken is as good as any in town, expertly skillet-fried, but who can resist the big pink ham with lustrous glazed sweet potatoes on the side, or the steamship round of beef displayed in the serving line, glowing pink and moist, ready to be lopped into juice-laden slices? Mashed potatoes are simple perfection, stout and veined with butter, and there are some two dozen other vegetables prepared every day, from farm-simple cooked carrots to green beans that are classic Americana—combined with mushroom soup, slivered almonds, and fried onion rings. The dessert display includes cobblers and dumplings, custards and puddings, ambrosias, jiggly meringue pies, and humble sugar-creams.

Aside from the spectacle of bounteous food, Laughner's long-standing appeal is civility. Dining rooms suggest old-world prosperity, outfitted with coats of arms and oil paintings of eighteenth-century European sea captains and saucy wenches in tasteful dishabille.

Mr. Dave's	
102 East Main St., North Manchester, IN (219) 982-4769	**$**
(closes midafternoon in winter)	**LD**

Indiana's best-known way station for tenderloins, Mr. Dave's cuts and breads its own pork patties and fries them to a crisp. The tiles of pork are then inserted into buns and dolled up with condiments. One of these is a superb indigenous sandwich, but modest-size enough that it is best eaten in pairs. Or, better yet, get a tenderloin and a burger on the side. Mr. Dave's hamburgers are a delight—not huge or opulent, just a good ol' burger, the kind you want in a good ol' Midwest sandwich shop.

Mr. Dave's has a drive-through window for pork-famished travelers in a hurry and also freezes tenderloins for shipping to homesick Hoosiers anywhere in the U.S.

Phil Smidt & Son	
1205 N. Calumet Ave., Hammond, IN (219) 659-0025;	**$$**
in Chicago (312) 768-6686	**LD**

Being in Phil Smidt's restaurant is like finding yourself in the parlor of a duchess who is formal but still has the people's touch. There are huge pink roses painted on the wall and all the napery is pretty pink, yet waitresses are battle-ax tough and will likely call you "Hon" or "Dear."

Generations of families have come to this lakeside eatery to roll up their sleeves and eat big plates of delicious lake perch, climaxed by a wedge of warm gooseberry pie à la mode. If the pink roses on the wall aren't your style—that is, if you prefer more muscular ambiance for your perch supper—Phil Smidt's also has seating in a dining room that affords customers a stunning view of Indiana steel mills and freight trains rumbling past.

Red Geranium	
at the New Harmony Inn, North and Brewery,	**$$$**
New Harmony, IN (812) 682-4431	**D**

Don't be surprised if dinner and a night's stay at the New Harmony Inn seem too good to be true. The town of New Harmony was designed to be perfect. Founded in 1814 by followers of George Rapp, who wanted to create a utopian society based on the principles of celibacy and communal property, this bucolic little village on the banks of the Wabash River is still a touch of paradise.

The inn's fine restaurant is called the Red Geranium, where there are a dozen good ways with beef on the dinner menu, including big slabs of prime rib that are char-broiled to maximum succulence, and tenderloin medallions marinated in olive oil and garlic known as "Steak Caesar." Potatoes are offered four ways: baked or hash browned, Lyonnaise or sautéed. Desserts range from ultrafancy (flaming cherries jubilee and baked Alaska) to one that is quite literally divine, known as "Heaven cake."

Romney Coffee Shop	
Intersection of US 231 and US 28, Lafayette, IN	**$**
(317) 538-2834	**BL**
Tues–Sat, D Fri only	

Breakfast is the big meal of the day in Lafayette's friendly local café, where the coffee starts flowing before dawn and biscuits emerge from the oven shortly after that. The biscuits are a ploughman's delight, served with thick, rib-sticking gravy, and if you are really hungry, with good hash brown potatoes, too. Wednesday and Saturday mornings, huge hot cinnamon rolls perfume the air.

Wendy Johnson-Niblick, who tipped us off to the pleasures of the Romney Coffee Shop, especially recommended the pork tenderloins, a crisp local treat. Other robust lunches we've enjoyed when taking a detour off I-65 include meat loaf (with poor mashed potatoes, alas) and chicken with noodles. Caramel raisin pudding and Amish vanilla pie are two memorable items from a long and appealing dessert menu.

Shapiro's

808 S. Meridian, Indianapolis, IN (317) 631-4041;	**$**
also at 2370 W. 86th St. 872-7255	**B L D**

Although many members of the staff speak with accents more like Clem and Betty Lou than Moishe and Yetta, Shapiro's food is genuinely Jewish. By *genuine,* we mean that the corned beef sandwich is superb. And we don't mean superb *for Indianapolis,* but by strict Lower East Side standards. Cushioned in rugged-cut rye is a mountain of hot corned beef, sliced thick but not cloddish, unctuous without seeming fatty, and with a mouth-watering equilibrium of peppery spice and melting tenderness.

Breakfasts in this modern cafeteria-style eatery include salami omelets, bagels and lox, and mighty good corned beef hash. One morning the server in the cafeteria line suggested turkey hash instead. "It smells soooo good," she said with a looping southern Indiana twang. "By, gol, I like it better 'n corned beef!" It is indeed delicious, with big shreds of turkey among drifts of potato, laced with onions, alternately crusty and moist. Another notable breakfast is eggs and matzoh, aka matzoh brei. Bite-size scraps of matzoh are sheathed in scrambled egg like a kind of jumbled French toast but with a distinctive unleavened munchiness: home cooking, in a broad bowl.

Snax

2413 E. 65th St., Indianapolis, IN	$$
(317) 257-6291	D

In a city where family-style chicken dinners have long set the culinary tone, Snax offers no full dinners at all. Instead, the menu at this eccentric bistro lists twenty-five dishes ranging from bread and pepper salad to panned spicy shrimp to spring risotto cakes. Ten small empty plates are piled up on every table, so you order a bunch of things and as they come from the kitchen, you portion them out and everybody has a little course. In some ways, such sharing *is* family-style dining, but the food is far from pan-fried chicken.

The menu changes seasonally and always includes lusty vegetarian items. Last autumn we enjoyed a crunchy root vegetable salad with piquant chile vinaigrette, shrimp and scallop gratin with pumpkin gnocchi, fall vegetable strudel in roasted red pepper oil, and southwestern pizza with chunks of sweet-sauced beef and a chewy cloak of asiago cheese.

Snax is a pert place with a bar separated from the dining room by a chain-link fence, like around a child's playground. Its inventive kitchen is shared with Something Different, an adjoining sister restaurant that serves fare that is similar but organized as normal meals. The staff wear T-shirts that say JUST EAT IT.

St. Elmo Steak House

127 S. Illinois St., Indianapolis, IN (317) 635-0636	$$$
(dress code)	D

St. Elmo Steak House recalls the clubby beef palaces every big midwestern city once had, frequented by local bigwigs and visiting dignitaries. Its bar room wall is lined with hundreds of photos signed by such diverse guests as Keith Richards, Jane Pauley, Ed Asner, and a wrestler identified as "the Original French Angel." There is even a shot of O. J. Simpson when he was best known for his athletic skills. Up front is a case filled with raw steaks, and adjacent to it is an open kitchen, scarcely bigger than that of a railroad dining car. Here meat is grilled and plates prepared by dexterous veteran chefs, then whisked to tables by tuxedo-clad waiters.

"May we suggest before dinner . . . a martini made with extra-dry vermouth?" asks the menu. The glacial stiffener makes a splendid companion to the house appetizer, six plump pink shrimp smothered with unbelievably explosive horseradish cocktail sauce. Cuts of beef range from mighty porterhouses to filets mignon capped with mushrooms. The sirloin, captioned "our favorite!" on the menu, arrives on a thick plate without so much as a garnish. It is a substantial strip of meat, glistening with juice, dense and full of flavor. On the side you get a baked potato or rough-hewn French fries. Ketchup is automatically brought to the table with the meal.

Teibel's

1775 Rte. 41, Schereville, IN	$$
(219) 865-2000	£𝒟

In this huge, institutional-looking eating establishment, the house specialty is perch, served filleted and glistening with butter. You get plenty on the plate—the proper term hereabouts is "a mess of perch"—and if for some crazy reason you don't like the tender sweet little slabs of lake fish, Teibel's offers alternative entrees of fried chicken or the other northern Indiana favorite, frogs legs.

Vogel's

1250 Indianapolis Blvd., Whiting, IN (219) 659-1250	$$
Tues—Sun	£𝒟

Vogel's lake perch, whole or boned to order, is radiant: firm, sweet-fleshed, enrobed in a chewy thin skin of seasoned crust. The whole ones are impeccable and are the better choice if you have the patience to work for your supper. Lightly cooked in the pan, the fish emits little puffs of buttery steam when you separate the meat from the bones; there is simply nothing fresher-tasting. The fillets are fine, too: ten are arrayed on a plate, pan-cooked, then boned and buttered just moments before they are served. If ten aren't enough, don't worry—the price of dinner includes another plateful.

The perch suppers are perfect, and Vogel's is an amazing place to visit for the decor alone, a cross between '50s Fontainebleau pomp and a gritty urban sensibility, something Liberace might have come up with if he had worked part-time as a steel smelter. In the cavernous Crown Room, red banquettes contrast with a striated avocado green rug; in the Aegean Room, Doric columns line the walls. In the vast vestibule, an immense stuffed bear roars when you come close.

IOWA

Breitbach's Country Dining

563 Balltown Rd., Balltown, IA	$
(319) 552-2220	ℬℒ𝒟

Who can resist a restaurant that boasts of being the only one on earth patronized by both Jesse James and Brooke Shields? Iowa's oldest eatery began as a stage stop; today, it is a big, efficient place with a real Midwest salad bar that boasts organic garden produce and a menu featuring Mississippi River catfish. The best time at Breitbach's is breakfast on Saturday and Sunday, when local farmers come in for plenty of coffee to accompany the weekend-only cinnamon rolls.

Clarksville Diner

504 Heivly St., Decorah, IA	**$**
(319) 382-4330	**BLD**

A consummate 1939 New Jersey diner trucked to Iowa's northeast corner in 1988 by chef Gordon Tindall, the Clarksville is a gleaming silver beauty with a menu of blue-plate specials (hot roast beef every Tuesday), crisp pork tenderloin sandwiches, and a *you tell me* omelet at breakfast. We especially recommend anything with syrup in the morning—pancakes, waffles, or French toast—because the syrup is 100 percent maple, harvested from a sugar bush in Castalia, Iowa, just south of Decorah.

Green Gables

1800 Pierce St., Sioux City, IA	**$**
(712) 258-4246	**LD**

The nice place in town, Green Gables is favored by local customers for its fried chicken basket, T-bones and pork chops, and fillets of walleyed pike, all served efficiently and politely from rolling carts pushed by uniformed waitresses. A comfy place to sit and soak up Sioux City ambiance, Green Gables also happens to feature one of Iowa's top soda fountains. You can have an adult supper of meat and potatoes, or even healthfully cooked orange roughy, a special attraction one recent night, and accompany it with a black-and-white ice cream soda, a chocolate malt, or a green river (lime soda), then top things off with a peppermint hot fudge sundae or the pièce de résistance, a goshawful gooey (marshmallow sauce atop vanilla ice cream and orange sherbet).

Maid Rite

116 Washington St., Decorah, IA	$
(319) 382-8865	£ D

Maid Rite is a franchise from another era, a simple town sandwich shop that serves a style of beef Iowans love. Known around the state as a loosemeats or a tavern, a Maid Rite sandwich is beef that is well-seasoned and well-cooked, with a pebbly consistency like a sloppy joe but without much slop, served in a burger bun. Various Maid Rite shops supplement the featured attraction with soup, chili, pie, or donuts; we especially like the Decorah outlet for its stylish presentation—the sandwich comes sheathed in wax paper with a small plastic spoon stuck in the topknot of the wrapper to help you scoop up meat that drips onto counter or table.

The Sandwich Shop

14 Benton Ave. W., Albia, IA (515) 932-7756	$
Mon–Sat	£

Tenderloin alert! If you are traveling through the Midwest hunting for tenderloin sandwiches (a worthy quest), be sure to stop in Albia and try one of the extremely tasty pan-fried pork patties served by Smitty's (aka the Sandwich Shop), an Albia institution since 1921. We are not absolutely certain it's the best on earth, but the pork is sliced thick and luscious and served loaded with pickles, onions, mustard, and ketchup. When marooned in the tenderloin-deprived Northeast, we dream of the simple pleasure of a Smitty's 'loin.

Stone's

507 S. Third Ave., Marshalltown, IA	$
(515) 753-3626	LD

Hearty, homey meals have lured travelers to Stone's for 110 years, since Ebson Weed Stone converted a disreputable saloon into a civilized restaurant for travelers. In 1910, it moved to its current location near the train tracks, where it became a favorite of railroad workers who telegraphed ahead so lunch would be ready when they pulled in to Marshalltown. Today, locals and tourists travel to the comfy dining parlors in the old building for a roast beef and baked ham buffet every Sunday, and such weekday comforts as chicken and noodles, pork loin, meat loaf, and the ever-popular (no kidding) tender beef heart with dressing. Every day of the week, the main attraction is dessert, lemon chiffon pie in particular, which is tart, fluffy, and amazingly tall.

The White Way

8th Ave., Durant, IA	$
(319) 785-6202	LD

Durant is the heart of the pork belt, where a dry chop or a gristly loin roast is practically a criminal offense. The White Way, which has won innumerable awards from the state's pork producers, is the place to taste it cooked properly. At about six o'clock each evening, the dining room is packed with townsfolk, most of whom seem to be easing their fork into thick Iowa chops smothered in gravy (that's after they have feasted on the cornucopic salad bar). A word to strangers passing through: reserve a slice of your favorite pie as soon as you sit down; by the end of the dinner hour, many of the homemade pies (including the divine sour cream raisin) are gone.

MICHIGAN

Caucus Club

150 W. Congress, Detroit, MI (313) 965-4970	**$$$**
Tues—Fri	**LD**

The first time we ate at the Caucus Club, we were sent there by a regular customer, who told us exactly what to eat and which waiter to ask for. When we informed the waiter about our mutual acquaintance, he instantly became our best friend and the best waiter we've ever had anywhere—suave, attentive, helpful, charming. The Caucus Club is that kind of place: for friends, and friends of friends, it is luxury incarnate, a classy, clubby restaurant where classy, clubby food is prepared with decades' worth of expertise.

The menu is an honor roll of great old gourmet wonders. There isn't a better Caesar salad anywhere. Steak tartare? The Caucus Club sets the gold standard. Prime steaks, double-thick chops, a mess of perch, corned beef hash: all these grand and hearty dishes are at their finest in this dark, exclusive place where Detroit's high rollers have dined since Cadillacs had tailfins. And honestly, the times we've gone to the Caucus Club as unknowns have been perfectly pleasant, with efficient if not coddling service. Our suggestions: make a reservation in advance, dress up, and tell them Henry Ford sent you.

Cousin Jenny's Cornish Pasties

129 S. Union St., Traverse City, MI (616) 941-7821	**$**
Mon—Sat	**BLD**

Miners who came from Cornwall to dig ore in Michigan's Upper Peninsula during the last century were known as Cousin Jacks; their wives were Cousin Jennies. These hardworking immigrants brought the Cornish pasty to the Northland, where it became a staple of local cookery. Pasties, which are essentially beef stew inside a flaky pastry crust, were favored by those who worked the mines because they were easy to carry and easy to eat, a hearty pocket meal.

Cousin Jenny's in Traverse City is a spanking-clean restaurant where the culinary theme is pasties, available in two sizes, both of which are big enough to require knife and fork. They are listed on the menu as "Gourmet Pasties," but the steak pasty is the traditional configuration, filled with beef, potatoes, onion, and rutabaga. In addition, you can get a meatless seven-vegetable pasty with cream and cheese; and there are always novelty pasties available, such as Italian (with pizza sauce and pepperoni) or German (Swiss cheese, ham, and sauerkraut in a rye-flavored crust). There are even hand-holdable breakfast pasties, starting at 7:30 am, filled with eggs, hash browns, and bacon or sausage.

Dale's Donut Factory

3687 South Lakeshore Dr., St. Joseph, MI	$
(616) 429-1033; also at 607 Broad St. in St. Joseph	BL
(616) 983-1007	

Cinnamon triangles, whole buttermilk coffee cakes or eat-it-now slices, gooey caramel pecan rolls and cinnamon pecan rolls, fritters, almond hearts, and a full battery of filled and holey donuts are the menu at Dale's, the donut factory of donut fans' dreams. The pastries hit the hot oil every morning at about 3 am, and the doors open shortly thereafter, making this an ideal stop for famished travelers along I-94 to hop off (exit 23) for a fresh donut fix. By sunup, nearly all the day's varieties are displayed, but not every good thing is made every day. Some Dale loyalists plan their visits for the weekend, when the dark chocolatey twists known as tiger tails are always in the lineup.

Edmund Place

69 Edmund Pl., Detroit, MI (313) 831-5757	$$
Tues—Sun	£D

The downhome food at Edmund Place is the real thing—high-seasoned meat loaf, succulent fried chicken, luscious pork chops accompanied by collard greens, mashed potatoes, and corn bread. The African-American staff makes you feel welcome, and it is a joy to partake of such homespun meals, expertly prepared. Located in a pleasant old home, Edmund Place is a beacon of civility and good taste and a worthy destination for anyone seeking true urban American soul food.

Gustafson's Smoked Fish

4321 Rte. 2 W, Brevort, MI	$
(906) 292-5424	BLD

Along Route 2, which hugs Lake Michigan in the Upper Peninsula, every motel offers freezers to guests who have fresh-caught fish to keep until they get home. For those of us needing immediate fish-eating gratification, there is Gustafson's.

It is not a restaurant, but this roadside convenience store sells food that is oh-so-ready-to-eat. Even with your eyes closed, you'll find it as you cruise along the shore road (we don't recommend driving this way) because a sugar maple haze from a quartet of smoldering smokers outside the shop perfumes the air with the unbelievably appetizing smell of whitefish, trout, menominee, chub, and salmon turning gorgeous shades of gold. Inside, coolers are arrayed with the firm-fleshed beauties, which you can buy by the piece, wrapped in butcher's paper. A big, moist hunk of freshly smoked freshwater fish, a fifty-cent stack of saltine crackers, a bag of cheese curds, and a beer, plus the scenic beauty of Lake Michigan's northern shore: what's better than that?

Ham Heaven

70 Cadillac Sq., Detroit, MI	$
(313) 961-8818	BL

Baked, fried, sandwiched, folded into an omelet, ground up for hash, or diced for salad, sweet pink ham reigns in this boisterous sandwich shop near the courthouse. The ham is especially good as the flavor agent of split pea or bean soup. The one dish we cannot resist is called a hamlet, similar to a hamburger: ham ground up with vegetables to form a patty that is fried to crisp succulence and served on a bun. Add a squirt of mustard and you truly are in ham heaven.

Ivanhoe Café

5249 Joseph Campau, Detroit, MI (313) 925-5335	$$
weekdays, D Fri only	L

This vintage family restaurant, patronized by generations of Michiganders who know it by its nickname, the Polish Yacht Club, used to be famous for the greeting Joe the bartender gave all who entered: "Hello, Iiiivanhoe!" We didn't get the salutation last time we visited, and the neighborhood outside has run down at the heels, but everything else about this comfortable old watering hole is exactly as it's always been. It is a place to eat fine corned beef and cabbage or kielbasa and kraut, hamburgers on pumpernickel bread, and perch served family-style, cooked up by the skillet-full and accompanied by crisp-fried potatoes.

Juilleret's

130 State, Harbor Springs, MI (616) 526-2821	$$
(closed late Sept to mid-May)	LD

Juilleret's is a good-time place, as rowdy as a small-town soda fountain when school lets out, its stamped tin ceiling reverberating with the noise of summering Michiganders sitting down to dinners of planked whitefish—Juilleret's specialty and one of the not-to-be-missed Great Lakes meals.

The snowy-fleshed sweet fish is heaped on the plank, pooled with butter, strewn with sliced tomatoes, parsley, and lemon, all surrounded by a wall of piped-on duchess potatoes. Even amid the commotion of Juilleret's free-for-all booths, there is something undeniably regal about a planked meal such as this, the exalted entree attended by its legions of vegetables and protected on all sides by sturdy spud ramparts.

When you have cleaned your plank, there is only one way to end the feast—with a soda jerker's specialty. You can get a black cow, a tin roof, a Boston cooler, or a bittersweet dusty sundae. Best of all, you can go with one of the Juilleret's doozies that has been popular for generations: a Thundercloud, in which layers of ice cream and bittersweet chocolate are topped with marshmallow and chopped nuts; or a Velvet, in which the same ingredients are whipped smooth like a milk shake, but so thick you have to eat it with a spoon.

Lafayette Coney Island

118 Lafayette St., Detroit, MI (313) 964-8198	$
8 am-4 am daily	

If it's three in the morning and the one thing you really crave before you greet the dawn is a brace of raunchy little wieners smothered in chili and raw onions with a cup of bean soup on the side dished out under glaring fluorescents, you better hope you're in Detroit. When it comes to déclassé frankfurters, Lafayette Coney Island—open nearly round the clock—is in a (dé)class by itself.

Lehto's Pasties

Rte. 2, St. Ignace, MI (906) 643-8542	$
(closed Dec 1 to Easter)	£𝔇

The best-known specialty of Michigan's Upper Peninsula is the self-contained meat and potatoes pocket meal called the pasty. Lehto's of St. Ignace, open since 1947, claims to be America's first pasty drive-in, and this old family-run stand is a delight for any fan of roadside regional cookery. The mighty Lehto's pasty, loaded with a melange of beef, rutabaga, onions, and potatoes, is fragile-crusted and immensely satisfying. It is sold wrapped and ready to go for customers in a hurry, but we recommend eating at the five-stool counter inside the little shop. It is a friendly place, and you have quick access to napkins. Eating a pasty with one hand while steering your vehicle with the other requires practiced dexterity.

The Log Cabin

Hwys. 2 and 41, Gladstone, MI	$$
(906) 786-5621	£𝔇

The Log Cabin is a cozy supper club with a small family of plaster lawn deer permanently grazing out front. Between quaffs of sweet manhattans, made with brandy, the Upper Peninsula way, we availed ourselves of the Log Cabin salad bar—an opulent array of composed salads that might give modern nutrition police conniption fits, but to us looked like midwestern Thanksgiving. There was Waldorf salad with big red strawberries, pea and ham salad, long noodles with mayonnaise salad, short noodles with even more mayo salad, and macaroni salad, also with mayo. The great main course hereabouts is whitefish; the Log Cabin's is perfectly broiled to ineffable tenderness, pulling into fragile white flakes when prodded with a fork.

We love the view from the dining room. At the end of one visit, we sipped another round of candied drinks, listened to a muted-horn instrumental version of "My Way" playing low on the Log Cabin sound system, and gazed out across the plaster deer to the tall grass waving in the sapphire shallows of Little Bay De Noc—a Great Lakes epiphany!

Polonia

2934 Yemans St., Detroit, MI (313) 873-8432	$
Mon–Sat	LD

Good Polish food is one of Detroit's primary culinary attractions, and there is no place better to savor it than at Polonia. This ancient tin-ceiling café, staffed by experts with thick accents and kindly dispositions, offers a golden opportunity to tuck into plump pierogi that are butter-slick and filled with seasoned mashed potatoes, hearty plates of kielbasa and kraut, jellied pigs' feet, bowls of pickly cabbage soup, and stuffed cabbage. Prices are low and portions are gigantic. If old-world fare is food for your soul, Polonia is a comfort-food gem!

Rattlesnake Club

300 River Pl., Detroit, MI (313) 567-4400	$$$
Sat D only, closed Sun	LD

Chef Jimmy Schmidt is one of American cuisine's shining stars, and the restaurant he owns in his hometown of Detroit is a must for any visitor who wants to splurge on great modern food. The riverside setting, with lots of white linen and fresh flowers, is contemporary and luxurious, a magnet for expense account diners and serious epicures alike. The menu changes daily and reflects the seasons, but you can always count on much local provender, from an old-fashioned mess of perch from the Great Lakes to Michigan morels with your rack of veal, as well as spiced baby back ribs that just might be the best anywhere. For dessert, the signature dish is white chocolate ravioli.

How to Spot a Great Small-Town Café

O ne of the joys of traveling Midwest back roads is eating in a small-town café. Not only are you likely to find terrific cinnamon buns in the morning and state-fair pie at lunch, you will also get a real flavor of life in the town. This is particularly true in the morning, when many cafés are ad hoc social centers for the exchange of news, gossip, political opinions, and amateur weather forecasts. Conversations tend to be communal, and there might be one large table where customers come and go, helping themselves to coffee refills.

Some signs of a great small town café:

- ☞ Police cars and pickup trucks in the parking lot
- ☞ A large round table at the front window, where customers can see the street
- ☞ A bakery case with pies displayed (bonus for any blue ribbons recently won)
- ☞ A pegboard where regular customers keep their coffee cups
- ☞ A collection jar near the cash register to help out a community member in need
- ☞ Place mats with advertising for the local garage, funeral parlor, and portrait studio
- ☞ Newspapers strewn about for customers to read
- ☞ A daily written menu with a long list of vegetables
- ☞ A motto (Flo's of Marseilles, Illinois, has this inscribed on its menu: "If I can't eat it, I won't serve it!")
- ☞ Peek in the kitchen. Old ladies wearing hair nets, up to their elbows in flour, are almost always a good sign.
- ☞ Hours of operation geared to hardworking clientele, such as from 5 am to 2 pm
- ☞ Roll down the car windows when you drive along Main Street and sniff. Good midwestern smells include cinnamon buns in Iowa, smoked fish in Michigan's Upper Peninsula, five-way chili in Cincinnati, and charcoal-cooked sausages in Wisconsin.

Rosenthal Orchard

off Rte. 31, Charlevoix, MI (616) 547-4350	$
seasonal hours, closed winter through spring	

This is not a restaurant, but hungry travelers need to know about Rosenthal Orchard, where the motto is "You pick or we pick." If you nab your own apples from the several dozen varieties available, you are rewarded with a refreshing glass of fresh-pressed cider. The orchard store has bushels of apricots, peaches, prunes, plums, and pears; but the main attraction, in late summer, is cherries—big, dark, sweet, plump Michigan beauties. You can pick those yourself, too, or buy bags of just-picked ones, washed and ready to eat.

Zingerman's Deli

422 Detroit St., Ann Arbor, MI	$
(313) 663-3354	BLD

A grandiose deli that serves every kind of sandwich the human race has devised—from Italian salami subs to brisket-and-schmaltz on rye and a pile of hot pastrami parenthesized 'twixt two potato pancakes. We get weak-kneed thinking of Zingerman's smoked whitefish salad, redolent of dill and red onion, piled on slices of freshly made onion-rye bread. The immense menu is a good hour's read, and ranges beyond sandwiches to such traditional old-world specialties as noodle kugel (a sweet pudding), cheese blintzes (cheese-filled crepes), and knishes (heavyweight dumplings). Or you can choose Thai noodle salad, Arkansas peppered ham, or Ratatouille with polenta. Brash, crowded, and invariably delicious, this one-of-a-kind place is an essential stop for all traveling eaters.

Zingerman's stocks a tremendous inventory of cheese, smoked fish, meats, breads, coffees, etc., for retail sale.

MINNESOTA

☆ ☆ ☆

Al's Breakfast

413 14th Ave. S.E., Minneapolis, MN	$
(602) 331-9991	𝓑𝓛

A l's Breakfast serves the best morning meal in town. It is a pint-size diner with an ancient counter of worn yellow linoleum and twelve stools permanently attached that form an aisle with the wall that is too small for any good-size person to pass through without turning sideways. In the front window of the restaurant behind the counter is a minuscule grill where the short-order cook flips pancakes, poaches eggs, and maintains a steady dialogue of wisecracks with customers and staff.

The buttermilk pancakes are superb, available with blueberries in the batter, and there are fine whole wheat cakes, too, but Al's fragile, free-form poached eggs have an uncommon savor that is hard to resist. Many customers get them in the classic eggs Benedict configuration, on Canadian bacon and English muffin halves, gilded with freshly made hollandaise sauce. Or you can get the hollandaise served over scrambled eggs and plates of potatoes. Some folks simply order a bowlful and use it as a dip for rye toast.

Tantalizing aromas billow from the grill up front of hash brown potatoes and corned beef hash. The hash has a briny, well-spiced smell and is thickly laced with shreds of potato. How it's served is up to you, either limp and glistening soft or fried to a brittle mahogany crisp.

Al's customers adore this place for its personality as much as for its food. "It is an organism," explained a friend of the house named John Marshall. "Good things happen here; people's lives change. If you want a car, or an apartment, or a sweetheart, come in and sit at the counter. Come in, have coffee, and chat a while. Pretty soon, I promise, you will get what you need. Al's has a life of its own, above and beyond any of us. We truly believe it is a crossroads of the universe."

Betty's Pies

215 Hwy. 61 E, Two Harbors, MN (218) 834-3367	$
(closed Nov through Apr; open weekends only in May)	B L D

Betty's serves first-rate sandwiches—ham salad on homemade rye is especially tasty—as well as homemade soup, hearty chili, and walleye pike from the cold waters of Lake Superior. But the main reason this little outfit is crowded all summer long with locals and tourists, dine-in and take-out customers, is dessert. There are crunchy cookies and lemon angel cakes that melt in your mouth, and about a dozen kinds of pie each day, including berries, fruits, creams, and custards. A beacon of delight on Lake Superior's north shore!

Café Brenda

300 1st Ave. N., Minneapolis, MN	$$
(612) 342-9230	D

Towering windows give this health-conscious dining room theatrical panache; but at table level, where framed botanical prints hang on clean white walls, the setting is serene, the sort of place that encourages a reverent attitude toward food. Tables are set far enough apart to make meals feel like private parties. We once saw a nutritionally compatible foursome toasting one another with glasses of microbrewed beer, then sharing shrimp satay, grain-and-bean croquettes, and plates of Moroccan vegetable couscous drizzled with peppery harissa sauce.

Chef and owner Brenda Langton recalled that when she started cooking in a St. Paul restaurant in 1976, "healthful ingredients took precedence over flavor." Twenty years have passed, and the meals she serves now are healthful but uncompromised. In this modern urban café, good flavors prevail.

Café Latté

850 Grand Ave., St. Paul, MN	$
(612) 224-5687	**LD**

Café Latté is an energetic urban cafeteria with many good dishes to recommend it, including glorious tossed-to-order salads, interesting soups (four each day), hearty stews, and a fresh bread selection that ranges from white chocolate scones to ten-grain loaves. The meal you eat will be satisfying and inexpensive, and it can be very healthful, but the thing that lures us with sweet tooths back is the spectacular selection of desserts, cake in particular. If the devil himself made them, they couldn't be more tempting. There is chocolate kahlua torte that nearly drips; an English pecan triple sec fudge cake so seductive that it ought to be arrested; strawberry rhubarb cheesecake and orange chocolate chunk cheesecake to swoon over. The pièce de résistance, and one of this planet's outstanding desserts, is a sprawling triple-layer "turtle cake," moist devil's food sandwiching gooey caramel studded with pecans, all blanketed with thick chocolate frosting.

Nye's Polonaise Room

112 E. Hennepin Ave., Minneapolis, MN	$$
(612) 379-2021	**LD**

Order a Polonaise Plate, and you get a small taste of nearly everything Polish that this kitchen makes: buttery pierogi, long pink sausages and kraut, hefty cabbage rolls, pork hocks, and spare ribs.

The meals are good, and the ambiance is rousing. But what thrills us most about this fine old supper club are the booths in the central dining room. They are shiny gold metal-flake vinyl, the kind of stuff that hisses quietly when you ease down on it. Here's the place to eat yourself silly, drink Polish pile drivers (vodka and Krupnik), and tap your toes to the rollicking Ruth Adams Band (Thursday through Saturday), which is billed as "The World's Most Dangerous Polka Band." Nazdrowie!

MISSOURI

Arthur Bryant Barbeque	
1727 Brooklyn Ave., Kansas City, MO	**$**
(816) 231-1123	**£D**

There was concern when Arthur Bryant died in 1982 that his legendary smoke house wouldn't survive without him. But it has, and although the floor isn't as slick with grease as it used to be and the beef isn't quite as oozingly moist, it is still a sensational place to eat barbecue. There are good ribs and sliced pork, but it's that beef brisket that makes us swoon—heaped into white-bread sandwiches, slathered with Bryant's hot, grainy opaque sauce, and accompanied by crisp French fries.

C&K Barbecue	
4390 Jennings Station Rd., St. Louis, MO	**$**
(314) 385-5740	**D**

Business is strictly take-out at this fine barbecue where strangers to soul food can sample a curious specialty found in few other cities: snoots. Snoots, which are pig snouts that are sliced and fried crisp and served drenched in barbecue sauce, are profoundly luscious, so much so that novice appetites might want to sample them as hors d'oeuvres rather than as a whole meal. What we like to eat at C&K after snoots are ribs—succulent and chewy, bathed in a peppery sauce that has an amazing ability to drip and spill onto the back seat as well as the front seat of your car. The ribs are served with potato salad (cool, tongue-soothing relief), white bread for mopping up the mess, and fine desserts that include chocolate cake, sweet potato pie, lemon cake, and caramel cake.

Despite the lack of amenities (or is it because of them?), this restaurant is de rigueur for anyone who wants to sample true St. Louis soul food, snoots and all.

Crown Candy Kitchen	
1401 St. Louis Ave., St. Louis, MO	**$**
(314) 621-9650	**£𝔇**

ach booth has a jukebox. Up front are cases of chocolates and a nickel scale that predicts your future. Behind the marble counter is a soda fountain where shakes are blended in tall silver carafes and multisauce sundaes are haloed with whipped cream and crowned with pecans, sprinkles, and cherries. This jovial 1913 ice cream parlor will concoct just about any confectionery pleasure you can imagine (and they serve sandwiches and fine chili dogs, too); the house specialty is a malt made with fresh bananas (with options of chocolate or butterscotch flavor). If you consume five malts in thirty minutes, you get them all free.

Jerre Anne Cafeteria	
2640 Mitchell Ave., St. Joseph, MO (816) 232-6585	**$**
Tues–Sat	**£𝔇**

neighborhood corner cafeteria that's been serving baked ham and beef hash for more than sixty years, Jerre Anne is also an excellent bakery. So even if you don't have all of fifteen minutes to load a tray with a hot meal of juicy roast brisket of beef (or any one of more than a half-dozen other entries) with potatoes, vegetables, rolls, salad, and all the trimmings, you could certainly stop by for an afternoon's supply of cookies, cake, and pastries.

Jess & Jim's

517 E. 135th St., Kansas City, MO	$$
(816) 941-9499	LD

Steak at Jess & Jim's is a Kansas City joy. In particular, we refer to the "Playboy strip" steak, the cut known elsewhere as a Kansas City strip—a boneless, pound-and-a-half sirloin carried from kitchen to table still sizzling on its platter. It is a tremendous thing of beauty, even more lovely once you slice down through its crust (the steak is griddle-fried) and watch the juices flow. On the side there is a monstrously delicious twice-baked potato or good crisp cottage fries.

Notes of warning: Jess & Jim's is often hideously crowded and accepts no reservations. Also, decor is nonexistent, service is brusque, salad is mediocre, there is no wine list and no dessert. However, concern about such imperfections evaporates at the first taste of steak.

Lambert's Café

2109 E. Malone, Sikeston, MO	$
(573) 471-4261	BLD

Billboards for Lambert's Café boast that it is HOME OF THE THROWED ROLL. From outside, it looks ordinary. Walk in the door and hot rolls are sailing through the air across the dining room, tossed by waiters from the kitchen to customers at tables, who gingerly split them open to let steam escape, then dip them into puddles of sweet sorghum molasses oozing on the tablecloths. Other eaters pop nubbins of fried okra down the hatch, spoon up heaps of beans and pepper relish, and drink iced tea from one-quart mason jars. Lambert's is one of a kind, and not just because its rolls are thrown and by the end of the meal everybody's table is a delicious mess of spilled and dripped food. Like the rest of the chow that emerges from the kitchen, those rolls are *good*—warm and fluffy—and Lambert's country ham with white beans and turnip greens is Ozark country cooking at its most toothsome.

Snead's Corner Bar-B-Q

801 E. 171st St., Belton, MO (816) 331-9858	$$
closed Mon and Tues	£𝒟

When we are in Kansas City with time for only one barbecue meal, we go to Snead's, a sprawling roadhouse beyond the edge of town. Handsome ribs, lean and juicy beef, ham that is sweet, and turkey that is tender—everything from the smoke pit glows with hickory flavor. The French fries are fresh and the beans have a nice tingle. We especially like Snead's "brownies," which are plates piled high with unbelievably savory burnt ends from the beef and/or ham; and the "log meat" sandwiches, a diced hash of all the hickory-smoked meats on a bun. Someday, we are going to order Snead's fried chicken. The menu warns that it takes forty-five minutes to prepare. Based on the excellence of everything else this kitchen produces, we suspect the chicken is on a par with KC's best.

Complimentary ice cream cones are provided at the end of each meal.

Stroud's

1015 E. 85th St., Kansas City, MO	$$
(816) 333-2132	𝒟

This dilapidated roadhouse on a bleak street south of the city serves four-star fried chicken—our choice as the best on earth. Dark or light, each piece of pan-fried meat is tightly enveloped in a red-gold crust imbued with the succulence of chicken fat exactly the way a crisp strip of bacon is charged with the nectareous goodness of pig fat. When you heft it in your hands (only oddballs use knife and fork) and penetrate the tender wrapping with your teeth, the flavor of sizzled skin is so profound that you might suddenly think you have never really tasted fried chicken before. With it come exquisite mashed potatoes, real pan gravy, and country-style green beans cooked to a fare-thee-well.

<u>Note</u>: A second Stroud's, in a lovely old house furnished with antiques, has a menu almost identical to that of the original except that fry-

frowners can get a skinless broiled chicken breast. It is at 5410 Northeast Oak Ridge Road in Kansas City, (816) 454-9600.

Midwest Splurges

Expensive, fancy, and/or fashionable regional restaurants that are worth it.

- Gibson's, Chicago, IL (p. 171)
- Tuttaposto, Chicago, IL (p. 180)
- Phil Smidt & Son, Hammond, IN (p. 185)
- St. Elmo Steak House, Indianapolis, IN (p. 188)
- Vogel's, Whiting, IN (p. 189)
- Caucus Club, Detroit, MI (p. 194)
- Rattlesnake Club, Detroit, MI (p. 200)
- Café Brenda, Minneapolis, MN (p. 204)
- Jess & Jim's, Kansas City, MO (p. 208)
- Karl Ratzsch's, Milwaukee, WI (p. 222)
- Rupp's Lodge, Sheboygan, WI (p. 226)

Ted Drewes

6726 Chippewa, St. Louis, MO	$
(314) 481-2652	£D

From its own freshly made custard, Ted Drewes concocts one of the world's greatest milk shakes, known as a "concrete" for its incredible avoirdupois. Forget using a straw, suction has no effect on this mighty substance. You practically could use a knife and fork. Customers who come on dates tend to use a spoon; guys in groups pour it down the hatch. Cones and cups of the first-rate custard are also available.

OHIO

★ ★ ★

Bun's

6 Winter St., Delaware, OH (614) 363-3731	$
closed Mon	BLD

A nice, homey, town dining room, Bun's descends from a family bakery that opened in Delaware in 1863. It still features dandy baked goods at a take-out counter (pecan loaves, butterscotch twists, Danish pullaparts, fudge cake, and breads and buns of all shapes and sizes), as well as a daily printed menu of heartland favorites, from ham salad sandwiches on Bun's-baked bread to meat loaf with escalloped corn and dark rye rolls. Prices are low, waitresses are friendly, meals are fresh and wholesome. Gee, it's great to eat American!

Camp Washington Chili

Hopple and Colerain, Cincinnati, OH (513) 541-0061	$
always open, except Sun	

For more than half a century, round the clock, Camp Washington has been a prime source of Cincinnati-style chili, which means thick, spicy meat sauce atop a bed of plump spaghetti, garnished with beans, shredded cheese, and chopped onions. Such a configuration is known as five-way chili; subtract the onions, cheese, and/or beans and you get three- or four-way. It is a wild, tasty meal, all the more pleasurable for the classic beanery surroundings: baseball trophies on display, ghastly fluorescent lights, worn (but clean) blue-and-white tile floor.

Beyond chili, Camp Washington is also a good place to have an archetypal Coney Island (a little wiener heaped with chili, cheese, and onions), as well as one of the tall double-decker sandwiches featured in all fine Cincinnati chili parlors.

Clark's Dining Room

Rtes. 40 and 13, Jacksontown, OH (614) 323-3874	$$
Tues—Sun	LD

On the old National Highway, Clark's is nearing its eightieth year in business. The vintage hostelry (rebuilt after a fire in the 1950s) has established its reputation on iron-skillet-fried chicken dinners with mashed potatoes and gravy, salad with great house dressing, all the vegetables you can eat, and Grandma Clark's homemade pie. In the few decades we've been customers, nothing has changed. Now run by a third generation of the family, Clark's has the same familiar, and familial, menu (with steak and ham added), and still employs personnel who have been part of the place for as long as anyone can remember.

Expect a considerable wait for a table, especially on weekends and holidays.

Doc's

18625 Main, Tontogany, OH	$
(419) 823-4081	LD

The only bar/restaurant in town that just recently acquired a gas pump" is how our northern Ohio tipsters, Jennifer Kinney and Michael Nagy, described the fine and funky short-order hash house known as Doc's. Customers come for a lunch of slim hamburgers sided by wicked cheese fries; roast beef with potatoes and gravy on the side; or just big plates of nothing but potatoes and gravy. "Real comfort food," the KinNagys advised, an assessment with which we wholeheartedly agree. They also recommended Doc's Saturday-night Mexican-food specials and its dartboard, which, as officers in the Bowling Green Dart Association, they lauded as "the real bristle-board kind."

Cincinnati's Ways with Chili

Cincinnati chili is a complex brew made with finely ground meat. It is served in chili parlors (preferably open-all-night ones) and bears little resemblance to the chili of Texas or New Mexico. When you order it, you must specify what "way" you want it:

- Two-Way Chili   Chili on top of noodles, aka "chili spaghetti"
- Three-Way Chili   Spaghetti topped with chili and grated cheddar cheese
- Four-Way Chili   Spaghetti with chili, cheese, chopped onions
- Five-Way Chili   Spaghetti with chili, cheese, chopped onions, and kidney beans

According to Timothy Charles Lloyd's treatise on the subject in *Western Folklore* several years ago, "the correspondence between the order of additional ingredients and higher-numbered ways follows a strict rule of cheese-three, onions-four, and beans-five." In other words, if you want spaghetti, chili, and onions *but no cheese,* you would never order a three-way with onions instead of cheese or a two-way plus onions. You would order a "four-way without cheese."

An exception to the rule is the combination of chili, beans, and spaghetti, which is known simply as "chili bean" rather than "five-way, no cheese, no onions."

Three-way chili is sometimes called a "haywagon."

Edgewood Inn

US 6 E and State Rte. 1, Pemberville, OH	$
(419) 287-4775	BLD

Thanks to the KinNagys of Bowling Green State University for tipping us off to the Edgewood Inn, which they described as an ideal eatery for anyone with a large appetite and a small budget. It is a meat-and-potatoes roadhouse, with both a lounge and a somewhat more civilized dining room where customers consume great platters of prime ribs (on weekend nights), corned beef, ham steaks, chicken, and gigantic "burritos supremo." The meal includes a shot at a copious, albeit predictable, soup and salad bar.

Flat Iron Café

1114 Center St., Cleveland, OH	$$
(216) 696-6968	£Ɖ

Going upscale can be a bad thing for a restaurant, especially one like the Flat Iron Café which earned its reputation as a blue-collar Irish pub in the Cleveland Flats. Although the neighborhood has spruced up and the bar's clientele has gone with it (you'll see more suspenders and designer shirts than work boots and dungarees), this is still a must-eat place as long as the day's supply of fresh-fried lake perch hasn't been exhausted. Sweet, crunchy, and addictive, these fillets are one of the Great Lakes' treasures, and a raucous pub like the Flat Iron is an ideal place to devour them.

Henry's

6275 Hwy. 40, West Jefferson, OH	$
(614) 879-9321	ℬℒ

With state fair pie and a pine-paneled dining room in a former gas station on an old road that the interstate has made obsolete, Henry's charms are abundant. Regular customers come to eat ploughman's lunch of ham and beans with corn bread on the side, or meat loaf and mashed potatoes, or roast beef with dressing and stewed tomatoes; but for most travelers, the great lure to this lonesome way station is dessert. It is quite literally blue-ribbon pie, having won top prizes at the state fair for years, and while the fillings are exemplary—whether fruit or cream—it is the crust that makes us swoon. Flaky and tender, ineffably flavorful, it is a truly elegant foodstuff. What a joy it is to be seated in one of Henry's weathered old Naugahyde booths and have a good American meal followed by such world-class dessert.

Nancy's Home Cooking

3133 North High St., Columbus, OH (614) 265-9012	$
Mon–Thur, BL Fri, B only Sat and Sun	BLD

Thanks to eater extraordinaire Mindy Pennington for tipping us off to this jim-dandy home café in her former hometown and advising us that the must-eat meal day is Thursday. That's when golden chicken-and-noodle stew gets ladled over mashed potatoes with green beans on the side. "C&N" is so locally famous that at noon one Thursday during the summer, we spent a good half hour waiting outside with scores of others eager to cozy up to supreme comfort food.

Another great Mindy tip was breakfast at Nancy's, where we started our day with a heap of sizzled-gold home fries and what's known hereabouts as the garbage omelet—green peppers, tomatoes, onions, ham, and cheese. Bravo!

Tony Packo's Café

1902 Front St., Toledo, OH	$
(419) 691-6054	LD

Taut little tube steaks are sliced lengthwise and heaped with fine-ground hot-spiced chili sauce. These infamous longitudinal sandwiches, eaten by most Tony Packo's habitués in bunches of three or four a shot, are wanton and wonderful foodstuffs, the perfect meal when only the raunchiest hot dog will do. They are what Buckeye-state homeboy Klinger of M*A*S*H (Jamie Farr) wanted to get discharged from the army for.

WISCONSIN

Aeppler Orchards

704 Concord Rd. Oconomowoc, WI (414) 567-6635	$
seasonal hours	

Aeppler Orchards feature more than two dozen varieties of apple, all of which are available singly, by the bushel, or in gift packs. They are also known for their brown apple syrup, a wondrous substance of apple juice and brown sugar boiled down to a thick, bracing concoction suitable for pancakes or as an unusual flavoring in cake and sweet bread recipes. For travelers without a kitchen handy the grand prize is freshly dipped taffy apples, available at the peak of apple season each fall.

Beernsten's Candy Store

108 N. 8th St., Manitowoc, WI	$
(414) 684-9616	£D

A seat in one of the beautiful black walnut booths at the back of Beernsten's is a time machine. The town sweet shop since 1932, this charming little confectionery also serves such lunch-counter sandwiches as grilled cheese, egg salad, or peanut butter and jelly, as well as franks and beans or macaroni. But the main attractions are old-fashioned soda fountain specialties. Here is the place to indulge in a Sweetheart (caramel, vanilla ice cream, marshmallow, crushed nuts), a Teddy Bear (chocolate ice cream topped with marshmallow), or a Sunset (strawberry and vanilla ice cream, pineapple, marshmallow, crushed nuts). We love the way fudge for hot fudge sundaes is served—in a separate shot glass so you can pour it on the ice cream yourself, measuring out just the right amount. The sundae comes with small, toasty pecans with just a hint of salt that perfectly balances the sweetness they adorn.

Up front, Beernsten's sells more than a hundred different kinds of hand-dipped candy including a chocolate cosmetology set (brush, mirror, hair dryer), smoochies (like Hershey's kisses, but bigger and more moist), raspberry and vanilla seafoam dainties, and a bon bon known as fairy food, which is a two-inch square of brittle spun sugar molasses enveloped in a sheaf of deep, dark chocolate.

Sheboygan Brats

Sheboygan brats are brightly spiced link sausages four to six inches long with taut skins and succulent insides made of pork or a combination of beef and pork—a not-to-be-missed Wisconsin delight. A brat (rhymes with hot) is always cooked over charcoal and almost always served in a sandwich, preferably a double sandwich (two brats), with pickle, mustard, onions, and enough butter that the sandwich drips. The brat's roll is as meaningful as the sausage itself; it should be tender inside so it can sop up large amounts of butter and have a supple leathery exterior—never brittle or crusty—that makes it easy to grip and transform the bun into a kind of mitt for holding onto all its ingredients.

Sheboygan brats are served at picnics and town affairs, and in most bars and bowling alleys. We like them best at

☞ Charcoal Inn, Sheboygan, WI (p. 219)
☞ Gosse's Drive-Thru, Sheboygan, WI (p. 221)
☞ Penguin, Manitowoc, WI (p. 224)
☞ Rupp's Lodge, Sheboygan, WI (p. 226)
☞ Tiny's, Sheboygan, WI (p. 227)

How to Grill a Sheboygan Brat

The fundamentals include locally made sausages (see sources, below), good hard rolls to put them in, and a grill with white-hot charcoal briquets or hardwood charcoal. It is traditional to steep the sausages in beer:

    4 cups beer
    4 large onions, sliced thick
    4 tablespoons mustard
    2 tablespoons ketchup
    12 bratwurst
    6 hard rolls (In the Northeast, we find fresh "Portuguese rolls"
        a good approximation of Sheboygan hard rolls.)
    sliced dill pickles, to taste
    additional mustard, to taste

Bring the beer to a simmer in a broad skillet with one of the onions, the mustard, and the ketchup. Put the brats in and simmer them about 20 minutes. Drain them, then grill them about 5 minutes over white-hot coals along with the remaining onion slices.

Bendtsen's Bakery

3200 Washington Ave., Racine, WI	$
(414) 633-0365	BL

Kringle, the delicate Danish pastry ring that has become a specialty of Racine, is not really restaurant food. Most townies buy it at a West Side bakery then eat it at home, where they butter it and consume it with a pot of coffee alongside.

Still, it's a swell car snack (if you don't mind crumbs), and Bendtsen's is a good place to pick up one for the road. Flaky, sweet, and laced with your choice of nut or fruit filling, kringle is addictive food. We especially like this particular shop because it always seems to have a little plate of bite-size kringle pieces on the counter for munching while you place an order. Also, Bendtsen's bakers are responsible for the World's Largest Kringle (photo evidence is posted on the wall).

Put a pair of brats in a hard roll, top them with some grilled onion, then sliced dill pickles and mustard.

To prepare the brats in advance:

Sheboygan butcher Chuck Miesfeld gave us this alternative recipe. Thoroughly cook them on the grill, without any steeping, then immerse them in a marinade of approximately these proportions:

12 ounces beer
1 large sweet onion, chopped
4 tablespoons melted butter

Keep the pan warm and, when ready to serve the brats, hoist them out of the liquid with tongs, put them in rolls, and apply your chosen condiments.

Mail-Order Brat Sources:

Poth's Sheboygan Bratwurst Co.: 1501 S. 8th St., Sheboygan, WI (414) 457-7424
Sheboygan's Meat Market: 1212 Pennsylvania Ave., Sheboygan, WI 1-800-733-GIFT

Charcoal Inn

| 1313 S. 8th St., Sheboygan, WI (414) 458-6988; | $ |
| also at 1637 Geele Ave. in Sheboygan 458-1147 | £𝒟 |

Nothing but a simple town sandwich shop, the Charcoal Inn is a leading source of the great Wisconsin sausage known as a brat. (Rhyme brat with hot; it's short for bratwurst.) It is served in a sandwich, and connoisseurs order a double. A Charcoal Inn double brat is brought to the table without a plate. It is wrapped in wax paper, which you unfold and use as a dropcloth to catch dripping condiments. Each brat is slit and flattened before getting grilled, which makes for easy stacking in the bun. These are brats from Henry Poth, the esteemed butcher shop just down 8th Street, and they are deeply perfumed with spices that burst into blossom when they sizzle over a smoky charcoal fire. Thick and resilient but thoroughly tooth-tender, they are as savory

Neighborhood Polish Restaurants

The American Midwest has a larger Polish-ancestored population than Poland. Chicago, Milwaukee, and Detroit are especially blessed with restaurants that serve true Polish food. Many of the staff scarcely speak English, and menus can be difficult to decipher; but you can count on friendly neighborhood ambiance, delicious old-world meals, and low-low prices.

- Busy Bee, Chicago, IL (p. 169)
- Irene's, Chicago, IL (p. 174)
- Crocus, Milwaukee, WI (p. 220)
- Polonia, Detroit, MI (p. 200)

as sausage can be, oozing a delectable blend of meat juice and the pure melted butter with which they are basted when they come off the grill.

For dessert after a brat, you need a torte. The Charcoal Inn's lemonade torte is a square about four by four inches wide and two inches high. It is white and smooth, sitting on a pallet of Graham cracker crumbs, and it tastes like a pint of cream that has been reduced, thickened, and sweetened. It is similar in texture to a cheesecake, but it is so pure and rich you want to call it cream cake.

Crocus

1801 S. Muskego, Milwaukee, WI (414) 643-6383	$
Mon–Fri, D Fri and Sat (hours vary seasonally)	£

White barszcz is a safe bet," the Crocus waitress says as we consider which of the day's five soups to have with our meal. "If you haven't been raised on czarnina, you might not like it." Czarnina is indeed a strange brew—syrup-brown and sweet, thick with little dumplings, beans, shreds of duck, and plump raisins—the hallmark of every neighborhood Polish restaurant in Milwaukee. Barszcz is a smoky harvest of sausage, ham, potato, and pieces of hard-cooked egg. We also like the aromatic dill pickle soup, which is pale porcelain green with little potatoes, and the red barszcz, a thin broth loaded with beets and onions.

After soup, this neighborhood tavern offers many fine Polish specialties, including braised beef roll-ups filled with a tangy bacon-mushroom mix, and pierogi stuffed with meat, cheese, or kraut and mushrooms. The potato pancakes are the star of the menu, with a refined, lacy texture and a fetching sour taste like something an expert grandmother would make—a fine companion to the fish fry Crocus has every Friday night.

Gosse's Drive-Thru

2928 N. 13th St., Sheboygan, WI	$
(414) 457-7784	£ D

Gosse's lets you enjoy Sheboygan bratwurst without leaving your vehicle. Just like at a franchise, you sit behind the wheel and holler into a microphone, then drive forward, pay, and pick up your sandwiches. (There are a handful of picnic tables outside the shack, which is hardly bigger than an ATM booth.) The brats are delectable porky patties, bathed in butter and adorned with pickle slices, raw onion, and mustard. It is also worth noting that perch is always on the menu. Nearly every restaurant around here serves it, but most do so only as part of the ritual Friday fish fry. It is remarkable fish for a fast-food type of operation, sweet and delicate, sheathed in a chewy golden crust.

Jessica's

524 E. Layton Ave., Milwaukee, WI	**$**
(414) 744-1119	**LD**

Jessica's is a 1950s-theme burger-and-malt shop with pink walls, a free jukebox, an Elvis clock, and an impressive soda fountain menu. Made with gorgeous creamy frozen custard, the shakes and malts are too thick for a straw; a "heavy" version adds an extra scoop of luxurious custard. We especially recommend the turtle sundaes—custard topped with hot fudge, caramel, toasted pecans, whipped cream, and a cherry—available in four sizes, ranging from Junior to Special, the latter big enough for two (or four) to share. Jessica's hamburgers come the Milwaukee way, with butter melting on top of the patty and sopping the top half of the bun.

Karl Ratzsch's

320 E. Mason St., Milwaukee, WI (414) 276-2720	**$$$**
(an early dining menu, from 4 pm to 6 pm, is under $15 per person)	**D**

This grand restaurant has been justly famous since 1904 for its German food, served by a staff of consummate professionals in a civilized dining room of dark woodwork, antique steins, and romantic murals. The old-world menu includes such stalwart classics as liver-dumpling soup, roast goose shank, beef rouladen, and sauerbraten with gingersnap gravy. There are five German beers on tap and a whole array of Kümmel, Kirschwasser, and Rumpleminze liqueurs for after dinner. Meals start with wonderful anisette and fennel rolls, and there isn't a more beautiful roast duck in the state of Wisconsin. But here's a secret: the non-German food is grand, too. Steaks and prime rib are utterly regal (get Ratzsch's thick, crusty potato pancakes on the side), and the whitefish is a Great Lakes treasure—tender, sweet, and juicy—served on a wood plank in a ring of mashed potatoes.

Kewpee Lunch

520 Wisconsin Ave., Racine, WI (414) 634-9601	**$**
closes at 6 pm	**BLD**

America's least-known hamburger chain has two shops in Lima, Ohio, two in Lansing, Michigan, and this one in downtown Racine, which is almost completely engulfed by a modern parking lot. Despite its modern Formica and clean orange Naugahyde decor, there is a nice antiquated vintage feel about this old burger shop, where a case along one wall is filled with Kewpee dolls. The root beer is home-made; the hamburgers are slim, lunch-counter classics (we recommend a double); and the house motto, inscribed on the paper napery, is inspired: "Hamburger, pickle on top, makes your heart go flippety-flop."

Kopp's Frozen Custard

Three locations: 5373 N. Port Washington Rd., Glendale, WI	**$**
(404) 961-3288; 18880 W. Bluemound Rd., Brookfield	**LD**
(404) 789-9490; and 7631 W. Layton Ave., Greenfield (404) 282-4312	

Kopp's, a joyful place with butter-basted burgers and merry eaters chowing down wherever they can find a place to lean, inside or out, is always mobbed. Sundaes are the specialty of the house.

The sundaes Kopp's makes are so elaborate that there is a brochure at the order counter with diagrams pointing out various ingredients and their place in the architecture of each concoction. The blueprint for the staggering Kopp's Special details pineapple and raspberry sauces, sliced bananas, hot fudge, toasted pecans, and a cherry on top.

The sauces are excellent and the toasted nuts are a revelation, but the foundation is the important part, and at Kopp's it is ivory-white custard made from pure, high-butterfat ingredients with none of the thickeners and stabilizers that gunk up ordinary ice cream. Custard like this is a Wisconsin passion. It is hypnotic to watch it ooze from great silver machines behind the counter. To taste it is to know why Kopp's has been a beloved Milwaukee institution since Elsie Kopp opened her first stand in 1950. Vanilla is superb—the true custard-head's choice—but Kopp's makes a new and different flavor every single day of the year. Last visit we had wonderful Palermo lemon, but it cannot surpass the glorious caramel apple with mixed nuts that was the featured attraction August 31, 1995.

Norske Nook	
207 W. 7th St., Osseo, WI	$
(715) 597-3069	BLD

Although the Norske Nook is a full-menu, meat-and-potatoes town café that even cooks up such Norwegian specialties as lutefisk and lefse at Christmas, most passersby hop off I-94 at Osseo for one reason only: to eat pie. There are always at least a dozen kinds on display, including sweet, buttery rhubarb, berries of all kinds, and mincemeat with rum sauce. Sour cream raisin pie is our personal favorite, cut into titanic slices, cream-sweet ivory custard full of plump raisins, heaped high with ethereal meringue, and piled into a wafer-crisp crust. With a cup of good coffee, this exhilarating pastry has become the Holy Grail for many traveling gastronomes.

Penguin	
3900 Calumet Ave., Manitowoc, WI	$
(414) 684-6403	LD

At this snazzy drive-in, Badger State burger hounds dine in the comfort of their vehicles, on little wire trays that hook onto the window brought to them by uniformed carhops. (There is also counter service inside.)

"Charco grilled" sandwiches are the specialty of the house, including deliciously spiced bratwurst, available as a single link or, in the locally preferred configuration, as a double sandwich. For the latter, two four-inchers with wicked char marks on their crackling crisp skin are split and stuffed into a rugged-crusted (but tender inside) hard roll.

Order a double brat with everything and the sausages are smothered with ketchup, diced onions, and a couple of pickle slices.

On the side, good onion rings and French fries can be had, but many customers, whose loyalty to Dairy State foods is inbred, choose cheese nuggets in their place. These are bite-size curds of buttery orange cheese enveloped in glistening golden coats of batter. Like charcoal-cooked brats, they are a local passion.

The other true Wisconsin taste at the Penguin is custard, which is as different from ordinary ice cream as champagne is from jug wine. Made fresh daily at the Penguin, it is an elegant off-white color, smooth as ivory, and richer than top cream. Get it plain in a bowl, atop a piece of pie, as the foundation for a sundae or a jumbo milk shake, or by the pint to savor for miles.

Real Chili

419 E. Wells, Milwaukee, WI	$
(414) 271-4042	£D

Green Bay–style chili is similar to Cincinnati chili: spiced ground meat atop layers of spaghetti noodles and beans. But Wisconsin's way is different. Once the bowl is assembled to your specifications with a mild, medium, or hot drift of sloppy meat atop its cushion of limp noodles and beans, the server garnishes it with a dollop of extra grease skimmed from the top of the pot. The spicy grease makes it all the more luscious. At Real Chili, a fine old parlor in downtown Milwaukee, you can have it topped with your choice of sour cream, cheese, and/or onions, accompanied by a bowl of crunchy oyster crackers to cleanse the palate between immersions in the nasty brew.

Rupp's Lodge

925 N. 8th St., Sheboygan, WI	$$
(414) 459-8155	£Đ

A plump grilled steak, bathed in butter, is what has drawn customers to this supper club in downtown Sheboygan for well over half a century. Start with a trip to the salad bar, which includes bean salads, pasta salads, pickled herring, cheese and sausage, slaw, corn niblets, and even little bowls of butterscotch pudding if you cannot wait for

Great American Steak Houses

We admire these places not just because they serve juicy steaks, good potatoes, and icy martinis, but also because they have ambiance well suited to eating red meat in abundance. That ambiance can vary dramatically—Doe's is funky, the Grill is swanky, Spark's is big-city brash, the Far Western is cowboy-casual—but every one, in its own way, will make you proud to be a carnivore.

- Ben Benson's, New York, NY (p. 58)
- Buckhorn Exchange, Denver, CO (p. 262)
- Cattlemen's Steak House, Fort Worth, TX (p. 289)
- Cattlemen's, Oklahoma City, OK (p. 283)
- Dodd's Town House, Indianapolis, IN (p. 181)
- Doe's Eat Place, Greenville, MS (p. 151)
- Dreisbach's, Grand Island, NE (p. 242)
- Eddie's, Great Falls, MT (p. 232)
- Far Western Tavern, Guadalupe, CA (p. 320)
- Gibson's, Chicago, IL (p. 171)
- The Grill, Beverly Hills, CA (p. 320)
- Jess and Jim's, Kansas City, MO (p. 208)
- Peter Luger, Brooklyn, NY (p. 66)
- Rainwater's, San Diego, CA (p. 328)
- Spark's, New York, NY (p. 67)
- St. Elmo Steak House, Indianapolis, IN (p. 188)
- Tea Steak House, Tea, SD (p. 248)

dessert. On the side, have a stack of crisp hash browns. Beyond steak, there is excellent charcoal-cooked bratwurst, roast duck is featured Saturday, perch and walleye Friday, and sauerbraten Wednesday. These hearty meals are served in a comfortable dining room with snug booths and a beautiful glassed-in kitchen along one side, and on weekend evenings, Don Van serenades from the piano bar. It is all very decent and midwestern, a place Rotarians in Sansabelt slacks take their wives on Friday night.

Solly's Coffee Shop

4629 North Port Washington Rd., Milwaukee, WI	$
(414) 332-8808	BLD

Solly's motto goes over big in Wisconsin, if not with today's nutrition police: "Food should be cooked with lots of love and lots of butter." The waitresses, who handle their chores without a pad and pencil, are pretty darn lovable, and there is butter in abundance on Solly's hamburgers, which fans refer to as sliders for their slippery, can't-stop-eatin'-'em unctuousness. They are itty-bitty burgers, topped with aromatic stewed onions and literally dripping with butter—a genuine taste of Wisconsin, especially when accompanied by one of Solly's thick malts, served in its silver mixing beaker.

Tiny's

1034 Michigan Ave., Sheboygan, WI	$
(414) 458-2551	LD

It seems like there is a tavern on every corner in Sheboygan, a city particularly well endowed with Wisconsin's fundamental Three Bs: beer, bratwurst, and bowling. Our search for the quintessential corner tavern took us to Tiny's, where the ambiance is flawless and the charcoal-cooked brats are delish.

Perch on a stool at a bar that has a shaggy rug to cushion your knees, drink Pabst from the tap, and admire the big softball trophy on display. The brats are massive sausages from the local Miesfeld Market, blushing pink with crackling crisp casing that bursts apart at first bite. They are generally sold in pairs, the twin tubes sticking out from both sides of a fresh hard roll, and unless you say otherwise, you get the works: pickle, mustard, ketchup, and a big raw onion slice. Presented in paper held around the sandwich by a single toothpick, this double brat is one of the best packages in a brat-crazed town—an impeccable combination of sausage and roll, with the added attraction of the exemplary taproom setting.

Watt's Tea Shop

761 N. Jefferson St., Milwaukee, WI	$
(414) 276-6352	£

Oh, what demure culinary charms there are to savor in the lunch-room on the second floor of George Watt & Son, a century-old shop that sells fine china and crystal, where the menu is a paean to the art of ladies' lunch. In Watt's tea room you can sip a Waterford spritzer (lemonade, lime, sparkling water) or a cold Russian (coffee, chocolate, whipped cream), munch a lovely little sandwich of minced chicken or ripe olives and nuts on tender-crumbed, freshly baked bread, and indulge in a slice of filled sunshine cake, made using the same good recipe that Watt's cooks have used for decades.

How polite is this ladies-lunch oasis? During one recent visit we picked up a brochure for "Etiquette Classes for Children" being given nearby, promising instruction in social skills for polite society: eye contact, "the personality of a handshake," enunciation, telephone manners, chewing gum (not!), and a list of theater-goers' no-no's that includes such controversial topics as "talking, humming, tapping fingers or toes, and opening cellophane-wrapped candies."

Great Plains

ALL-AMERICAN

MONTANA

NEBRASKA

NORTH DAKOTA

SOUTH DAKOTA

WYOMING

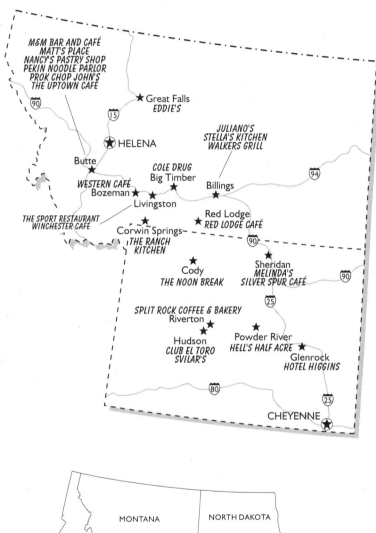

M&M BAR AND CAFÉ
MATT'S PLACE
NANCY'S PASTRY SHOP
PEKIN NOODLE PARLOR
PROK CHOP JOHN'S
THE UPTOWN CAFE

★ Great Falls
EDDIE'S

JULIANO'S
STELLA'S KITCHEN
WALKERS GRILL

★ HELENA

Butte ★

COLE DRUG
Big Timber
★

Billings
★

WESTERN CAFÉ
Bozeman ★

Livingston ★

Red Lodge
★ *RED LODGE CAFÉ*

THE SPORT RESTAURANT
WINCHESTER CAFÉ

Corwin Springs
THE RANCH
KITCHEN

★
Cody
THE NOON BREAK

Sheridan ★
MELINDA'S
SILVER SPUR CAFÉ

SPLIT ROCK COFFEE & BAKERY
Riverton
★

Powder River ★
HELL'S HALF ACRE

Hudson
CLUB EL TORO
SVILAR'S

Glenrock
HOTEL HIGGINS

CHEYENNE
★

MONTANA

NORTH DAKOTA

IDAHO
(not shown)

WYOMING

SOUTH DAKOTA

NEBRASKA

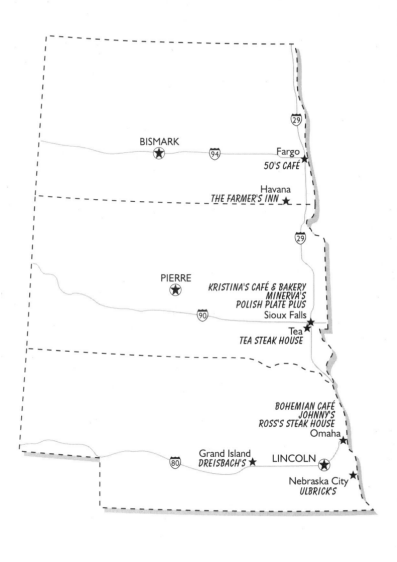

BISMARK

94

Fargo
50'S CAFÉ

Havana
THE FARMER'S INN ★

29

PIERRE

KRISTINA'S CAFÉ & BAKERY
MINERVA'S
POLISH PLATE PLUS

90

Sioux Falls
★

Tea
TEA STEAK HOUSE

BOHEMIAN CAFÉ
JOHNNY'S
ROSS'S STEAK HOUSE
Omaha
★

80

Grand Island
DREISBACH'S ★

LINCOLN

Nebraska City
ULBRICK'S ★

GREAT PLAINS

MONTANA

Cole Drug

136 McLeod, Big Timber, MT (406) 932-5316	$
Mon–Sat 9–5	

There is a swell restaurant for epicures in the unspoiled community of Big Timber at the old Grand Hotel, and there is a jim-dandy tavern called the Timber Bar, where the American cheese poppers go great with a night's worth of beers or brandies. But the place that wins our heart is the soda fountain at Cole Drug. The food menu is limited to hot dogs, Polish sausages, cheeseburgers, and soup with crackers, but the ice cream special menu is spectacular. Sidle up to the bar and plow into a Sweetheart (chocolate ice cream topped with caramel, marshmallow, peanuts, and whipped cream), or a Montana milk shake (made with ice cream, syrup, and peanut butter), or, if you're really hungry, a Big Timber. That's nine scoops of ice cream, six different sauces, whipped cream, and nuts.

Eddie's

3725 2nd Ave., Great Falls, MT	$$
(406) 453-1616	£D

Eddie's menu features many Italian specialties, including homemade ravioli that regular customers extol, and nice-looking chicken and fish and even salad, but there is one spectacularly good reason to come to Great Falls (other than the Charles M. Russell Museum): Eddie's campfire steak. "Campfire" means marinated, which they'll do to any size steak. Our preference is the king tenderloin: big and juicy and easy to slice (but not *too* easy), one of these beauties is just what an appetite demands in Big Sky country. It is all the tastier for Eddie's impeccable supper-club ambiance, which includes slick upholstery in gold metal–flaked red vinyl.

Juliano's

2912 7th Ave. N., Billings, MT (406) 248-6400	$$
Mon–Fri, D Wed–Sat	£

Juliano's outdoor patio is one of the nicest places in Montana to enjoy a civilized summer meal, perfumed by the breeze, under umbrellas outside the old stone house that was once a livery stable. Any time of year, chef Carl Kurokawa's interesting menu is a joy for anyone in search of sophisticated New American meals. We have savored such hors d'oeuvres as battered chicken and grapefruit salad, pan roasted portobello mushroom with summer vegetable broth, and seared peppered ostrich on field greens with cranberry vinaigrette. Memorable beefy dinner entrees include a gorgeous garlicked strip steak served with corn fritters, as well as a most unusual lobster-rich fried rice topped with steak. One day at lunch, we swooned over the freshwater savor in a grilled slab of flathead whitefish and also enjoyed an impeccably fine hamburger on a fresh-baked bun.

Great Plains Splurges

Expensive, fancy, and/or fashionable regional restaurants that are worth it.

- ☞ Eddie's, Great Falls, MT (p. 232)
- ☞ Uptown Café, Butte, MT (p. 239)
- ☞ Winchester Café, Livingston, MT (p. 241)
- ☞ Dreisbach's, Grand Island, NE (p. 242)
- ☞ Johnny's, Omaha, NE (p. 243)
- ☞ Ross's Steak House, Omaha, NE (p. 243)
- ☞ Minerva's, Sioux Falls, SD (p. 246)
- ☞ Hotel Higgins, Glenrock, WY (p. 250)

M&M Bar and Café

9 N. Main, Butte, MT	$
(406) 723-5552	BLD

The M&M Bar is a radiant vision of the West, with its chrome facade and a dazzling neon sign looming over the street. The interior is a fluorescent-lit, high-ceiling cavern, weathered by decades of use. To the left is the consummate drinking person's bar, its stools occupied by a clientele of regulars and irregulars including part-time cowboys, old-time miners, frocked and unfrocked priests, ladies and women who used to be ladies, winners and losers; their faces are a stunning group portrait of a town long ago known as the Richest Hill on Earth but now cursed by one guidebook as "the ugliest town in America."

At the lunch counter to the right, customers eat ground-round hamburgers with lanky French fries, husky slabs of liver 'n' onions, hot roast beef sandwiches with mashed potatoes, or swollen spaghetti noodles topped with strong red sauce and accompanied by a roasted quarter chicken. Thursday is pasty day at the M&M, when steaming behemoth baked dough crescents filled with beef, potatoes, and onions are served under a surge of brown gravy with a cup of vegetable soup and a dish of thick, cream-style cole slaw. Service is lightning fast and diner-friendly and prices are rock bottom; regulars simply sign their lunch checks and pay at the end of the month.

When it began in 1890, as Martin & Mosby, the M&M stayed open twenty-four hours, seven days a week, because the mines operated nonstop. To this day it has no lock and it never closes—a reminder of the days when Butte was a flourishing round-the-clock metropolis.

Matt's Place

Montana St. and Rowe Rd., Butte, MT	$
(406) 782-8049	LD

Pristine and painted white, Matt's is a vest-pocket drive-in restaurant over a half century old. It is tiny, without room for tables, just a short curved counter and a bright red, waist-high Coke machine, the kind in which the bottles tinkle when you pry open the top to fetch one.

No jukebox plays; your serenade comes from the back kitchen—the sound of hamburgers sizzling slowly on a grill—and from the low chatter of other customers. One afternoon we were entranced by a quartet of elderly Butte ladies, with immaculately coiffed white hair in tidy permanent waves, who came in for pork chop sandwiches with heaps of honeytone French fries and pink strawberry milk shakes.

The soda fountain behind the counter is fully equipped with six wands for blending shakes, dispensers for syrup, and three tall seltzer spouts; the menu lists root beer float, ice cream sodas, malted milks, and nut sundaes. The hot food menu features chili con carne and all sorts of hamburgers, including a Wimpy special (two patties on one bun) and a hamburger with an egg on top.

Nancy's Pasty Shop

2810 Pine, Butte, MT (406) 782-7410	$
Tues–Sat	£Ð

Nancy's is an eat shack that sells mighty fine pocket meals at a short counter inside or at a take-out window for workers on the go. Pasties were originally brought to America from Cornwall; miners carried them down to the mines and ate them for lunch. They became a staple here in Butte and are now one of the Treasure State's signature dishes. There are several reputable places in town to eat them, including Joe's and Gamer's, but we like Nancy's best of all. Huge, with a lush crust that cleaves into see-through flakes if you rub it in your fingers, each pasty weighs at least a couple pounds and is loaded with a mouthwatering, onion-flavored melange of coarse-cut beef and little chunks of potato. Not only are they simple and delicious food, easily eaten out of hand, these pasties are an edible tradition, an authentic taste of a culture brought West by those who worked the mines.

Pekin Noodle Parlor

117 S. Main, Butte, MT	$
(406) 782-2217	D

Pekin Noodle Parlor is a relic of Butte's boom days as a mining town, when the small street out back was known as China Alley. An ancient sign on the wall says FAMOUS SINCE 1916.

Climb a small dark staircase to the second floor of the antique building and you will be escorted to your own curtained dining cubicle. The setting suggests exotic intrigue, like an old Montana version of the Shanghai Express. When the food comes from the kitchen, it is announced by the rumble of the waitress's rolling trolley along the wood-plank floor; the curtain whisks aside, and behold! Here is a vista of foreign food the likes of which most devotees of Asian cookery forgot about forty years ago.

Chop suey and chow mein are mild, thick, and harmless; fried shrimp are girdled by a pad of breading and served on leaves of lettuce with French fried potatoes as a garnish; sweet and sour ribs drip pineapple-flavored syrup; and the house specialty, noodles, come in a shimmering clear broth with scallions chopped on top. Get the noodles plain or accompanied by strips of pork, beef, or chicken served on the side in a little bowl with half a hard-boiled egg.

The after-dinner drink menu-that-time-forgot includes separators, stingers, White Russians, and pink squirrels. The thing to drink before a meal is a ditch—Montanese for whiskey and water.

Pork Chop John's

8 Mercury St., Butte, MT	$
(406) 782-0812	LD

Pork chop sandwiches are now sold in many Montana restaurants, but the place they were invented, and the cognoscenti's choice, is a hole in the wall on Mercury Street known as Pork Chop John's. Although minuscule, John's is easy to spot by the sign hanging out over the street, which portrays three smiling pork chops named Wholesome, Healthful, and Delicious.

The sandwiches are patties of ground pork, breaded and fried to a crisp and served "loaded," which means topped with pickle chips, mustard, and onions. (Mayo, cheese, and ketchup are also available, but must be specified.) They are a savory splurge—crunch-crusted and luscious inside. Enjoy them at John's small counter or at one of three alfresco tables on the sidewalk, from which you have a view of the cramped back street that was the heart of Butte's once-thriving (but now extinct) Chinatown.

The Ranch Kitchen

Hwy. 89, Corwin Springs, MT	$
(406) 848-7891	BLD

This rustic, family-style restaurant serves healthful fare—sandwiches on tweedy whole grain bread, fruit-sweetened sweet rolls, hearty soups, pastas, stir fries, and fresh berry pies. One day at breakfast, we delighted in hot peach muffins and bowls of warm oatmeal topped with puckery-sweet berry syrup. Such nutritionally enlightened fare is rare in restaurants in this part of the world, the sign of an unusual culinary consciousness. Only if you stop next door at the Cinnabar General Store and browse through the religious books for sale does it become apparent that the Ranch Kitchen does indeed have a different slant on life. Like everything for miles around in Paradise Valley, it is owned and operated by Elizabeth Claire Prophet's Church Universal and Triumphant, which apparently believes in eating well right up until the forthcoming apocalypse.

Red Lodge Café

16–18 South Broadway, Red Lodge, MT	$
(406) 446-1619	BLD

Where the locals eat (and tourists, too), the Red Lodge Café is a comfy old-fashioned lunchroom with a stamped tin ceiling, wagon wheel chandeliers, and painted murals of local scenery (white water, the Beartooth Mountains) separated by varnished wooden totem poles. It is a good place to eat a buffalo burger or a regular cow burger, and a midday special we like is tuna noodle casserole (a classic, with pale canned peas on the side). On one occasion, we were surprised and delighted by mighty tasty chicken stir-fry on rice.

The time that's best in this place is just after six in the morning, when the clientele is mostly working Montanans, the whole wheat, blueberry, buckwheat, or sourdough pancakes are piled high, and table-to-table gabfests are conducted about the hot topics of the day.

The Sport Restaurant

114 S. Main, Livingston, MT	$
(406) 222-3533	LD

A real western café/bar known in rowdier times simply as the Beer Hall, the Sport now makes a specialty of burger toppings, which range from beefy chili to a slice of pineapple for the marinated teriyaki burger, plus a long list of "NYO" (name your own) hamburger adornments that include hot or mild peppers, salsa, salad dressing, and assorted cheeses. Proprietor Suzanne Schneider also offers a fine pork chop sandwich ("John's original" her menu says, referring to Pork Chop John's of Butte, where it was invented) and delicious malts and shakes dispensed in tall silver beakers. For dessert, there's apple or peach pie, made from Suzanne's grandmother's recipe. The pie is cut in big homey squares, like shortcake, and demands a scoop of ice cream as its companion.

The Sport's dining room decor is a hoot: there are mounted animal heads and an extraordinarily long rattlesnake skin, a couple of old shotguns hanging in nooses from the ceiling, and stacks of vintage magazines and newspapers for customers to browse.

Stella's Kitchen

110 N. 29th St., Billings, MT	$
(406) 248-3060	BLD

Stella's is a modern lunchroom with a bakery in back. Its glass cases are filled with homey loaves of sunflower wheat bread, sticky fritters and dumplings, and sour cream coffee cake.

Stella's serves three meals a day; the best one is breakfast, especially if you like warm cinnamon rolls. Stella's offers two sizes: regular, made with whole wheat flour, packed with raisins and cinnamon-sugar, with sugar frosting glistening on top, and large, which is the size of a cake for six. Caramel rolls are similarly immense, made with white flour and enveloped in sticky, mahogany-colored glaze.

"Monster cakes"—twelve-inch flapjacks—were put on the menu, Stella says, when "I had a cook who simply could not make a small pancake. So we gave up and raised the price." You have your choice of buttermilk, wheat, applesauce and cinnamon, blueberry, or blueberry wheat; portions range from one to four, and if you eat four in a single sitting, you get a free cinnamon roll.

Uptown Café

47 E. Broadway, Butte, MT	$$
(406) 723-4735	LD

Started in the mid-1980s by Susan Phillips, Barbara Kornet, and Guy Graham, this friendly bistro is now known far and wide for such fashionable dishes as grilled citrus-marinated halibut and chicken Arthur with artichoke hearts and sun-dried tomatoes. Such sophisticated food is rare in Montana; to find it prepared so well is a bonanza.

When we stopped in, Susan was busy making pesto because she had just gotten a batch of good basil, Guy was planning nightly specials that included seared tuna with mango and ginger salsa, and salmon on a julienne of summer vegetables, and Barbara guided us through the café's monthly lunch calendar, which ranges from chicken pot pie and stromboli to pasta puttanesca and Thai beef stir-fry. We delighted in a grandmotherly sausage onion soup, turkey Devonshire with zesty twice-baked potato casserole, and desserts that included a drop-dead delicious chocolate rum pound cake, creamy Bavarian apple tart, and intensely fresh black raspberry pie. It is easy to understand why, even in the winter when it's fifty degrees below zero, customers drive to the Uptown Café from as far as Red Lodge, 227 miles away (actually, not too long a trip by Montana standards).

Walkers Grill

301 N. 27th St., Billings, MT	$$
(406) 245-9291	D

As soon as you tear into the breadbasket at Walkers, you know a good meal is coming your way. Crusty, faintly sour, and with a soulful chew, this is bread that is pure and simple yet an emblem of real culinary expertise. You cannot watch the bread being baked, but you can see the young masters at work in Walkers' exhibition kitchen at one end of the handsome subterranean dining room, where the modern meals are prepared in a whirl of activity.

From the comfort of "James Beard's meat loaf" with shiitake mushroom gravy and creamy mashed potatoes to Thai rock shrimp pasta sauced with a blend of cilantro and coconut milk, the far-reaching menu is a joy to browse. Pizzas, cooked on quarry tiles, have true Mediterranean character; half-pound hamburgers, accompanied by French fries and homemade ketchup, are flawlessly all-American.

Walkers is the kind of place where some people come to splurge and celebrate; others eat supper here several times a week, simply because it is the best dining room in eastern Montana.

Western Café

443 E. Main St., Bozeman, MT	$
(406) 587-0436	BLD

A cowboy hash house once known as Eat-A-Bite, the Western has been operated for the last twenty years by Dick and Alice Mierva, who inherited its prized recipe for cinnamon rolls from the former owner. The summer morning we stopped in the counter was packed, its surface worn bare at uniform intervals on either side of each stool where customers have rested their elbows for years.

Besides superb cinnamon rolls, the thing to eat is pie. In a state where pies are the pride of every town café, the Western's are outstanding. Timed by baker Annie Robinson to be carried from the kitchen at the end of the lunch hour, there are magnificent meringues, dense fruit pies, Dutch apple, and egg custard. The custard, when it is still slightly warm at one o'clock, jiggles precariously and is nursery sweet—food fit for a toothless god.

Winchester Café

In the Murray Hotel, 201 W. Park, Livingston, MT	$$
(406) 222-2708	BLD

Montana celebrities have gravitated to the Murray Hotel for decades. Movie director Sam Peckinpah lived upstairs (and was reputed to fire his six-gun through the ceiling when on drinking binges); Calamity Jane stayed here. Today's clientele is a motley mix of residents, pilgrims, and local literary lights. In the bar, kids play electronic games and adults drink the Montana favorite, ditch—whiskey and water. Late at night, it is not uncommon for the barroom philosophizers to raise a little hell.

The Winchester Café, located off the lobby, has a flowered rug on the floor, a wine list that fills two sides of a piece of parchment paper limp from handling, and a menu that offers turkey Oscar, shrimp scampi, and penne, as well as a range of hamburgers, sandwiches, and salads at lunch. At suppertime, a trout special is everything it ought to be in angler's paradise—chunky-fleshed, sweet and moist, gilded with maître d'hôtel butter. One late summer special, rack of lamb, came under a rich cordovan-colored sauce made from local huckleberries. Wine was served in brandy goblets. "The hotel took all our wineglasses for a function," the waiter apologized.

NEBRASKA

Bohemian Café

1406 South 13th St., Omaha, NE	$$
(402) 342-9838	£D

Several years ago, while traveling through eastern Nebraska, a radio jingle lured us to the ethnic enclave of south Omaha. "It's dumplings and kraut today at the Bohemian Café," the appetizing advertisement said; and sure enough, that night in this unpretentious old-world eatery, we savored not only dumplings and kraut, but also mighty platters of tender boiled beef with dill gravy and masterfully cooked, crisp-skinned duck. We have never eaten at the Bohemian Café on Friday or Saturday night, but we want to in the worst way. That is when the hearty food is served to the lilting strains of an accordionist.

Dreisbach's

1137 S. Locust, Grand Island, NE	$$
(308) 382-5450	£D

Well-marbled, dry-aged beef has been earning Dreisbach's a loyal clientele since 1932. The restaurant has been transformed from a farmhouse into a roadhouse with all the charm of a truck stop, but no one comes for atmosphere. They come for meat. Tenderloins, T-bones, filets mignon, sirloins, and New York strips are all available, served with hot baking-powder biscuits and honey, salad with killer-garlic dressing, and lengthwise-thin-sliced potatoes topped with cheese (known as sunflowers). All-you-can-eat fried chicken is also on the menu, as is rabbit (a legacy of beef shortages during World War II), but if you are a traveler with an appetite along I-80 anywhere near Grand Island, it is steak you want.

Johnny's

4702 S. 27th St., Omaha, NE	$$
(402) 731-4774	£D

Johnny's has been Omaha's stockyards steak house for three-quarters of a century. Once a café for cowboys and cow shippers, it is now a grandiose restaurant with well-upholstered chairs, broadloom carpets, and modernistic chandeliers. We love the baronial ambiance, especially because it is balanced by service that is as folksy as in any small town café, courtesy of waitresses unafraid to call you "Hon" and to scold you if you don't finish your T-bone but then want dessert. Beef, of course, is what to eat: Johnny's has every cut of steak you've ever heard of, plus liver, tongue, oxtail, and the like, all nicely cooked with decent accompaniments (except the mashed potatoes, which we don't like). Dessert is corny and ingratiating: crème de menthe sundaes, gooey turtle pie, and clear blocks of Chuckles-colored Jell-O.

Ross's Steak House

909 S. 72nd St., Omaha, NE (402) 393-2030	$$
(reservations required on weekends)	£D

Every year, the management of Ross's pays top dollar to purchase Nebraska's champion steer; and every night, customers put on their fine-dining attire to come to this immense, ornate restaurant to eat some of the finest red meat in cow country, at reasonable prices. Select your own steak, and then, while it's cooking, you and your date can twirl around the dance floor to work up an appetite, of which you'll want plenty when the meal arrives.

Ulbrick's	
Rte. 75, Nebraska City, NE (402) 873-5458	$
(reservation advised)	D

What road wanderer doesn't have a soft spot for restaurants located in former gas stations? Ulbrick's is one of the best, a decrepit-looking but utterly upright culinary mecca in the midlands. Its divey looks make it all the more fun for the crowds of boisterous fans who gather around the oilcloth-covered tables lined up in the back room to gaily plow through platters of crisp-fried chicken. The delicious bird is preceded by a battery of heartland "salads," served family-style, most of which could double as dessert crowded as they are with marshmallows and mandarin orange pieces; one, called "frog eye salad," is made of tapioca pudding and bite-size Funmallows in all the colors of the rainbow. Alongside the superb chicken come platters of creamed corn, creamed cabbage, ultracreamed chicken and noodles, and green beans cooked the country way—until tooth resistance is but a memory.

NORTH DAKOTA

✫ ✫ ✫

50's Café	
13 S. Eighth St., Fargo, ND	$
(701) 298-0347	BLD

Unable to find a truly compelling meal in Fargo, we were delighted to eat tasty half-pound hamburgers at the 50's Café. They are hand-formed jumbos, available with all the fixin's imaginable from chili and cheese to pizza sauce or avocados. The configuration we like best is called the Big Bopper, with bacon, cheese, tomato, lettuce, onion, and salad dressing, plus French fries and cole slaw on the side. Available beverages include real malts, and there is a short list of sundaes, sodas, and banana splits available from the 1950s soda fountain. (However, our recommendation for dessert is to sneak a few doors up Eighth Street to Widman's Candy Shop, where the "hot air" candy—spun molasses sheathed in chocolate—is celestial and where you can enjoy such health food Great Plains confections as chocolate-covered wheat, chocolate-covered sunflower seeds, and chocolate-covered potato chips.)

The Farmers' Inn	
Havana, ND	$
(701) 724-3849	ℬℒ

Across from the grain elevators in the tiny town of Havana, the Farmers' Inn is owned and operated by a consortium of local farmers. The ladies of the town, and some of the men, take turns flipping flapjacks and cooking eggs in the morning, then making a hearty meal in the middle of the day. The menu changes according to who's on duty. We can speak highly of Murdean Gulsvig's sausage patties and pancakes in the morning, and the pork roast with mashed potatoes, dressing, and gravy that his wife, Doris, cooks for dinner. And don't forget to sign the guest register: it's an event when someone from out of town stops by. And for those of us who make the trip, it's no less an event to sit down for a meal elbow-to-elbow with the good people of Havana, North Dakota.

SOUTH DAKOTA

Kristina's Café & Bakery

334 S. Phillips Ave., Sioux Falls, SD (605) 331-4860	$
(call for limited dinner hours)	B L

Kristina's serves the best coffee in Sioux Falls, strong and spicy. Although it tastes European (or at least Seattlean) in character, cups of it are refilled generously while you dine, service reminiscent of a good mid-American café. Downtowners occupy Kristina's bare wood tables to read the daily paper (spread out for the taking on the counter) and to savor their morning cup accompanied by toasted Italian bread, maple-frosted wheat-cinnamon rolls hot from the oven, or flaky scones. Heartier breakfasts include omelets, baked egg casserole with smoked turkey and melted cheese, and delightful buttermilk pancakes with soft, sautéed apples in the batter and maple butter on top.

Minerva's

301 Phillips Ave., Sioux Falls, SD (605) 334-0386	$$
Mon–Sat	L D

Like many growing cities, Sioux Falls is ringed with franchised restaurants, but the food you want to eat, served in human-scale surroundings, is downtown. In business since 1977, yet with a handsome patina that feels way older than that, Minerva's is a wood-and-tile floor establishment with white-clothed tables, ample booths, and a friendly staff that aims to please. It is *the* fine-dining place in town, where customers come for deluxe rib-eye steak—aged and cut on premises—or fresh walleye pike, pan-fried or broiled. Atlantic salmon is always on the menu, and Copper River salmon from Alaska is often available in May and June. While high rollers may feast on a half a honey-glazed roast duck or Cajun fettucine, many regulars come to avail themselves only of the salad bar. It is a sparkling heartland buffet of composed salads that range from ham or pasta to creamy pink Jell-O, plus fresh fruit, and Maytag blue cheese dressing for the lettuce.

A statue of Minerva, the Roman goddess of wisdom and war, presides over the bar. The same people who run this place also operate Minerva's Market Café at 1716 Western Avenue, an upscale market that serves three meals a day and has a large selection of fancy foods and meals to go.

Polish Plate Plus

2909 E. 10th St., Sioux Falls, SD	$
(605) 332-1011	£Ð

Have you been here before?" asks the hostess in a thick Polish accent. If you say you haven't, she'll guide you along the buffet line, pointing out which pierogi are filled with sauerkraut and which with spicy ground meat and which are filled with cheese and hot jalapeño peppers(!). She explains that you should take sour cream to accompany the potato pancake and points out how well the sauerkraut goes with the short lengths of Polish sausage. There isn't room on a plate for everything on display—we regretfully passed up the cabbage rolls and Hunter's stew—but it's hard not to find satisfaction at this inexpensive old-world buffet.

The restaurant itself is a strange one; it's as clean as a new franchise, with little in the way of decor except for a few dolls in peasant garb and a display of Polish currency near the door. If you are a first-timer, you will get a punch card to record your visits. After twelve times, you get the thirteenth meal free; plus you get two-dollar tokens to play in the East Side Casino at the back of the Polish Plate Plus building.

Tea Steak House

Tea, SD	$$
(605) 368-9667	£D

Off the interstate in the tiny town of Tea, steak-lovers congregate at tables covered with seafoam green oilcloth to slice into handsome T-bones, sirloins, and filets mignon. The Tea Steak House, a low-slung, wood-paneled restaurant that shares a building with O'Toole's Bar, is one of the top beef dens of the Great Plains. Dress-up clothes are not required, but it is a weekend-splurge kind of place. On Friday nights (when fried perch joins the meaty menu), the dining room is packed with couples, families, and star-crossed carnivores on big dates.

Service, by women in nylon uniform blouses, is instantaneous. Iceberg lettuce salad arrives in a little wood-grain plastic bowl along with a silver server with three dressings you ladle on at will. The steaks are tender and juicy, available charbroiled over coals or grilled in a pan. Of the three types of potatoes, French fried and baked are nothing notable, but the hash browns, soft inside with a hard-crusted surface, are delicious. Every table is outfitted with ketchup and Heinz 57 Steak Sauce.

It is a midlands meal of the highest order. And who can resist a restaurant with this motto printed on its menu: "We're Glad You Brought Your Sugar to Tea."

WYOMING

Club El Toro

132 S. Main, Hudson, WY	$$
(307) 332-4627	D

Club El Toro is a wonderful restaurant in the tiny town of Hudson that is a destination for beef eaters from miles around. Every evening, this commodious supper club teams with happy families and friends who come to glide their knives into gorgeous rib-eyes, sirloins, and filets mignons, as well as some of the largest and tastiest prime ribs anywhere. The savory red meat is served as part of a full-course feast that includes relish tray, salad, a plate of ravioli, and Serbian stuffed cabbage known as sarma, plus excellent cowboy potatoes (spicy French fries). On weekend evenings, couples glide across the dance floor to the keyboard stylings of Carl F. Baxter. A delicious, only-in-America experience!

Hell's Half Acre

Hwy. 20–26, 5 miles west of Powder River, WY	$
(307) 472-0018	BLD

You won't have a big choice of places to eat between Casper and Riverton. In fact, you'll have none. But may we suggest that rather than starve along the way you stop at Hell's Half Acre for a snack? We make this suggestion because you will likely want to drive right past. This ramshackle tourist attraction, built around a geological anomaly that spews hot vapors, frankly looks like a rather scary roadkill café. And the day we walked in, the steam-table spaghetti that had been basking in the open for God-knows-how-long didn't do a lot to reassure us. However, the hamburgers we ordered were very tasty. In particular we enjoyed the devil burger, topped with melted Swiss cheese and chopped mild green peppers, served on a nearly elegant toasted and buttered bun, with excellent French fries on the side, and a genuine milk shake, blended as we watched, to wash it down.

We must admit that it wasn't only the devil burger that won our hearts. Decor at Hell's Half Acre includes jaw-droppingly tacky velveteen wall rugs showing bulldogs shooting billiards and brave matadors fighting bulls. The attached souvenir shop is one of the last places in America that still sells original, linen-finish postcards (of interesting nearby rock formations), not to mention rubber tomahawks and toy guns for the little 'uns.

Hotel Higgins

416 West Birch, Glenrock, WY (307) 436-9212	$$
(breakfast for overnight guests)	D

The kitchen of this immaculate time capsule of frontier elegance is a beacon of fine dining; locals drive for miles to eat beef steaks and prime ribs or to indulge in the occasional "rib night," when tender baby back pork ribs are available with chutney brandy, sweet and sour sauce, or traditional barbecue sauce. The dining room's main attractions are epicurean meals with entrees such as shrimp scampi, veal Madeira crème, salmon Marseille, and tarragon chicken. International Nights feature full-course meals from other parts of the world. Indonesian Night, for instance, starts with gado-gado (tofu and vegetable salad), is followed by beef rendang (cubed round steak slowly roasted all day with coconut milk and lemongrass) with yellow rice, and concludes with kueh prol aanas (pineapple bread pudding). Such a meal is a curiosity anywhere in America; in Glenrock, Wyoming, it's a wonder.

Melinda's

57 N. Main, Sheridan, WY (307) 674-9188	$$
Tues–Sat, D Wed–Sat	BL

Melinda's is a friendly, brick-wall café with many things to recommend it, including drippy-sweet caramel rolls in the morning, clever pastas at suppertime, and a repertoire of afternoon (3 pm to 5 pm) snacks, soups, and salads. What we like best is a bowlful of comfort Melinda calls the TLC Special: a heap of lumpy mashed potatoes topped with chicken noodle soup, accompanied by a few slices of fresh-baked bread.

Supper can be as traditional as a grilled steak or stuffed pork chops, or you can eat more adventurously and start with whole roasted garlic bulbs (squeeze the tender cloves onto Melinda's fresh-baked bread) or grilled shrimp marinated in basil and lime, and then move on to an honest plate of fresh, grilled halibut, moist and savory, served with spicy hash brown potatoes on the side.

There is a full bar and a short wine list, and whole wheat and

French bread are available by the loaf to go. Along with the Silver Spur (p. 251), Melinda's is one of two great places in town for breakfast: fresh pastries, lusty biscuits with sausage gravy, healthful granola, and delicious strong-brewed coffee and espresso.

The Noon Break

927 12th St., Cody, WY	$
(307) 587-9720	BL

It's laid back and far enough off the beaten path for few tourists to find it, but the main reason to come to the Noon Break is green chile. There are two kinds available, regular and "Code 10," the latter a hot jalapeño soup made with little chunks of pork sausage, available in a cup or bowl or as the topping of a tasty burrito in a bowl.

There are a few more excellent reasons to find this small café. One is the happy breakfast hour, when regulars sip endless amounts of coffee with platters of huevos rancheros, buckwheat pancakes, or biscuits and gravy. Another is the fact that many of the zesty Mexican dishes on the short menu are in fact heart-healthy, such as the red and green chilies, posole topped with yogurt rather than sour cream, burritos stuffed with beans or potatoes.

One last reason we like this kooky place, which is strewn with newspapers and magazines and decorated with old Wyoming license plates, is a lunchtime item listed as "Louie's Ethnic Plate." It's a Spam sandwich, grilled to order, with potato chips on the side.

Silver Spur Café

832 N. Main St., Sheridan, WY	$
(307) 672-2749	BL

The counter and back-room tables of this elbow-to-elbow little diner are where good citizens of Sheridan gather every morning starting at 6 am. They come for hearty muffins, griddle cakes, and eggs, accompanied by cups of coffee that get topped off or refilled approximately every thirty seconds by the staff of highly opinionated wait-resses who took over the old café when former owner Jan Drake passed away last year. The staff and steady customers welcome strangers into cross-counter colloquies about local news and politics, weather and sports, and all the other subjects that a good dose of morning caffeine brings to mind.

Split Rock Coffee & Bakery

108 S. 3rd East, Riverton, WY (307) 856-4334	$
Mon–Fri	BLD

Culinarily speaking, Wyoming's raison d'être is beef. Although it is great to be a carnivore in the Cowboy State, here's a little tip in case you need a respite from animal protein: whole grain meals at the Split Rock Bakery. This little shop, which happens also to be an outpost of espresso, cappuccino, and all manner of modern caffeinated potions, has wheaty cinnamon rolls, healthful muffins, and oat-bran bagels in the morning, as well as noontime sandwiches that range from bizarre meatless garden burgers and tempeh rubens to perfectly tasty egg or tuna salad, cheese, or avocado. For dessert, there is a different low-fat yogurt flavor every day. It's an odd experience, but we have to admit we find it a pleasant diversion from an all-cow diet.

South-west

ALL-AMERICAN

ARIZONA

COLORADO

KANSAS

NEVADA

NEW MEXICO

OKLAHOMA

TEXAS

UTAH

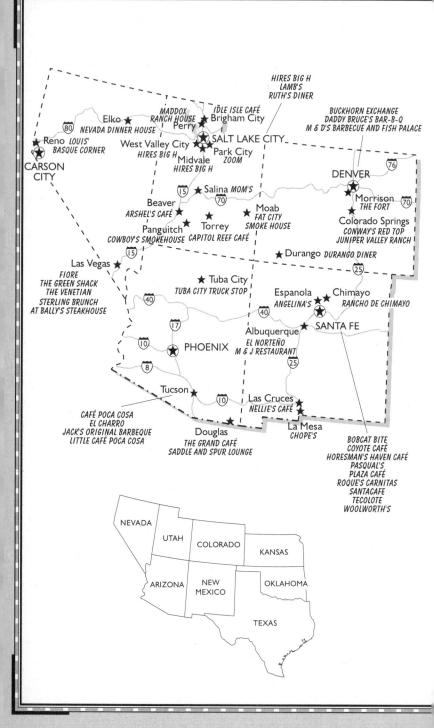

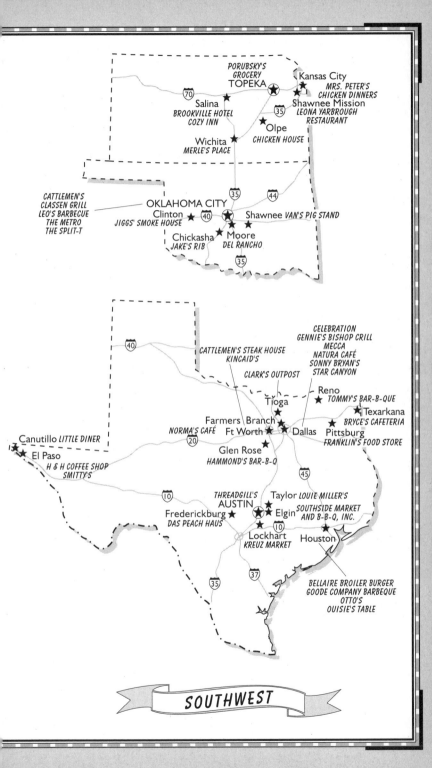

PORUBSKY'S GROCERY
TOPEKA
Kansas City
MRS. PETER'S CHICKEN DINNERS
Shawnee Mission
LEONA YARBROUGH RESTAURANT
Salina
BROOKVILLE HOTEL
COZY INN
Olpe
CHICKEN HOUSE
Wichita
MERLE'S PLACE

CATTLEMEN'S CLASSEN GRILL
LEO'S BARBECUE
THE METRO
THE SPLIT-T
OKLAHOMA CITY
Clinton
JIGGS' SMOKE HOUSE
Shawnee VAN'S PIG STAND
Chickasha Moore
JAKE'S RIB DEL RANCHO

CELEBRATION
GENNIE'S BISHOP GRILL
MECCA
NATURA CAFÉ
SONNY BRYAN'S
STAR CANYON
CATTLEMEN'S STEAK HOUSE
KINCAID'S
CLARK'S OUTPOST
Tioga
Reno
TOMMY'S BAR-B-QUE
Texarkana
BRYCE'S CAFETERIA
Farmers Branch
NORMA'S CAFÉ
Ft Worth
Dallas
Pittsburg
FRANKLIN'S FOOD STORE
Canutillo LITTLE DINER
El Paso
H & H COFFEE SHOP
SMITTY'S
Glen Rose
HAMMOND'S BAR-B-Q
THREADGILL'S
Taylor LOUIE MILLER'S
AUSTIN
Frederickburg
DAS PEACH HAUS
Elgin
SOUTHSIDE MARKET
AND B-B-Q, INC.
Lockhart
KREUZ MARKET
Houston
BELLAIRE BROILER BURGER
GOODE COMPANY BARBEQUE
OTTO'S
OUISIE'S TABLE

SOUTHWEST

ARIZONA

Café Poca Cosa	
88 East Broadway, Tucson, AZ	$$
(602) 622-6400	£D

You never know exactly what you'll find at Café Poca Cosa, one of the most inventive Mexican restaurants in the American Southwest.

The menu changes daily, depending on what ingredients are available and what chef Suzana Davila is in the mood to cook. Customers request her picadillo or pork roast stuffed with plums and chipotle chilies; a stash of hibiscus flowers inspires a fragrant meal called chicken tropicale; a farmer will arrive in the morning with a basket of smoky pasilla chilies she can use to make quesadillas with a breathtaking wallop.

There is much good beef: carne asada with fiery habanero peppers; grilled steak strips flavored with chipotles; carne asada barbacoa steeped in beer and spiced with chilies. Molés include pollo en molé negro, a strange blend of chili's heat, chocolate's richness, and the zip of cinnamon. Molé verde is as verdant as the negro is earthy, with an exotic herbal hue.

Tamale pie is prepared in a variety of ways and can be a vegetarian's delight. It is made of cream, cheese, and corn masa whipped into a tender custard—sometimes around veins of green chile, sometimes not. It is luxurious, but with an honest virtue of the corn that is its essence.

El Charro

311 N. Court, Tucson, AZ	$
(520) 622-5465	£ 𝔇

E l Charro—since 1922—is a fortress of Mexican-American food, much of it built around delirious tasty carne seca (air-dried beef), a specialty of Mexican cattle country. This beef, which is dried out back in a cage that hangs in the Arizona air above the patio, fills fabulous burritos, chimichangas, tacos, and enchiladas.

One of the most unusual things about El Charro is its emphasis on nutritionally enlightened fare. Even items on the menu that don't seem like they are diet food are made with an eye toward good nutrition: chili sauce is made without oil; almendrado (Mexican custard) is cholesterol-free. If you are serious about eating healthy, you can order tasty frijoles enteros (whole beans) in lieu of frijoles refritos (beans that are mashed and fried with lard); nonfat yogurt can be had instead of sour cream. Vegetarians come for enchiladas made with mushrooms instead of meat.

Still, most customers come to El Charro to indulge appetites and to party hearty. It is noisy and sociable, almost always packed with tourists, Tucsonians, health nuts, and burrito hounds who spoon up fiery salsa picante with corn chips and drink Tecate beer served in the can with a wedge of lime on top. Its wall decor is legendary—a kaleidoscope of straw sombreros and rawhide bullwhips, and years' worth of El Charro calendars, many of which feature melodramatic scenes of Mexican horsemen (known as charros), proud steeds, and pretty maidens all making flirty eyes at each other amidst stormy landscapes.

The Grand Café

1119 G Ave., Douglas, AZ (520) 364-2344	$$
(breakfast starting late in the morning)	£ 𝔇

A beacon of bordertown hospitality, the Grand Café serves such Sonoran-style dishes as broad flour tortillas with melted cheese on top and limp grilled green onions on the side, steamy husk-enveloped green-corn tamales, and red or green chili beef, plus shrimp scampi and an off-the-menu dark molé that attracts devoted fans from miles away.

There is a small dance floor at the back of this main street café, which is the sort of festive place that encourages you to punctuate the moment between your appetizer of queso fundito (a hot skillet full of melted cheese) and the carne asada (a broad chuck steak served with four-alarm pico de gallo) with a quick twirl with your partner. On especially festive days, proprietor Vanessa Quintana will add to the merriment by dressing up as Marilyn Monroe, a woman she deeply admires and impersonates in local parades.

Jack's Original Barbeque

5250 E. 22nd St., Tucson, AZ	$
(602) 750-1280	£D

On the whitewashed walls of Jack's dining room is a snapshot history of this eatery, from its birth in June 1950 at its first location to its current incarnation as a serve-yourself smoke house, where the motto is "Taste the Wisdom." Despite its fame, Jack's remains a modest place, where food is presented on throwaway plates and a sign implores, IF YOUR TRAY FALLS IN THE TRASH BIN, PLEASE TELL US.

We especially like the hot links with taut skin and spicy insides served with cumin-flavored chili beans. An order of sliced pork provides tremendous variety—some pieces as wickedly luscious as bacon, others like a tender slice from the middle of a loin. And the sloppy joe, a Thursday special, is glorious, like the best school lunch anyone ever imagined, dark, long-cooked shreds of beef in zesty barbecue sauce. Whatever you eat, follow it with sweet potato pie that is super sweet and spiced like Christmas.

Little Café Poca Cosa

20 South Scott Ave., Tucson, AZ no phone	$
	BL

Eight oilcloth-covered tables are packed in this closet-size café, which brims with sombreros and serapes and is presided over by Luis Dávila, who makes each meal a party. "Musica, musica!" he cries when the mariachi music on his tape machine runs out. Ask to see his kitchen and he shows you the chili colorado and chili verde bubbling on his little cookstove in back. Ask him what's good for breakfast and he will suggest such Sonoran fundamentals as huevos rancheros puddled with salsa, huevos Mexicanos scrambled with tomatoes, onions, and chilies, and machaca con huevo, which is moist shreds of beef with bits of green chili in a thin veil of scrambled egg.

At lunch, Señor Dávila makes smoky sweet beef shreds in pepper sauce known as barbacoa, pollo ranchero (a hearty stew with tomatoes, peppers, potatoes, and onions), and pollo Acapulco (a gallimaufry of broccoli, cauliflower, peas, carrots, and onions). The beverage selection is outstanding: lemonade made with fresh limes, jugo de duranzo (peach juice), and the south-of-the-border cooler called horchata. It looks like milk, but it's nondairy (it is made from rice) and has a refreshing perfumy sweetness.

Tuba City Truck Stop

Junction of Rtes. 160 and 264, Tuba City, AZ	$
(520) 283–4975	BLD

Housed in a cinderblock building with the words LET'S EAT on its outside wall, the Tuba City Truck Stop is a reservation café frequented by Native Americans who linger at the tables sipping coffee and reading the *Navajo Times.* Many wear Levi's and T-shirts, but a surprising number are dressed traditionally—women in velvet blouses and turquoise-nugget necklaces; men with long hair wrapped in the traditional Navajo bun.

It is possible to eat authentic Native specialties in this old joint—mutton and hominy stew, for example, or chewy fried bread that

A Tequila Treatise

Here is the correct right way to drink tequila: open the bottle, pour some into a glass, and swallow it.

We risk being obvious only because so many more elaborate methods have been invented for drinking tequila and for getting drunk on it. The most popular one, known as the Mexican itch, is to bracket hammered-back shots of it with licking salt off the base of one's thumb and squeezing a wedge of lime between one's teeth, a slavering ritual that makes the tequila-drinker sound like a bulldog sucking up a mouthful of Jell-O. It is also frequently slugged back neat alongside a bottle of beer—a bordertown boilermaker. For a slammer, the liquor is combined in a glass with champagne, tonic, or soda, banged on the table a couple of times until it fizzes, then gulped in one greedy, effervescent swallow. It seems fair to say that in none of these examples is the act of tequila-drinking an expression of connoisseurship or gentility; the point is to ingest the stuff fast and get drunk.

Tequila doesn't necessarily deserve its rowdy reputation. Like fine Kentucky bourbon, it is distilled with care and precision. The best, made from the heart of the agave plant, is aged in smoke-flavored, wax-lined barrels until it is as suave as good cognac. However, such smooth tequila is fairly rare, and most drink-till-you-drop brands are about as tasty—and as effective—as chloroform. Tequila in the U.S. has always had a certain outlaw swagger about it, conjuring up images of dusty cantinas where cowboys go to pass out on the floor, shoot holes in the ceiling, or fall in love with a pretty senorita (or all three, in reverse order).

The most fearsome tequila is mezcal con gusano, known as mescal, which is made without the polish of double-distilling and aging and with the added attraction of a dead maguey worm (that's the "con gusano" part, and it is actually a caterpillar) submerged in the bottom of the bottle. The worm, which feeds on the agave plant, was originally packaged in mescal as proof that there was enough alcohol in the booze to preserve it. It is widely believed to induce hallucinations, or at least to make whoever drains the bottle's dregs into an ornery son of a buck. In fact, the worm is considered by protozoa connoisseurs to be so excellent that mescal is sometimes drunk by the shot with chaws of lime and heaps of crushed, mummified worms on the side to lick in lieu of salt.

Tequila's bellicose reputation has mellowed in recent years, thanks mostly to the popularity of frozen margaritas, which has helped establish its image as a fun libation for civilized middle-class people. Whipped into a frothy confectionery cooler the color of folding money and about as sweet as a green river, tequila nowadays needn't seem any more dangerous than sloe gin.

CLASSIC MARGARITA

With a curiously tropical taste, this is the way margaritas used to be made before everybody had a blender. They were invented sometime in the 1930s, but they didn't get popular until students at party schools, mostly in the West, discovered their seductive powers in the 1960s. Most modern, nonblenderized margaritas contain considerably less Triple Sec than this original recipe.

$1^1/_2$ ounces freshly squeezed lime juice
$1^1/_2$ ounces Triple Sec
$1^1/_2$ ounces tequila
salt poured into a saucer

Mix lime juice, Triple Sec, and tequila. Moisten the rim of a short, 6- to 8-ounce glass and dip it in the salt. Put a few ice cubes in the glass. Pour in the mixed drink. Stir, taking care not to wash away the salt. Drink immediately.

FOAMY, BLENDERIZED MARGARITA

This recipe makes enough for four really big drinks.

1 cup tequila
1 cup freshly squeezed lime juice
$1/_3$ cup Triple Sec
1 tablespoon sugar (or more, to taste)
crushed ice
lime wedges for garnish
salt poured into a saucer

In a blender, combine tequila, lime juice, Triple Sec, sugar, and ice. Blender-ize at medium-high speed just long enough to make a frothy mixture. Taste and add more sugar, if desired.

Use a lime wedge to moisten the rims of four 8-ounce glasses. Dip the rims in salt. Give the mixed drink a quick last shot in the blender and pour it into the prepared glasses, garnishing each with a lime wedge.

Serve immediately.

CHIMAYO COCKTAIL

This is the recipe for the house drink at Rancho de Chimayo (p. 279), where they make it with cider squeezed from local apples.

1¹/₂ ounces tequila
1 ounce apple cider
¹/₄ ounce lemon juice
¹/₄ crème de cassis
cracked ice

Combine all ingredients in a shaker. Mix vigorously and pour into manhattan glasses, either with ice or strained.

makes good munching with coffee—but the best dish in the house is the Navajo taco. A café staple throughout the region, it is a late-twentieth-century melting-pot combination of meat-and-bean chili, melted cheese, lettuce, and tomato chunks atop a puffy pedestal of Indian fry bread.

COLORADO

☆ ☆ ☆

Buckhorn Exchange

1000 Osage, Denver, CO	$$
(303) 534-9505	£D

Holder of Colorado Liquor License #1 (issued in 1893), outfitted with a museum's worth of antique firearms and furniture, and decorated with a dazzling menagerie of some five hundred game animal trophies shot by former owner Shorty Zietz, the Buckhorn Exchange is no mere frontier-themed restaurant or historical relic. It happens to be a fine place to eat.

At lunch, hamburgers, salads, and sandwiches are consumed without ado by a cadre of regular customers inured to the stare of a thousand glass eyes and the creak of wood floors where Buffalo Bill once trod. Tourists like us cannot help but gape and wonder, and then tuck into a serious ranch meal. We like to start with hearty ham and bean soup or an order of Rocky Mountain oysters (sliced, fried calf testicles), move on to beef steak or buffalo prime rib or savory trout with crunchy cottage fried potatoes on the side. Top it all off with crumb-topped apple pie and cinnamon hard sauce, and you have eaten a true-West meal.

Conway's Red Top

1520 S. Nevada, Colorado Springs, CO (719) 633-2444;	$
other locations are 3589 N. Carefree and 390 N. Circle Dr.	£𝔇

Hamburger heaven: six-inch-wide patties are sandwiched in high-topped buns, plain or with Velveeta cheese, or with chopped onions and barbecue sauce. Relatively thin, so much so that the degree of doneness is simply not an issue; these are nothing like the plush "gourmet" burgers that sell for near double-digit prices in swankier restaurants. They are wide-load versions of old-time lunch-counter hamburgers, offered at Conway's on a menu that also includes good navy bean soup, beef stew, and, of course, shoestring French fried potatoes.

Daddy Bruce's Bar-B-Q

1629 East 34th Ave., Denver, CO	$
(303) 449-8890	£𝔇

Daddy Bruce Randolph came to Denver from Arkansas, via Texas and Arizona, so the barbecue in the restaurant he established is fundamentally southern-style, meaning sweet and sloppy and impossible to stop eating. There are ribs, chicken, and brisket, all infused with a peppery, garlicky red sauce with that unmistakable Dixie panache. Alas, the balmy sweet potato pie that was once Daddy Bruce's trademark dessert seems to have been dropped from the menu.

Durango Diner

957 Main Ave., Durango, CO	$
(313) 247-9889	*BLD*

A tip of the Stetson to Gail Zweigenthal, editor-in-chief of *Gourmet* magazine, for alerting us to the Durango Diner, where—according to the menu—"locals have been gathering to eat and talk for decades." Supper in this big, comfortable café includes unalloyed diner fare like fine hot roast beef dinners and hefty French dips, as well as food with a Southwest regional twist (the wild turkey sandwich is available with mashed potatoes and green chili). But the grand meal of the day is breakfast. One huge pancake, made with or without blueberries, blankets a plate and tastes great. There are classic huevos rancheros and breakfast burritos as well as awesome omelets, including one called the "kitchen sink," heaped with green chili. That good green chili is also available to take home, by the pint, quart, or gallon.

The Fort

Hwys. 8 and 285, Morrison, CO	$$$
(303) 697-4771	*D*

In the atmospheric adobe-walled Fort, with an inspiring view of Denver's lights in the distance, you eat old-time frontier vittles prepared in a sophisticated modern kitchen. Buffalo steaks and sausages, Rocky Mountain oysters, and local trout are all found on a fascinating, deluxe menu that serves up a large portion of culinary history as the side dish to every meal. For all its prairie ambiance, the Fort is an eminently civilized theme restaurant and a good place to splurge for anyone whose appetite for big beef steaks is whetted by the storybook romance of the American West.

Juniper Valley Ranch

Hwy. 115, about 15 miles south of Colorado Springs, CO	$$
(719) 576-0741	D
L on Sunday (limited hours in fall, closed in winter, reservations advised)	

Juniper Valley Ranch has not changed since 1951. New generations of the same family have taken over since the early days of Grandma Ethel and Aunt Evelyn's reign, but the menu has remained precisely the one they instituted: family-style dinners of skillet-fried chicken or baked ham en casserole, accompanied by hot biscuits and apple butter, stewed okra, and riced potatoes. You start with spiced cider or consommé, and finish with cake or cobbler. It is a homey, civilized meal, served at mismatched tables in an ancient red mud house hidden by juniper and skunk brush.

M & D's Barbecue and Fish Palace

2004 E. 28th Ave., Denver, CO	$
(303) 296-1760	LD

Despite its name, M & D's is *not* palatial; but the soulful fish that attracts customers from near and far is fit for royalty. Dine here in plain but comfortable surroundings, or get the satisfying meat-and-potatoes meals packed to go: pork chops, meat loaf, succulent chicken with well-cooked, deeply seasoned southern-style vegetables. The real star of the menu is barbecue—pork or beef, served in an unwieldy sandwich or as part of a platter with all the fixin's.

KANSAS

☆ ☆ ☆

Brookville Hotel

KS 140 15 miles west of Salina, KS (913) 225-6666	$$
daily, L Sunday	D

People drive for hours, from as far away as Wichita and Kansas City, to eat at the Brookville Hotel, which has been serving celebration-size meals in the Kansas prairie since 1897, when Brookville was the roundhouse town for the Central Pacific Rail Line. The fancy old Victorian dining room is crowded every Sunday with families and friends passing and grabbing serving platters heaped with skillet-fried chicken, mashed potatoes, creamed corn, baking powder biscuits, and gravy. It's an eat-till-you-drop affair: whenever serving platters start looking empty, they are filled again.

Chicken House

Hwy. 99, Olpe, KS	$
(316) 475-3386	LD

Off the Kansas Turnpike south of Emporia in the small cattle country town of Olpe, Leonard and Theresa Coble built a restaurant some forty years ago. It burned to the ground in the mid-1970s, and the new, modern eat-place was constructed, but the Cobles' reputation for good fried chicken has never wavered. The crunchy pieces of bird are accompanied by fried onion rings and honey wheat-nut bread, followed by creamy pies. It's a Kansas meal that packs the capacious new restaurant almost every night, most especially for Sunday lunch.

Cozy Inn

108 N. 7th, Salina, KS	$
(913) 825-9407	LD

A hamburger landmark, the Cozy Inn started selling sliders—America's original itsy-bitsy wimpies—in 1922. Each tiny tile of meat is grilled with onions, then served inside a steamed bun with a dill pickle slice and a blob of mustard. Six or eight make a meal-size portion. Most customers buy them by the sack to take home, but it is a mesmerizing sight to sit at the minuscule counter, where you can see the grill man flip and garnish patties with supreme finesse, and where the oniony aroma of the grill adds an indescribable *je ne sais quois* to the dining experience.

Leona Yarbrough Restaurant

2800 W. 53rd St., Shawnee Mission, KS	$
(913) 722-4800	LD

Emily Post would have felt comfortable lunching off floral-trimmed dinner plates in this gentle establishment, a longtime bastion of heartland cooking with a feminine touch. Leona Yarbrough's kitchen cuts no corners; from homey chicken noodle soup and fresh-baked bread to old-fashioned lattice-top apple pie, the food served here is honest, inexpensive, and delicious. The menu is printed daily; our fond memories include dinners of braised lamb shank, turkey divan, and excellent fried chicken, and for lunch impeccable egg salad sandwiches on toasted whole wheat bread with potato soup on the side and blackberry cobbler for dessert.

Merle's Place

440 N. Seneca, Wichita, KS	$
(316) 263-0444	£D

We slice our meat thin and pile it high!" boasts the menu at Merle's, a vintage-1935 beer bar that was turned into a civil little eatery about a decade ago. Nothing exotic about the sandwiches served here: just good ham, roast beef, pastrami, or turkey on thick-sliced white, wheat, or rye, served hot or cold, with a full array of condiments, potato chips, and a robust dill pickle. Put a tall, cold beer on the side and you will see just how pleasant life can be.

Mrs. Peter's Chicken Dinners

4960 State Ave., Kansas City, KS	$
(913) 287-7711	£D

Mrs. Peter's is known for a ritual Kansas City meal: creamy cole slaw and marinated vegetables followed by heaps of fried chicken, mashed potatoes, gravy, long-cooked green beans, biscuits with honey butter and strawberry rhubarb sauce, and pie or a sundae for dessert.

The ambiance is country-craftsy. Waitresses wear granny dresses and frilly bonnets; a dainty gift shop up front is tended by a little old lady who folds white cloth napkins when not waiting on customers. When we left two pieces of chicken on our serving platter at the end of a big supper, our waitress, Nell, said, "Whenever I go on a bus trip with the church choir, I stop here first and get chicken to bring along. Please, take these pieces with you for a midnight snack." Such a nice place!

Porubsky's Grocery

508 N.E. Sardou, Topeka, KS	$
(913) 234-5788	£

If you are lucky enough to be in Topeka between October and March, take the opportunity to taste Charlie Porubsky's chili. This seasonal brew, a specialty since Charlie and his wife, Lydia, opened the store in 1947, has inspired cadres of loyalists, including Kansas governors and senators whose pictures and encomia line the walls. Any time of year, the thing to eat in this friendly old tavern is a sandwich—piled-high pastrami or whatever cold cut you want, accompanied by fire-hot pickles that Charlie makes himself with a blend of horseradish, pepper, and mustard.

NEVADA

☆ ☆ ☆

Fiore

3700 W. Flamingo Rd. (in the Rio), Las Vegas, NV	$$$
(702) 252-7777	D
(reservations recommended)	

Every top casino in Las Vegas has at least one super-deluxe restaurant with high prices and white-glove service. Some are silly (at Bacchanal in Caesars Palace, "wine goddesses" feed grapes to male customers and massage their necks); and despite their exotic themes (ancient Egypt at Isis in the Luxor, South Pacifica at Kokomo's in the Mirage), most serve meat and potatoes—of the highest quality, mind you—to customers who are out-of-towners with money to burn. Fiore is a wonderful exception, a swank bistro with a truly interesting menu and elegance more convincing than the Disney World standards that prevail elsewhere.

You *can* get meat and potatoes—a black Angus medallion, dusted with white truffle, is magnificent; lamb is roasted to perfection over olive wood—and your meal can include plenty of tableside folderol, from Caesar salad to crepes suzette, as well as intermezzo sorbet spritzed with Dom Pérignon and ornamented with edible flower petals. All meals are augmented by the offerings of a bread hostess who comes to the table with a basket with interesting slices, such as olive bread, Parmesan cheese bread, pesto bread, accompanied by a dish of herbed extra-virgin olive oil. The menu changes all the time, but our fondest recollections are of huge New Orleans shrimp with red chili and thyme, seared ahi tuna enlivened by a splash of 100-year-old Balsamico, and yummy garlic mashed potatoes served with rotisserie chicken.

Diners' perks are of a level found only in Las Vegas—tables are equipped with little purse rests so milady needn't leave her bag on the floor; fine cigars are proffered with cognac after dinner on a climate-controlled terrace. If you strike it rich, or if you simply want to splurge on the best casino meal in town, this is the place.

The Green Shack

2504 E. Fremont, Las Vegas, NV (702) 383-0007	$$
(reservations advised)	D

Hoover Dam workers were the original customers of the Green Shack, one of the rare Las Vegas landmarks where nothing changes. It is still the humble supper club it always was, and it is still known for country cooking. Fried chicken is the meal on which the Shack's reputation rides: skillet-cooked to crusty succulence and accompanied by genuine mashed potatoes and hot biscuits with a pitcher of honey. In a city of pageantry and excess, such a meal—or the excellent grilled chicken livers or gizzards—makes a convincing reality check. The clientele is almost exclusively locals, who crowd the old saloon in such numbers that getting a seat on a weekend night or around the holidays can be a problem.

Louis' Basque Corner

301 E. Fourth St., Reno, NV	$
(702) 323-7203	£Ɗ

Just a few blocks from the casinos' glitter, Louis and Lorraine Erreguible's high-spirited dining room provides customers with a taste of Pyrenees cuisine as developed by Basque cooks and chuckwagon chefs in the American West. A twist of French style (crusty bread), a jot of Spanish spice (in the paella or tripe stew), and a whole lot of garlic are the fundamental elements of the hearty meals spread across Louis's bright-clothed tables. From barley soup to garlicked salad to exotica like chicken Basquaise or shepherd's stew to hefty steaks or pork chops, the tasty meals seem to go on forever. To wash them down, you want hearty red wine; the only thing Louis does not provide is a goatskin flask to squirt it from.

Nevada Dinner House

351 Silver St., Elko, NV	$
(702) 738-8485	Ɗ

Frontier culture west of the Rockies was enriched by Basque shepherds, cowboys, and chuckwagon cooks. On Silver Street in Elko's old downtown, a few good restaurants express that heritage by serving cordial family-style meals (help yourself from the serving bowl).

The Star Hotel and Biltoki are both good places, but after a wonderful week of trying them all (at the Cowboy Poetry Gathering, which is held here every January), we decided we like the Nevada Dinner House best. It is a casual eat-place with a spacious bar and speedy waitresses, where the food is basically western and the seasoning is Basque. Simply put, that means nearly everything but the liquor and ice cream is shot through with garlic. Meals start with powerhouse salads—no exotic greens or any such wussy ingredients, just good ol' iceberg lettuce—glistening with a delicious lemony vinaigrette. From that, you move on to old-world casseroles and steaks or chops or falling-off-the-bone garlic chicken accompanied by mouth-watering mashed potatoes (are they garlicked, too?!). Start the meal, or finish it, or accompany it with Picon punch, the high-octane Basque *digestif* made of brandy, Picon liqueur, and a twist of lemon.

Sterling Brunch at Bally's Steakhouse

at Bally's Casino, 3645 Las Vegas Blvd. S., Las Vegas, NV	$$$
(702) 739-4111	
Sunday brunch	

Buffets are a Las Vegas thing. Most are bulk-feeding opportunities for gamblers who want maximum food for minimum money; but Bally's Sunday brunch is something else. The quintessence of casino opulence, it *does* offer tons of food, but this is terrific food. Omelets are made to order while you watch, and so is sushi; there are heaps of caviar and warm blinis, smoked salmon, freshly opened oysters and clams on the half shell. And there are also meats: rack of lamb, veal and lobster strudel, salmon steak, beef tenderloin. Pies, tortes, cakes, and pastries are supplemented by warm peach Martinique à la mode. Champagne glasses are kept full of Piper-Heidsick. Ladies get bussed on the hand by the tuxedoed maitre d' when they arrive and receive a long-stemmed rose on their way out. Ridiculous and wonderful: this is Vegas incarnate.

The Venetian

3713 W. Sahara Ave., Las Vegas, NV	$$
(702) 871-4190	*D*

No sybarite should visit Las Vegas without sampling an appetizer called neckbones a la Venetian, a great, messy bowl of inelegant scraps long simmered in pungent wine marinade. It is finger food: pick your way through the heap of pork parts, worry each piece in your mouth, finding tender nuggets of succulent meat and licking bones clean, and use good, fresh bread to mop up the pungent sauce. Another irresistible Venetian exclusive is sautéed spinach and broccoli greens with lots of garlic and oil. Such earthy fare, which is just the beginning of a vast menu of old Italian favorites from honest pastas to scampi fra diavolo and a grand grilled veal chop (with cannoli for dessert, of course!), has made this comfy roadside grotto a beloved haunt of native Las Vegans and visitors for more than forty years. It is a homey place, about as close as this city gets to a neighborhood eatery: waitresses are fast and friendly; brick and stucco and a Venetian mural on the wall create a charming ambiance reminiscent not of Italy but of America circa 1950, when going out to eat Italian food was a romantic adventure.

NEW MEXICO

★ ★ ★

Angelina's

Española, NM	$
(505) 753-8543	L D

There are ordinary tables in the middle of Angelina's dining room, but the choice seats are around the perimeter, in small, semiprivate eating areas, each of which is outfitted like a different old-West place: a teepee, a hacienda, a jail, a bank. It's fun decor, with none of the corporate slickness of a theme restaurant, but what's really great here is the food. Classic northern New Mexican fare includes zesty huevos rancheros, bowls of pure, fire-hot red and green chile (this is the land of chile with an "e"), carne adovada, and puffy sopaipillas on the side.

Southwest Splurges

Expensive, fancy, and/or fashionable regional restaurants that are worth it.

- ☞ The Fort, Morrison, CO (p. 264)
- ☞ Fiore at the Rio, Las Vegas, NV (p. 269)
- ☞ Sterling Brunch at Bally's Steakhouse, Las Vegas, NV (p. 272)
- ☞ Coyote Café, Santa Fe, NM (p. 275)
- ☞ Santacafe, Santa Fe, NM (p. 280)
- ☞ Cattlemen's, Oklahoma City, OK (p. 283)
- ☞ The Metro, Oklahoma City, OK (p. 286)
- ☞ Cattlemen's Steak House, Fort Worth, TX (p. 289)
- ☞ Star Canyon, Dallas, TX (p. 302)
- ☞ Zoom, Park City, UT (p. 310)

Bobcat Bite

Old Las Vegas Hwy., Santa Fe, NM (505) 983-5319	$$
Wed–Sat	£Ð

You can spend nearly fifteen dollars for a beefsteak in this ancient but utterly pristine roadhouse restaurant, and a swell steak it is, with excellent spuds on the side. There are pork chops and a ham steak, too, but we like to come to Bobcat Bite for a cheap bowl of chile (in the winter only) or a sandwich. There isn't a tastier green chile cheeseburger for miles: high-class meat, mild but tasty chile, plenty of cheese, and potato chips all served in a plastic basket lined with wax paper.

The honest food is all the tastier for the nostalgic (but in no way preciously so) ambiance of the tiny dining room, which is like a set from *They Drive by Night*. If Bogie came in for a cup of java and a ham sandwich, no one would look twice.

Chope's

Hwy. 28, Las Mesa, NM	$
(505) 233-9976	£⧝

A boisterous café-bar favored by planters, horticulturists, and chili-heads, Chope's is surrounded by fields of peppers on the vine. All the specialties star the hot pod—complex blue-corn enchiladas, bowls of pure red or green chile, steamy stuffed cornmeal pockets known as gorditas—but the dish that speaks most eloquently of the local crop is chile rellenos, which features whole stuffed chilies with stems still attached. They come as a trio on a plate, filled with balmy cheese, breaded, and fried crisp. If you have only thought of chile as a spice to use with caution, these rellenos will convert you. They are a celebration of chile's profound flavor, which is even more remarkable than its heat.

Coyote Café

132 W. Water St., Santa Fe, NM	$$$
(505) 983-1615	⧝

By elevating vernacular southwestern fare to gourmet status (duck tamales; red chile onion rings; blackened tomato salsa), Mark Miller has made the Coyote Café a beacon of high-fashion food in America. Some locals resent him and his immensely successful restaurant as an invasion of West Coast show-biz sensibility. He argues that the inspiration for his imaginative dishes is ancient Pueblo food that might have been enjoyed by twelfth-century cliff-dwelling Indians. Unless you are a culinary anthropologist, the ego-clash is a silly debate, because the fact is that there are many wonderful things to eat at Coyote Café, from delectable sea bass tacos to tenderloin of pork with red chile chutney. The noise level in the fanciful high-desert-decor dining room is deafening or convivial, depending on your mood, and the clientele is an interesting mix of local high rollers, serious foodie pilgrims, and hapless tourists gasping for air when they taste just how hot the (delicious) chilies rellenos are.

Note: The Rooftop Cantina at Coyote Café serves similar fare at somewhat lower prices and is open for lunch from April through October. On the first floor, there is a great retail store specializing in chilies and related products.

El Norteño

7306 Zuni SE, Albuquerque, NM	$
(505) 256-1431	L D

Soft taco heaven! The menu in this pleasant family-run restaurant lists well over a dozen things you can wrap in the big wheaty rounds of flatbread, including not-for-the-squeamish cabrito (goat) and lengua (tongue), as well as the tastiest barbacoa (charcoaled meat) anywhere. Get two or three different kinds, top them with exhilarating pico de gallo, and have the waiter keep a few cold bottles of beer in an ice bucket by your booth. It all adds up to an authentic taste of northern Mexico, and one of the great bargain meals in Albuquerque.

Horseman's Haven Café

6500 Cerrillos Rd., Santa Fe, NM (505) 471-5420	$
Mon–Sat, BL Sun	B L D

Situated in a gas station near the interstate, this extremely humble café serves some of the tastiest New Mexican food anywhere, and at rock-bottom prices. At the counter or in one of the half-dozen little booths, customers are surrounded by equine art: statuettes, paintings, and wall plaques of horses, as well as horsemen ranging from Mexico's vaqueros to Hollywood's John Wayne.

Breakfasts are splendid arrays of food: colossal burritos loaded with eggs and bacon and topped with cheese and chile; fiery carne adovada (tender chunks of chile-marinated pork) with eggs, potatoes, and a warm homemade tortilla on the side. The lunch and dinner menu features enchilada pies of beef, chicken, carne adovada, or cheese; tacos on blue corn tortillas; and one of the finest—and hottest!—green chile cheeseburgers anywhere.

M & J Restaurant

403 Second SW, Albuquerque, NM	$
(505) 242-4890	LD

Also known as the M & J Sanitary Tortilla Factory, this airy lunch-room across from the bus station is one of the most memorable cheap-eats experiences in Albuquerque. The boisterous dining rooms are outfitted with spacious booths and rough-textured walls covered with love letters to the restaurant written by satisfied customers from around the world. The carne adovada just may be the best in the West, especially when loaded into a burrito; the chilies rellenos and stuffed sopaipillas are exemplary; and the blue corn enchiladas are *magnifico!* Even old-fashioned ordinary-looking tacos, in hard corn shells, are extraordinarily tasty, and the chips (made here) and hot salsa that begin the meal are impossible to stop eating.

Nellie's Café

1226 W. Hadley, Las Cruces, NM (505) 524-9982;	$
a spin-off restaurant, Little Nellie's Chile Factory,	BLD
is located at 600 E. Amador, 523-9911	

The motto is "Chile with Attitude," which is what you get at Nellie's and Little Nellie's, a pair of cheeky urban chile parlors where the price is low and the spice is right.

The original Nellie's has long been famous for the heat of its chile-based menu: feverish red salsa with chips start off the meal, enchiladas topped with a hot red or hotter green elixir of the pods, and burritos smothered with chile sauce. However, the kitchen's secret weapon has no chile in it whatsoever. It is the refried beans that accompany nearly everything: silk-smooth but with just enough bits of unmashed legume to make the texture interesting and the taste irresistible.

Despite its rough-around-the-edges personality, Nellie's serves some specialty dishes with high style. For tacos al pastor, corn tortillas are arrayed with neat little hills of shredded meat festively garnished with chopped tomatoes, slices of radish, wedges of avocado, fresh jalapeños, green onion, and sprigs of cilantro. Even the giant chile cheeseburger is a thing of beauty. Instead of being covered with a mash of chopped peppers as is customary, Little Nellie's Chile CBs come with whole cooked and peeled pods—a rousing complement to meat, cheese, and bun.

Pasqual's

121 Don Gaspar Ave., Santa Fe, NM	$
(505) 983-9340	BLD

Pasqual's is a modest corner café with terrific food. At mealtime in this crowded, split-level dining room, you are lucky to find a seat at a small table or at the large shared one where a local yokel or a stranger from just about any part of the world might break bread with you. For breakfast, we love the pancakes, the blue-and-yellow corn-meal mush, big sweet rolls, and giant bowls of five-grain cereal with double-thick cinnamon toast on the side, accompanied by immense bowls—not cups—of latté. And for lunch, we can never resist the expertly made soups. Little things mean so much: good, fresh bread for sandwiches; earthy roasted chilies on quesadillas; even the coffee is a tasty surprise. After a few meals at Pasqual's, it is easy to feel affection for its unpretentious, sometimes clamorous ambiance. This is a restaurant with an adventurous character that perfectly complements the good stuff from the kitchen.

Plaza Café

54 Lincoln Ave., Santa Fe, NM	$
(505) 982-1664	BLD

The oldest restaurant in Santa Fe (since 1918), the Plaza is a modest luncheonette that caters more to locals than the tourist set. It serves Greek diner standards (souvlaki, Greek salad) as well as New-Mex specialties including chilies rellenos, posole with pork, menudo, and really delicious sopaipillas that are available every day starting at about eleven. Fresh and hot and almost painfully flaky, these little golden pillows are wonderful to eat plain—they are nearly as light as air but with a satisfying bready crust—and are great for dunking, dipping, and mopping in the Plaza's fine red or green chile.

Rancho de Chimayo

Rte. 520, Chimayo, NM	$$
(505) 351-4444	£D

Up a winding two-lane road into the hills above Santa Fe is the ancient village of Chimayo. The Jaramillo family have lived here for over a century and their home is now a restaurant. Rancho de Chimayo has with wide plank wood floors, hammered tin chandeliers, a capacious fireplace, and a menu of native foods seldom found on ordinary Tex-Mex or southwestern menus. Chili peppers are used in nearly all the good things the Jaramillos serve, from cheese and chile omelets to chile-topped sirloin steak. The best dish is carne adovada (chile-marinated pork), its heat dampened by airweight sopaipillas (pillowy triangles of fried bread) dipped in honey. The place can get overrun by travelers, but there is still something magical about an outdoor table in the high desert air, with candlelight and roving musicians adding to the romance of the Southwest.

Roque's Carnitas

Washington and Palace, Santa Fe, NM no phone	$
(closed in winter)	£

Roque's is a jolly little chuckwagon that serves a great sandwich. Folded inside a sturdy flour tortilla that has been heated on a grate over a charcoal fire is succulent beef, and plenty of it—top round thinly sliced and seasoned, sizzled on a grate along with onions, chilies, and fiery jalapeño salsa. Dining accommodations are park benches in the plaza; your companions are hungry pigeons. Roque, a fifth-gener-

Tex-Mex Lex

A handful of helpful menu terms in Spanish, pigeon-Spanish, Mexican, Cal-Mexican, and Tex-Mexican.

Ajo	Garlic
Carne adovada	Beef or pork marinated in hot chilies
Carne seca	Air-dried beef (a Tucson specialty)
Carne verde	Beef with green chile
Cebolla verde	Green onion, usually grilled in Arizona
Chile con carne	Beef with red chile
Chile colorado	Red chile
Chimichanga	A deep fried burrito
Chorizo	spicy pork sausage
Fajitas	Grilled beef (or chicken), served sizzling with vegetables and tortillas
Flauta	Flute—a tortilla rolled around beef or chicken
Frijoles refritos	Refried beans
Gordita	Cornmeal pocket filled with meat and/or cheese, grilled

ation Santa Fean and a fount of local lore, goes to Mexico each winter, where he runs a pizzeria. To our noses, the smell of his sizzling carnitas on the Santa Fe plaza is as much a sign of spring as singing robins and blooming lilacs.

Santacafe

231 Washington Ave., Santa Fe, NM	$$$
(505) 984-1788	LD

Santacafe is very, very stylish, and the food is very, very delicious, especially the chile-spiked brioche at the beginning of the meal, and the peppery dumplings and smoked pheasant spring rolls with dipping

Huevos rancheros	Eggs with salsa, always accompanied by tortilla and frijoles refritos
Menudo	Tripe soup (a hangover cure)
Mole poblano	A rich sauce of chile, chocolate, and spices (many variations)
Tostada	Crisp-fried corn tortilla, topped with cheese or guacamole
Quesadilla	Tortillas layered with cheese and heated

Some Common Fillings for Tacos

Al carbon	Charcoal-grilled beef or pork
Al pastor	Roast pork
Carne asada	Roasted beef
Carnitas	Small pieces of pork (in California) or beef (farther east)
Frijoles enteros	Whole beans
Hongos	Mushrooms
Lengua	Tongue
Picadillo	Seasoned ground beef
Pollo	Chicken

sauces. The kitchen is renowned for combining southwestern flavor with Asian style, but the meal we remember best is one autumn's all-vegetable plate—the very image (and flavor) of a utopian harvest, including all sorts of beans and legumes and the sweetest ear of roasted-in-the-husk corn on the cob.

The old adobe restaurant is a real beauty, and dining here is romantic—indoors is cozy, intimate, elegant; the courtyard is more festive. With a loved one or good friends, a meal at Santacafe is a Santa Fe experience to remember.

Tecolote	
1203 Cerrillos Rd., Santa Fe, NM	**$**
(505) 988-1362	**BL**

A casual, family-style café where breakfast is king: atole piñon hot-cakes, made with blue cornmeal and studded with roasted piñon nuts; French toast made from cinnamon-raisin or orange poppy seed bread; corned beef hash atop a hot tortilla, smothered with red or green chile; the "sheepherder's breakfast," which is spuds and jalapeño peppers cooked on a grill until crusty brown, then topped with two kinds of chile and melted cheddar cheese. The only thing wrong with this place is waiting for a table on weekend mornings.

What Is Chili?

Chili is a fighting word. Devotees to each regional variation swear by their own and damn all others. In the interest of world peace and good eating, here is a rundown of the basic kinds.

Chili Mac: A midwestern urban variant of ground beef in a spicy tomato sauce mixed with spaghetti or elbow macaroni and beans (Bishop's Chili Hut, p. 168)

Cincinnati Chili: Sweet-spiced, finely ground, saucy beef layered onto limp spaghetti noodles, crowned with grated cheese and chopped onion, oyster crackers on the side (Camp Washington Chili, p. 211)

Green Bay (Wisconsin) Chili: Meat and bean chili gilded with a ladle full of hot-spiced oil (Real Chili, p. 225)

New Mexican Chile: Beanless and meatless—a pure puree of pods; always spelled chile and served on the side with other dishes and with soft tortillas for mopping and sopping (Chope's, p. 275)

Texas Chili: Beanless, made with coarse-ground beef or small beef chunks, usually simmered in beer with hot peppers; beans may be served on the side (Franklin's Food Store, p. 292)

Woolworth's

58 E. San Francisco, Santa Fe, NM	$
(505) 982-1062	BLD

Here in the heart of New Mexico's fashionable capital city is a rare outpost of very unfashionable dime store cuisine, a secret eating place seldom found by tourists but loved by long-time citizens. Traditional lunch-counter meals include tom turkey with dressing, meat loaf with gravy, and corn dogs to go; but here, too, are such classics of the plebeian New Mexican kitchen as chile cheeseburgers and burritos. The pièce de résistance is Frito pie, a trough of crisp corn chips blanketed with red or green chile and a heap of shredded orange cheese. Dine at a store-long counter on an orange-upholstered stool under bright fluorescent lights, or do as generations of Santa Feans have done—carry it into the plaza and enjoy it as you stroll.

OKLAHOMA

Cattlemen's

1309 S. Agnew, Oklahoma City, OK	$$
(405) 236-0416	BLD

In the old (and still thriving) stockyards, Cattlemen's is one of America's best places to eat beef. Its sirloin steak is supremely hedonistic—slow-aged and fast-broiled, with a delirious flavor that flows and flows. There are plenty of other good cuts of beef on the menu, as well as the Oklahoma favorite, lamb fries—testicles of young lambs that are sliced and deep fried.

Breakfast is a special time here: no tourists, plenty of genuine cowboys and truckers who are their spiritual heirs, and a menu that features crusty breakfast steaks and platters of brains and eggs.

Beyond great chuck, this place has another dazzling attraction: an immense illuminated mural in the front dining room shows cattlemen on horseback many years ago, riding among a vast herd of bovines.

Classen Grill	
5124 N. Classen, Oklahoma City, OK	**$$**
(405) 842-0428	**BLD**

We like lunch and dinner at Classen Grill—excellent burgers, debonair grilled fish, sophisticated pastas—but breakfast wins our eternal loyalty. Start the day with taquitas (tortilla-wrapped packets of eggs, cheese, and vegetables) or chinook eggs (salmon patties topped with poached eggs) accompanied by a block of lush cheese grits. Insatiable appetites go for "biscuits debris"—two big ones split open and mounded with gravy choc-a-bloc with ham and sausage chunks, cloaked with melted cheddar cheese. On the side you get potatoes, either home fries or Classen potatoes, which are mashed, seasoned with garlic, and rolled into little balls, then deep fried until brittle gold on the outside. The result is a kind of prairie knish.

Del Rancho	
301 W. Main St., Moore, OK	**$**
(405) 794-4131	**LD**

Del Rancho is a restaurant chain with a handful of branches in central Oklahoma. We're not usually partial to chains, but two things endear this one to us: especially crisp chicken-fried steak (the house specialty), and a weird, old-fangled service system in which each booth telephones its order to the house operator, who then conveys it to the kitchen. A few moments later, it is delivered by a waitress.

Chicken-fried steak connoisseur Karl Rambo of Norman, Oklahoma, originally recommended Del Rancho to us as a convenient stop for interstate travelers. Mr. Rambo advised that in his experience, the Del Rancho in Moore is the one with the best food.

Jake's Rib

100 Ponderosa, Chickasha, OK	$
(405) 222-2825	£D

Jake's serves Paul Bunyan portions of barbecue. It is a polite town café with a television so customers can watch sportscasts as they eat, and a menu that offers mammoth platters of pork ribs, pork chunks, sliced brisket, hot sausage links, and smoke-flavored pink bologna steaks. Side dishes are abundant, too, including curly-Q fries, fried okra, and pinto beans, plus colossal glasses full of iced tea or cold beer.

Jigg's Smoke House

exit 62 off I-40, Clinton, OK	$
(405) 323-5641	£D

This friendly shack by the side of the highway has a single table (made of a construction spool) where customers enjoy excellent barbecue sandwiches of juicy hacked pork in a tangy tomato sauce stuffed inside burger buns. Jiggs's is also an outpost of genuine beef jerky. Using an ultraslow, smoke-drying process, raw beef is reduced to enormous, leather-textured flaps of jerky that smell of smoke and meat for days. It takes two big hands to bend one and a healthy set of teeth to rip off a chaw. Chew, chew, chew—the salty cured flavor inundates the mouth with more intensity than a plug of Copenhagen Skoal.

Leo's Barbecue

3631 N. Kelley Ave., Oklahoma City, OK	$
(405) 427-3254; also at 6816 N. Western	£D

Leo's beef is so coarsely hacked that a portion of it, on a platter or in a sandwich, contains some outside chunks with crunchy blackened edges and others that are velvet-soft and dripping natural juice. Sauce is dark and demonically hot with a vinegar punch—good not only on the meat but on the small, buttery baked potato that accompanies all sandwiches and meals. Leo's also offers pork ribs, hot links, and a locally favored treat, bologna. Before you dismiss barbecued bologna as a smoke-house aberration, you need to try it here. This is not bubble-gum-colored supermarket lunch meat; it is a thick-sliced, dark-pink slab with wicked zest, dense and powerfully smoky. We don't like it better than the beef, which is superb, but it *is* interesting.

The Metro

6418 N. Western, Oklahoma City, OK	$$
(405) 840-9463	£D

A chic bistro where the walls are decorated with posters of French wine labels and the tables are covered with thick napery and clean butcher paper, Metro is an oasis of culinary savoir faire in the meat-and-potatoes belt. Even here, the beef is grand—they make a smoked tenderloin hors d'oeuvre, grilled fillets stuffed with mushrooms and shallots, and a Roquefort burger with pommes frites or lacy fried onions on the side. But the real lure (aside from a list of twenty-five wines by-the-glass and an inventory of essenced vodkas from cilantro/serrano to vanilla bean) is such urbane creations as acorn squash cakes with orange-glazed shrimp and scallops. A menu of seasonal fare is redesigned every two months; last year, it featured roast quail salad, braised tilapia with aromatic herbs, and a dessert feuillete constructed to hold wine-marinated spring berries. Year-round, there is one dessert we can never resist: bread pudding with bourbon sauce. "I don't drink bourbon," revealed the waitress when she brought us a serving of this dark, cinnamon-scented treasure in its liquory pool, "but I sure like to eat it!"

The Split-T

57th and N. Western, Oklahoma City, OK	$
(317) 842-0331	£ⅅ

The Split-T is a sports bar with a TV in each of the four corners of each room, just beneath the ceiling. One of a number of joints in Oklahoma City that serves weird and wonderful hamburgers, it is known for one called the Caesarburger: a broad patty on a big bun with a full inch of sopping Caesar-flavored stuff piled inside. We say "stuff" because the condiment is a sort of cross between salad and sauce. The combination of this zesty cool garnish and hot beef is inspired. It comes wrapped in paper, but copious spillage is inevitable.

Van's Pig Stand

717 E. Highland, Shawnee, OK	$
(405) 273-8704	£ⅅ

Pork shoulder, slow-smoked in the hickory pit, is cut into big, tender chunks and exuberantly sauced, then served with curlique French fries or a "Vanized" potato (cut open and filled with garlicky sour cream). It's a superb meal, simple and cheap, and impossible to duplicate in the northern half of the U.S. Meaty pork ribs and sliced beef brisket are also available in this pleasant little barbecue, where the citizens of Shawnee have come to dine for decades.

TEXAS

★ ★ ★

Bellaire Broiler Burger

5216 Bellaire Blvd., Houston, TX (713) 668–8171	$
Mon–Sat	£ D

The Broiler Burger, a long-respected fast-food joint on Bellaire at Bissonnet, has just what you need if you are a hungry soul in search of a classic 1950s fix. The burgers are thin and cooked through and through, and delicious! The shakes are real, and the French fries are good enough to shame any of us who, at one time or another, have settled for franchised burger-joint spuds.

Bryce's Cafeteria

2021 Mall Dr. (exit 222 off I-30), Texarkana, TX	$
(903) 792-1611	£ D

Conversation overheard waiting in line at Bryce's Cafeteria:

"This is the finest food in Texarkana."

"No," a stranger up the line turns to reply. "This is the finest food in Texas."

"I say it's the best in all the South," a third pipes in.

It is hard not to wax rhapsodic waiting at Bryce's Cafeteria, because the waiting line takes you past an array of swoonfully appetizing food, the likes of which has made this place famous since it opened for business some sixty years ago.

There are more vegetables arrayed for the asking than most of us Yankees see in a year. Feast the eyes on purple-hulled peas, fried green tomatoes, red beans, turnip greens cooked with chunks of ham, buttered cauliflower, sauced broccoli, along with a full array of potatoes, cheesy macaroni casseroles, and rice casseroles. Among main courses, fried chicken is stupendously crunchy, and big slabs of sweet ham are sliced to order. For dessert, we like Karo-coconut pie, hot blueberry cobbler, and banana pudding made with meringue and vanilla wafers.

The entire experience is a culinary dream, complete with a smartly uniformed dining room staff (to help old folks and invalids with their trays and to bus tables), and servers who address all men as "sir" and women as "ma'am."

Cattlemen's Steak House

2458 N. Main St., Fort Worth, TX	$$$
(817) 624-3945	LD

Big, beautiful steak is the lure of Cattlemen's, where walls are hung with portraits of prize-winning cattle. Porterhouse, T-bone, sirloin, filet mignon: whatever cut you like, it is broiled hot and fast to pocket all the juices and served with potato and a salad with good blue cheese and sesame dressing. Service can be offhand and fellow diners might be rowdy (in the stockyard since 1947, Cattlemen's draws lots of tourists as well as rodeo folk and ranchers from the outback), but who can worry about such petty concerns when relishing a flavorful forkful of corn-fed, aged beef?

It's nice to walk off a meal with a stroll around the stockyards district, which is populated by a vast number of saddle, boot, and tack shops.

Celebration

4503 W. Lovers Lane, Dallas, TX	$$
(214) 351-5681	LD

Housed in a low-slung stone ranch house in a residential neighborhood, Celebration is a real discovery, for both its ambiance and its good food. The handsome wood-paneled walls are decorated with Indian rugs and evocative black-and-white photographs of contemporary Texas ranch hands, cattle, and life on the range. In the small dining rooms, a meditative calm prevails as gentle western music plays quietly in the background.

Where to Eat Chili and Where to Eat Chile

Although Texas is famous for chili, and Texans tend to be persnickety about it (no beans, please!), genuine chili parlors scarcely exist anymore in the Lone Star State. The closest thing we have found to old-fashioned chili with beef and spices is at sausage shops in and around the East Texas town of Pittsburg, like Franklin's Food Store (p. 292), where the bowl of red is hot and deliriously greasy, and the dining experience is like being in a Walker Evans photograph.

In New Mexico, chile is spelled with an "e" at the end as tribute to the pod from which it is made (the state's co-vegetable, with the pinto bean), and it is served in many, if not most, restaurants but practically never as a main dish. Bowls of pureed chile pods, with only minimal spice, come alongside meals as a dunk for tortillas; chile is used to marinate pork or beef for carne adovada; whole pods are stuffed for chile rellenos and roasted for the tops of cheeseburgers. During autumn's harvest, roadside stands sell chile sandwiches, which are freshly roasted and peeled pods packed between slabs of hearty bread.

The best place to taste chile is in the southern part of New Mexico where it is grown, especially at Chope's (p. 275), a café surrounded by chile fields and patronized by generations of planters.

In this gracious environment, Celebration serves magnificent home cooking. Pot roast is cooked until ridiculously tender; its profound beefy juices are retrieved and served in a little bowl alongside mashed potatoes that are still a little chunky and freckled with potato skin. Meat loaf is perfumed with spice, lean and beefy. Each piece of fried chicken is massive, nutty-crusted on the outside and dripping moist within. The vegetable selection varies with the season. We have enjoyed an autumn casserole made of sweet, bite-size chunks of squash cooked al dente and veiled in garlic and cheese; and spinach glistening with butter and seasoned just enough to highlight its natural vigor.

Waitress Stephanie offered her advice about dessert. "I'll be honest with you. The coconut cream pie is the best," she said. We wouldn't call her wrong, for this pie is a beauty with a deliriously coconutty filling; but the chocolate cake is equally awe-inspiring. It is a double-layer one, moist and thickly iced, and so tall that it is difficult to cut without carefully positioning the fork on top and gliding it smoothly down through the six inches of devil's food.

Clark's Outpost

Hwy. 377, Tioga, TX	$
(817) 437-2414	£𝕯

Clark's beef is so delightful to look at with its blackened crust and rosy insides glistening with juice that you want to pick it up in your fingers and fondle it before savoring its incomparable taste. A fine old store with western-theme decor and checked tablecloths, Clark's serves other barbecued things, including pork and pork ribs, and there are some really strange and tasty side dishes—deep-fried corn on the cob and sliced and fried bull's testicles. But it's the beef that is essential.

Das Peach Haus

Hwy. 87, Fredrickburg, TX (210) 997-0359	$
seasonal hours	

We love Das Peach Haus as a happy antidote to the exceptionally greasy (but irresistibly delicious) chili and hot links of Franklin's Food Store (see p. 292). This part of Texas Hill Country is famous for its luscious peaches and for the roadside fruit stands where you can buy fresh-picked ones. You can also get Fischer and Wieser peach preserves, made from proprietor Mark Wieser's mother's family recipe, peach butter for spreading on toast or biscuits, and peach honey, which is the consistency of chocolate syrup and is suitable for flavoring everything from peachy-keen milk shakes to the glaze on a country ham. Peach season generally lasts all summer long, sometimes starting as early as May.

Franklin's Food Store

115 Jefferson St., Pittsburg, TX	$
(903) 856-2784	BLD

When you walk into Franklin's Food Store, you are going back a hundred years. Hot link sausages are cooked each morning in a pit just inside the swinging doors. Sit on the wooden bench at the table with its view of the open kitchen. The sausages are served with a sharp knife to cut them and a basket of saltines to sop up grease. Slow fans wafting above seem hardly to disturb the lugubrious East Texas air, perfumed by bowls of beanless chili, Frito pie, and chicken-fried steak sputtering in oil. Even when Franklin's is full at lunch, eerie calm prevails: eating such extravagantly oily food induces a meditative state.

"It is an acquired taste," the waitress reassured us when we forked up half a hot link and our eyes bugged at the visceral savor of the meat. "Some people think they're greasy," she said. "I think they're juicy." Pittsburg hot links are not for the timid epicure, that's for sure; but anyone with a taste for genuine Americana, Texas-style, will relish Franklin's, grease and all.

Gennie's Bishop Grill

321 N. Bishop Ave., Dallas, TX	$
(214) 946-1752	£

IF OUR PRICES WERE HIGHER, WE'D BE FAMOUS says the movable-letter menu above the buffet line at Gennie's Bishop Grill. The management is disingenuous. Since it opened in 1970, Gennie's has become quite famous among American café connoisseurs to whom this modest lunchroom is a blue-plate shrine.

Service is cafeteria-style; the line is short and functional. Grab a tray from a pile that includes some plain ones and some with the insignia of an apparently defunct Sirloin Stockade, take a sheaf of silverware wrapped in a paper napkin, then slide toward the food. Tell the server what you want from a selection of that day's three or four entrees. When available, garlic chicken is a must: oozing juice, slipping off its bones as you lift it, fragrant with spice, it is a deeply sensuous eating experience. On the side, you want corn bread stuffing, which is soft and sweet. You also want greens, limp and heavy, sprinkled with peppery vinegar. As for potatoes, Gennie's sweets are brightly flavored, cooked until all tooth resistance is gone; mashed potatoes are glorious—whipped smooth, crowned with a spill of well-peppered cream gravy. Other frequent entrees include spicy beef and macaroni, chicken-fried steak, meat loaf, and liver 'n' onions. All meals are accompanied by your choice of a crisp corn bread muffin or a yeasty round-topped dinner roll that is excellent for mopping up the last streaks of gravy.

Note: Rosemarie's, a sister restaurant of Gennie's, is located just up the road in Oak Cliff at 1411 N. Zangs Boulevard, (214) 946-4142. Rosemarie is the person who makes the fabulous peanut butter pie served at both restaurants.

Goode Company Barbeque	
5109 Kirby, Houston, TX	$
(713) 522-2530 or 523-7154	£🅓

J im Goode's restaurants have become a small constellation of North Stars in East Texas. Smokehounds from near and far come to the barnlike buildings to pig out on crunch-crusted pork ribs, melt-in-the-mouth brisket, chicken, ham, duck, or turkey with peppery pinto beans and luscious jalapeño cheese bread on the side. The food is sensational, the ambiance is downhome (neon beer signs, stuffed armadillos, cordwood stacked by the outside walls), and the prices are low. Only one problem: the crowds can be daunting, especially on weekend nights.

Other stars in the Goode galaxy include the Goode Company Seafood restaurant at 2621 Westpark for boiled crawfish and gumbo and the Goode Company Hamburger and Taqueria restaurant at 4902 Kirby.

Chicken-Fried Steak

To our knowledge, no one has pinpointed the origin of chicken-fried steak, one of the fundamental foodstuffs west of Kansas City. If you are a culinary newbie, you need to know that it isn't chicken, and it isn't steak, and chuckwagon law requires that it be eaten with mashed potatoes and gravy. Technically, it is a cheap piece of beef, breaded and fried like chicken. Culinarily, what it becomes—in the hands of an expert cook—is supreme southwestern comfort food.

We suspect that its origins probably have something to do with the large number of Germans and middle Europeans who settled in the Texas Hill Country, bringing with them a recipe for wiener schnitzel, but finding themselves with tough beef instead of tender veal. Probably some time during the Depression, when times were lean, these ingenious cooks learned to pound the tar out of a cheap cut of beef (classically, using an old-time Coke bottle as a sledgehammer) until it was tender. Then they battered the meat, dredged it in eggs and flour, and skillet-fried it, making gravy from the drippin's.

Make no mistake: chicken-fried steak can be hideous, and we don't recommend ordering one in just any café. But at a restaurant like Threadgill's in Austin (p. 303) or Gennie's in Dallas (p. 292), it is a taste of Texas transcendence with its gnarled tan crust rising in a thousand crisp bubbles melded to the meat so that every mouthful is a perfect mix of crunch and chew. Cut it easily with the edge of a fork, then push the forkful through your gravy. With a heap of black-eyed peas, biscuits, and a tall glass of iced tea (presweetened, natch), this is a four-star Lone Star meal.

H & H Coffee Shop

701 E. Yandell, El Paso, TX (915) 533-1144	$
Mon–Sat	BL

H & H Coffee Shop is a hospitable, Mexican-accented cook shop that adjoins the H & H Car Wash, so you can enjoy the sight of vehicles being soaped and toweled while you eat huevos rancheros, burritos, enchiladas, or—Saturday only—menudo, the tripe and hominy stew renowned for its power to cure a hangover. The house salsa, served with nearly everything, is made from finely chopped jalapeño peppers that play reveille on the tongue. H & H is an archetypal hole-in-the-wall, the sort of place you wouldn't likely stop to eat unless you were let in on the secret.

Hammond's Bar-B-Q

US 67, Glen Rose, TX (817) 897-3321	$
Fri–Sun	£ D

In this sawdust-floored country restaurant, you will feast on Texas barbecue—chopped or sliced beef brisket, big hot sausage links, ham, or ribs, accompanied by pinto beans, mustardy potato salad, and Texas toast (thick-sliced white bread cooked in the pit). About that fine beef, A. J. Hammond says he cooks it as slowly as humanly possible, letting it imbibe the flavor of hickory smoke for a full day and a half. The result is meat so tender you literally cannot pick up a piece without it falling into tender shreds, meat so succulent you want to suck on it rather than chew.

Kincaid's

4901 Camp Bowie Blvd., Fort Worth, TX (817) 732-2881	$
Mon–Sat	£ D

Kincaid's added actual tables awhile back, which diminished the thrill of having to dine on your feet, standing wherever you could find a place among the helter-skelter grocery store shelves. Despite the new amenities in this old grocery store, Kincaid's world-renowned half-pound hamburger, dripping juice and stuffed into a warm bun that oozes condiments, remains pure and good and true.

Kreuz Market

208 S. Commerce St., Lockhart, TX (512) 398-2361	$
Mon—Sat	£𝔇

Kreuz (pronounced "Krites") has been smoking meat since the beginning of the century, and they don't even have plates; but they do twist up the ends of the butcher paper so the meat's juices don't spill when you carry it from the pit to a table. Beef is accompanied by white bread or saltines; and there is a condiment bar with onions, tomatoes, and jalapeño peppers. Kreuz used to be equipped with knives shackled to wood posts; but the sharp knives have been removed and now the management supplies plastic ones. They are not necessary for this meat, which is unspeakably tender, eager to fall apart as soon as you lift it from the paper.

Little Diner

7209 7th, Canutillo, TX	$
(915) 877-2176	£𝔇

This off-the-beaten-path café, which shares a building with a public coin-op Laundromat, serves flautas and gorditas that may be the best in West Texas.

Flautas, which means flutes, are tightly rolled, crisp-fried tortillas packed with either seasoned chicken or beef. The chicken is moist and savory; the beef is brisket, cooked until falling-apart tender, then hand-shredded. About the size of a hefty asparagus stalk, this well-nigh perfect piece of food is finger fare: pick it up and crunch away; juices from inside will dribble down your chin. Gorditas are sandwich pockets made of cornmeal, griddle-cooked and stuffed. They have an earthy corn taste and moist insides with just a hint of flaky crispness all around their skin.

Also known as the Canutillo Tortilla Factory, the Little Diner makes flour tortillas every day and corn tortillas (thin and thick) every other day. Both are sold by the dozen across the counter.

Louie Muller's

206 W. Second St., Taylor, TX (512) 352-6206	$
Mon–Sat	£D

The walls of this establishment, which was a school gymnasium many decades ago, were once green. But they have been aged in cooking smoke so long that they have developed a resinous patina that looks like tortoiseshell. Louie Muller's dining room—one of the supreme shrines of Texas barbecue—is outfitted with communal wooden tables and is generally as quiet as a cathedral, separated from the kitchen by a counter reminiscent of a chancel rail. Back there is the pit—a long metal box holding a grate where briskets cook slowly over burning hickory and oak until the meat is so tender it jiggles like Jell-O. There are no balanced meals, no *plats du jour* here. Order beef by the pound or hot sausage links; they are served on butcher paper atop a molded plastic cafeteria tray. Tote it yourself. Few dining experiences are simpler, or more heavenly.

Mecca

10422 Harry Hines Blvd., Dallas, TX	$
(214) 352-0051	B£D

Mecca is a happy-go-lucky roadhouse plastered with Dallas Cowboys souvenirs, a mounted jackalope, 8 × 10 glossies from celebrity patrons, and wisecracks in the form of bumper stickers (WILL ROGERS NEVER MET AN AUDITOR) and photocopied manifestos ("I have P.M.S. and a handgun," says a snarly cartoon character. "Any questions?"). A squadron of feisty waitresses rules the loose-jointed dining room; and while these good ol' gals never hesitate to share a piece of their mind, they also take care of you like mother hens.

"You see that part of your chicken-fry?" says ours, pointing to the breakfast steak on the plate she carries to our table. It is enveloped in a golden crust, but one bit along the edge is crustless. "That worried me," she says, cocking her brow and giving a gimlet eye to the offending area. "You tell me if it tastes fine. If not, I'll raise hell."

It tastes delicious, even the crustless part, a Lone Star delicacy, tender and beefy, sheathed in breading that cracks into flakes when pressed by fork or knife. Its natural companion is gravy, which comes in a bowl so you can spoon it on and use it as a dip for shreds of Mecca's proud, puffy biscuits.

Cinnamon rolls are a house specialty. Each is a coil of sweet baked dough veined with cinnamon and frosted, about six inches across and two inches high, served hot and sopped with melting margarine that forms a golden pool on the plate. Immense and ungainly, one roll calls for a half dozen cups of coffee to wash it down. No problem: in this joint, waitresses tote coffeepots with the proficiency of a quick-draw artist twirling a Colt .45.

Natura Café	
2909 Mckinney Ave., Dallas, TX (214) 855-5483	**$$**
brunch Sat and Sun	**£ D**

The menu of Natura Café is entitled "New American Taste Indulgence with No Regrets," and it comes supplemented by a breakdown of the calories, fat, protein, cholesterol, and carbohydrates in every dish served, as well as a promise that the air in the restaurant is "filtered, ozonated and constantly circulated." Conspicuous health policies in no way inhibit the high spirits of this gathering place, where hip young urbanites crowd the bar up front, munching vegetable tamales and venison quesadillas accompanied by fresh-squeezed six-vegetable juice and whooping it up just as hard as their beer-guzzling, taco-eating counterparts do elsewhere.

Nor does high nutritional consciousness diminish the flavor of Natura's fine square meals: lean meat loaf (320 calories) with scallion and rosemary-flavored mashed potatoes (a mere 160 calories); slow-roasted chicken with herbed potatoes (623 calories); and tacos loaded with succulent chunks of red snapper (576 calories) and accompanied by a peppery corn and tomato relish. Sandwiches include three kinds of burgers: beef, bison, or tuna, all served on fresh onion rolls.

Hamburger Honor Roll

In our book, there is no one Platonic hamburger. This honor roll includes dramatically different ones, from Hackney's juicy football-size patty to the flat little sliders of the Cozy Inn. Furthermore, although none of the restaurants are very fancy, some are considerably more déclassé than others (we're thinking of Kewpee Lunch).

- ☛ Cassell's, Los Angeles, CA (p. 314)
- ☛ Conway's Red Top, Colorado Springs, CO (p. 263)
- ☛ Cozy Inn, Salina, KS (p. 267)
- ☛ Goldyburgers, Forest Park, IL (p. 172)
- ☛ Hackney's on Harms, Glenview, IL (p. 172)
- ☛ Kewpee Lunch, Racine, WI (p. 223)
- ☛ Kincaid's, Fort Worth, TX (p. 295)
- ☛ Louis Lunch, New Haven, CT (p. 7)
- ☛ Phillips Grocery, Holly Springs, MS (p. 154)
- ☛ Solly's Coffee Shgop, Milwaukee, WI (p. 227)
- ☛ The Sycamore, Bethel, CT (p. 11)

Norma's Café

3330 Beltline Rd., Farmers Branch (near Dallas), TX	$
(214) 243-8646	𝓑𝓛𝓓

Norma's is a good ol' roadhouse with plenty of personality expressed by signs that hang everywhere:

- LIFE IS LIKE A BLUE PLATE SPECIAL. YOU PICK OUT THE ENTREE AND THE SIDE ORDERS FOLLOW.
- THE DISHWASHER IS THE CREDIT MANAGER. HE IS LOOKING FOR A FEW GOOD MEN.
- YES, WE HAVE GRITS.

The cuisine is haute southwest diner, from giant breakfasts of chicken-fried steak, biscuits, and cream gravy to country catfish or meat loaf with real mashed potatoes at lunch. The long list of burger options is crowned by an "atomic chili cheeseburger" strewn with slices of hot jalapeño pepper. Crinkle-cut French fries are also available in a nuclear configuration, heaped with meaty chili, melted cheese, peppers, and red onions. And of course you can get a hand-dipped milk shake on the side. All this fine food is eaten to the tune of a vintage jukebox featuring the hits of Elvis and Richie Valens. On the way out, the last sign you see says, YOU ARE ABOUT TO RETURN TO THE HARSH REALITY OF THE REAL WORLD.

Otto's

5502 Memorial Dr., Houston, TX	$
(713) 864-8526	£ D

Smoked brisket, hot links, and ribs are dished out in a pine-paneled dining room on one side of Otto's; on the other side, hamburgers are served. The burgers are lunch-counter mainstays—thin, cooked-through, and enveloped by soft, spongy buns—and the barbecue is juicy and full-flavored, served with a tangy sauce on the side. Either way, you get a quick, cheap meal that has been satisfying Houstonians for nearly fifty years.

Ouisie's Table

3939 San Filipe Rd., Houston, TX	$$
(713) 528-2264	£ D

Just the right mix of uptown savoir faire and downhome Texas comfort food make Ouisie Cooper's lunchroom a treasured destination in Houston. The hamburger is deluxe; a bowl of simple but elegant black beans, garnished to a fare-thee-well, is a memorable meal; and the BLT sandwich, including a fried egg and jalapeño-spiked mayonnaise, is born again. There is a fresh pasta each day, a glorious grapefruit and avocado salad, and black magic cake to set a sweet tooth spinning. Specials are written on a large blackboard; every local gastronome knows that Tuesday is Ouisie's chicken-fried steak day.

Smitty's	
6219 Airport Rd., El Paso, TX (915) 772-5876	$
Mon–Sat	£𝕯

Decor at Smitty's consists of neon beer signs. But if it's beauty you crave, order any dinner platter. Feast your eyes on the smoke-cooked brisket, so tender and moist it seems to melt on the tongue; gaze upon the sweet Texas beans, the slaw, and the magnificent, crusty hunks of German fried potato. Then, after you have feasted your eyes, dig in and really feast. It is superb Texas barbecue, with fiery jalapeño peppers on the side. Located in a strip mall near the airport, Smitty's is our favorite place to while away time waiting for a flight, and the first place we go when we fly into El Paso from any barbecue-deprived part of the country.

Sonny Bryan's	
2202 Inwood Rd., Dallas, TX (214) 744-1610;	$
other Dallas locations are 302 N. Market 744-1610,	£𝕯
325 N. St. Paul 979–0102, Plaza of the Americas Hotel 871-2097,	
4701 Frankford Rd. 447-0102, Macy's Food Court at the Galleria Mall	
851-5131	

Wedge yourself into a school desk and feast on what cognoscenti consider the best urban barbecue in Texas. Profoundly beefy slices of tender brisket are heaped into gigantic sandwiches, well-sauced and sold with good side dishes such as French fries and pork and beans, as well as tumblers of iced tea.

Only the original Bryan's on Inwood has the school desks and the classic bare-bones atmosphere of an old Texas smoke house *(and it still tends to close midafternoon),* but all the johnny-come-lately branches of Bryan's dish out smoky brisket that is as good as it gets. We are especially appreciative of the Frankford Road location, just off the Dallas Parkway. Zooming from the airport toward an appointment in Plano one day awhile back, we had no time for a meal. We hopped off the six-lane, scarfed down a quartet of brisket sandwiches, and headed north again, thanking the good Lord we were chowing down in Texas once again.

Southside Market and B-B-Q, Inc

1212 US 290 W, Elgin, TX	$
(512) 281-4650	£Ð

Although the brisket (and even the mutton) is exemplary, the sausages, known hereabouts as Elgin hot guts, are what have made the Southside Market a benchmark of smoke-pit quality since 1882. They are all-beef tube-shaped beauties, served with crackers, breathtaking hot sauce made of vinegar and spice, and potato salad and beans. Alas, the colorful old market is shuttered, and Southside now inhabits an airplane hanger–style building on the highway; but despite the lost ambiance, the sausages remain superb.

Star Canyon

3102 Oak Lawn, Dallas, TX (214) 520-7827	$$$
(reservations required)	£Ð

In a gorgeous dining room with an Old West motif (look up at the Texas town names branded on the ceiling), get in a proper frame of mind with a dazzling cowboy martini at the bar, then pleasure your palate with chef Stephan Pyles's always inventive—but never meretricious—new-Tex cooking. Cornmeal-crusted catfish, served with bacony black beans and rice, is a dish to die for; and we once actually ate a stupendously satisfying meatless dinner of grilled vegetables with a wild-flavored mushroom tamale on the side. Of course, the wood-grilled steaks are impeccable. And for dessert, you want chocolate brioche bread pudding with Sambuca-chocolate sauce.

Threadgill's

6416 N. Lamar, Austin, TX	$
(512) 451-5440	£ D

Threadgill's is a hoot. A huge rambling roadhouse loaded with neon beer signs and much Janis Joplin memorabilia (she started her career here on hootenanny night in the 1960s), it is a stronghold of Texas food.

The chicken-fried steak is sublime: a broad slab of beef with a golden crust that's all puckered and puffed, audibly crisp when you crunch down, yet melt-in-the-mouth rich. Push a piece through Threadgill's creamy, pepper-flecked gravy, and fork up some smooth mashed potatoes. Complete this lovely picture with black-eyed peas, a steaming biscuit or square of corn bread, a tumbler of iced tea, and a wedge of cool buttermilk pie for dessert, and you have a quintessential blue-plate feast.

The kitchen's motto is "We don't serve all you can eat. We serve more than you can eat." Meat loaf is massively sliced and smothered with chunky Creole sauce. Sheaves of smoked and glazed ham are piled on a plate under a great spill of Jezebel sauce (named for its sweet and tart blend of horseradish, mustard, and apple jelly). The deep-fried chicken liver platter is one of the most astounding plates of food available anywhere, described on the menu as "more than anyone can eat!"

Despite such excesses, Threadgill's also happens to be a good place to practice nutritional virtue. "Victory with Vegetables" says one side of the menu, where the twenty-three different side dishes Threadgill's offers every day are listed. Many customers come only to eat vegetables: a selection of three, five, or nine, heaped together on a single oval trencher like great colorful globs of paint on an exuberant artist's palette, is called a "vegetable orgy."

Tommy's Bar-B-Que

Rte. 82, Reno, TX (903) 785-2808	$
Tues–Sat closes at 7 pm	**BLD**

East of Paris, Texas, there is a barbecue shack with so much stuff on the walls that it is almost difficult to pay attention to the excellent pit-cooked brisket, hot sausage links, spicy smoked bologna, and tongue-teasing red sauce.

Even before you walk into Tommy's, you know there is someone here with a passion for detail: the small front windows are brimful of taxidermied small game. On the walls inside are rodeo photos, steer horns, horseshoes, collectible cowboy-themed clocks, an autographed picture of Reba McIntyre, a formal portrait of John Wayne, and a funny cartoon that is captioned "Arkansas Motorcycle" and shows a cow wearing socks: *Cow-a-socky.* What all these items have in common, of course, is that they celebrate cowboy heros, cowboy work, and cowboy humor. The food, including silk-smooth sweet beans and a mighty spicy all-beef chili, is cowboy to the core, too.

UTAH

Arshel's Café

711 North Main St., Beaver, UT	$
(801) 438-2977	**BLD**

Arshel's Café is a pleasant highway diner with frilly curtains in its window that serves homey hot lunches and hamburgers with fresh-cut French fries. But it's Arshel's pies that snare travelers on their way to or from the parks and canyons of the southland. The lemon meringue is famous, but we were more impressed by crunchy boysenberry with a crumb top, and peanut butter chocolate with a cool, smooth ribbon of fudgy cream mounted atop a pebbly layer of chunky peanut butter.

Capitol Reef Café

360 W. Main St., Torrey, UT	$$
(801) 425-3271	B D

A sophisticated oasis in a spectacular landscape far from everywhere, Southey Swede's dining room (with low-cost lodgings and a nice bookstore attached) is a healthy-eater's destination. It is really quite amazing in a region where meat and potatoes rule to plow into the cornucopic ten-vegetable dinner salad or to find such well-made stir-fries and meatless pastas. Breakfast juices are fresh-squeezed, and espresso is available. At suppertime, beef, chicken, trout, and wonderful shish kebab are also on the menu for vegetable-frowners.

Cowboy's Smokehouse

95 North Main, Panguitch, UT (801) 676-8030	$$
(closed in winter)	L D

B eef brisket, pork ribs, chicken, and turkey are slow-smoked to succulence in this colorful eatery where the walls are covered with the business cards of friends and fans, and the decor is mounted heads of moose, elk, and deer.

Each table is equipped with a bottle of peppery-sweet, cinnabar-red sauce, but tasty as it is, we recommend savoring the meat pure and unsauced—especially the brisket, which spends a leisurely half-day imbibing warm smoke. Served in slices, each piece has a chewy, blackened rim (delicious to gnaw), and within that crusty exterior is beef that is as soft as brisket can get without disintegrating. Ranch beans are available on the side—simple, peppery, al dente, and there is tasty fruit cobbler for dessert; but it's the barbecued meats and the open-fire-grilled dinner steaks that emblazon the Smokehouse on Utah's good-eats map.

Fat City Smoke House

36 South 100 West, Moab, UT	$
(801) 259-4302	£D

Our thanks to Alex Tanford, roving barbecue sleuth, for clueing us in to this fine way station for all sorts of barbecue, but especially sausage. Made on the premises, the sausages are available in two configurations—red hot (but not really incendiary) and garlic (whoo-eey, pass the Breath Assure!). Both are delicious in their own way, served in sandwiches or as part of a plate with potato salad, Texas toast, and a choice of cowboy beans, a sweet potato, a baked potato, or dirty rice. In addition to smoky links, the Fat City pit also yields succulent beef brisket, pork ribs and baby back ribs, slow-cooked chicken, ham, and turkey. Top it all off with a serving of silky sweet potato or buttermilk pie.

For travelers on the go, box lunches are available.

Hires Big H

425 South 700 East, Salt Lake City, UT (801) 364-4582;	$
other locations are at 835 E. Fort Union Blvd., Midvale,	£D
561-2171; and 2900 W. 4700 South, West Valley City, 965-1010	

This bright, cheerful root-beer-and-burger drive-in offers a choice of carhop service or indoor tables. The hamburger, served in a little paper pouch, is a handsome quarter-pound of beef with lettuce, tomato, and special sauce on an extraordinarily fresh floury-topped sourdough bun. There are plain burgers, onion burgers, Roquefort burgers, bacon burgers, and pastrami burgers; and there are excellent French fries or cheese fries or chili cheese fries on the side. Cokes are available with vanilla or cherry syrup added. For what it aims to be, Hires Big H is just about perfect.

Pie Palaces

Why is pie so especially good when traveling? Even for those of us who don't eat much of it back home (we personally lean more to cake and cookies), pie eating is one of the true pleasures of any road trip. For a lone wedge with a cup of coffee to break up a long stretch of highway, or as the climax of a meal, here is a baker's dozen of pie stops worth inscribing in your little black book.

- ☛ Betty's Pies, Two Harbords, MN (p. 204)
- ☛ Buntyn, Memphis, TN (p. 92)
- ☛ Dodd's Town House, Indianapolis, IN (p. 181)
- ☛ Duarte's, Pescadero, CA (p. 318)
- ☛ Family Pie Shop, Devalls Bluff, AR (p. 122)
- ☛ Henry's, West Jefferson, OH (p. 214)
- ☛ Laughner's, Indianapolis, IN (p. 184)
- ☛ Moody's Diner, Waldoboro, ME (p. 19)
- ☛ Norske Nook, Osseo, WI (p. 224)
- ☛ The Owl, Parksley, VA (p. 105)
- ☛ Pope's Café, Shelbyville, TN (p. 101)
- ☛ Stone's, Marshalltown, IA (p. 193)
- ☛ The White Way, Durant, IA (p. 193)

Idle Isle Café

24 South Main St., Brigham City, UT	$
(801) 734-9062	£𝕯

Here is the sort of honest town café once found on main streets all across America, but now a rarity treasured by all who yearn for honest food served in a setting of utmost civility. You can have a lovely burger and a malt at the marble and onyx soda fountain; but the choice seats are in the polished wooden booths, each outfitted with a ramekin of Idle Isle apricot marmalade for spooning onto the fleecy, oven-warm rolls that come with dinner. The menu is nothing but expertly prepared blue-plate fundamentals, including divinely tender pot roast with mashed potatoes shaped like a crater to hold gravy as well as such daily specials as Wednesday braised beef joints, Friday trout, and Saturday prime rib.

You must save room for dessert, either Idleberry pie—a resonating dark purple blend of blue, black, and boysenberries—or baked custard pudding—which is simply the tenderest comfort food that one can imagine.

Lamb's	
169 South Main St., Salt Lake City, UT	**$$**
(801) 364-7166	**BLD**

When we tell you that Lamb's is basically a diner, we mean it in the nicest possible way. Open all day every day but Sunday since 1919, it has a long counter up front and a dining room in back, a swift staff of uniformed waitresses, and a menu with something for everyone. You can breakfast on bacon and eggs, milk toast, or grilled mountain trout; eat a lunch of ham on white or liver 'n' onions, and splurge on a deluxe steak dinner (or more of that fine river trout). Accommodations include plush tall-backed booths; and among the civilized amenities is a sound system programmed to soothe and comfort valued customers.

Maddox Ranch House	
1900 S. Hwy. 89, Perry, UT	**$$**
(801) 723-8545	**LD**

Look for the futuristic spinning sign by the side of the highway and you will find *the* place north of Salt Lake City for eating immense steaks. OVER 4000 HEAD OF CHOICE BEEF USED ANNUALLY, a sign outside boasts. In business since the 1940s, Maddox is big and popular (you'll likely wait for a table). In the old days, the feed lot was adjacent to the restaurant, allowing customers to look out the window at future steaks on the hoof as they dined. Meals include corn sticks and potatoes, as well as pure drinking water drawn from Maddox's own well.

For those on the go, Maddox has a drive-in adjacent to its restaurant. Here the menu is such classic car-fare as burgers, chicken baskets, long dogs, and cream pies, accompanied by a beverage called
"Fresh lime," which is Sprite doctored up with lime squeezin's and
sugar.

Mom's	
10 E. Main, Salina, UT	**$**
(801) 529-3921	**BLD**

Mom's is a vintage crossroads café in an old cow town. Locals as well
as travelers congregate in its aqua-upholstered booths for three
meals a day, dished out by energetic uniformed waitresses while Mom
sits at her desk in the back of the dining room overseeing everything.
The menu is basic meat and potatoes. We like the hamburgers and the
liver and onions, the latter available, according to the menu, only
when the liver is absolutely fresh. For breakfast, there is lush-crusted
chicken-fried steak; and there are scones—Utah's own flaky version of
the deep-fried dough pastries known in New Mexico as sopaipillas.
Mom's scones come hot from the kettle accompanied by a squeeze bottle of honey-butter.

Ruth's Diner	
2100 Emigration Canyon, Salt Lake City, UT	**$**
(801) 582-5807	**BLD**

Ruth's is a diner with a sense of history. Opened in 1930 by Ruth
Evans, who developed a reputation as one of the crankiest Pall
Mall–puffing hash-slingers in the West, it was bought by a new generation in 1979 and has since become a beacon of sophisticated urban
fare. You can still get a hamburger—Ruth's specialty—but burgers at
the new Ruth's are available with pasta salad on the side, and topped
with Cajun spice and/or blue cheese, fresh guacamole, or melted Swiss.
And while Old West biscuits and gravy continue to be a featured at-

traction of the breakfast menu, you can also eat a luxuriant "Rutherino" omelet with pasta, pesto, cheese, and hollandaise sauce. The dinner menu ranges from liver and onions to Chinese chicken salad and paillard of pork in lemon shallot caper sauce. Recommended: chili rellenos or roasted garlic chicken.

(Under the same management, the Santa Fe Restaurant adjacent to the diner is a little swanker and features a "private club" where customers can circumvent Utah's strict liquor laws.)

Zoom	
660 Main St., Park City, UT	**$$**
(801) 649-9108	**£ D**

*Z*oom is an agreeably casual "roadhouse grill"—come for a sandwich and a beer, sit outside on a heated patio, gab forever over coffee. Yet the setting is western chic (Utahan Robert Redford owns it) and the food smacks of New American creative zeal.

The clever menu is divided into small plates and main plates, so you can have a quick snack of crunchy-topped baked macaroni and cheese or a grand supper of Cuban rubbed pork with papaya relish and black beans. Sandwiches include a thick black Angus burger and a grilled portobello mushroom on focaccia; entrees vary from impeccable leg of lamb served on a bed of minty lentils with yogurt sauce and cheese-dusted pita crisps to ridiculously messy, falling-off-the-bone Detroit-style ribs.

The one dish we cannot resist is grilled tri-tip steak—a cut of beef favored in old vaquero country west of the Rockies. Sided by Zoom's mess o' greens—vivid, tart, incredibly toothsome—this robust platter strikes us as the kind of protein-rich fare that health-food experts used to prescribe for anemic urbanites in need of red meat and fresh air.

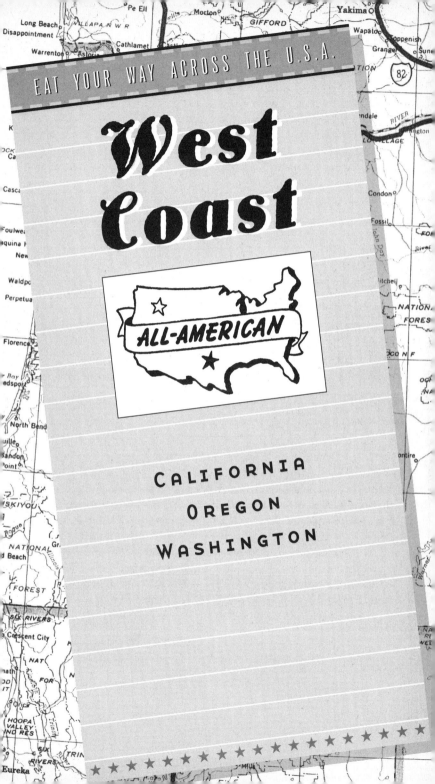

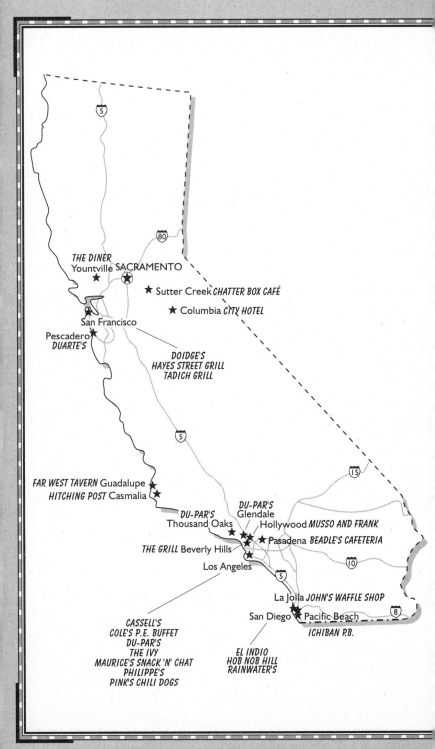

5

80

THE DINER
Yountville SACRAMENTO
★   ★

★ Sutter Creek *CHATTER BOX CAFÉ*

★ Columbia *CITY HOTEL*

San Francisco
★

Pescadero ★
DUARTE'S

DOIDGE'S
HAYES STREET GRILL
TADICH GRILL

5

FAR WEST TAVERN Guadalupe ★
HITCHING POST Casmalia ★

DU-PAR'S   *DU-PAR'S*
Thousand Oaks   Glendale
                Hollywood *MUSSO AND FRANK*
THE GRILL Beverly Hills ★ Pasadena *BEADLE'S CAFETERIA*

15

Los Angeles

5

10

La Jolla *JOHN'S WAFFLE SHOP*
San Diego ★ Pacific Beach
ICHIBAN P.B.

8

CASSELL'S
COLE'S P.E. BUFFET
DU-PAR'S
THE IVY
MAURICE'S SNACK 'N' CHAT
PHILIPPE'S
PINK'S CHILI DOGS

EL INDIO
HOB NOB HILL
RAINWATER'S

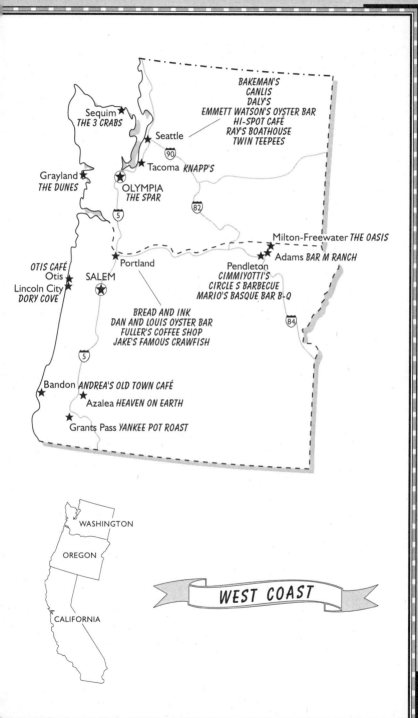

CALIFORNIA

Beadle's Cafeteria

825 E. Green St., Pasadena, CA	$
(818) 796-3618	£D

Beadle's is a reasonably priced cafeteria that showcases such stalwart dinners as leg o' lamb, pot roast with potato pancakes, and baked ham every Sunday. Hash—beef, turkey, or corned beef—is often on the menu. Roast turkey with aromatic sage dressing, mashed potatoes, and gravy is served five days a week. "People seem to expect Thanksgiving dinner," manager Jane Arvizu told us as she watched a customer vacillate between colorful confetti Jell-O and a dish of carrot-raisin slaw, then finally choose both.

Cassell's

3266 W. Sixth St., Los Angeles, CA (213) 480-8668	$
Mon–Sat	£

Beautiful hamburgers, one-third or two-thirds of a pound of freshly ground beef, rosy red inside a glistening charred crust, are piled onto fresh sesame buns—a mouth-watering presentation, to which you add your own condiments from a buffet. These include *homemade* mayonnaise, high-quality tomatoes, red relish, Roquefort dressing, peach halves and pineapple chunks, and an epicurean potato salad. Cassell's is a rudimentary restaurant—nothing to look at and too crowded any time after noon, with bare-bones seating on a small patio—but its burgers just might be the world's best.

Chatter Box Café

Main St., Sutter Creek, CA	$
(209) 267-5935	B L

This tiny main street café opened for business in 1946, and while the decor is pure nostalgia, the food is a cut above. Enlightened burgers topped with anything from blue cheese or green chilies to sweet Jamaican relish are served on bakery rolls with high-quality condiments and fresh-cut French fries on the side. Breakfast is a bonanza: interesting omelets, delectable corned beef hash, a gold-country version of San Francisco's New Joe Special (ground beef, spinach, and onions scrambled with eggs), and a choice of *ten* different kinds of sausage, including spicy andouille, bratwurst, kielbasa, and bangers. Muffins are oven-hot, as are cinnamon rolls . . . but come early, because the good breadstuffs can vanish well before breakfast ends at 11 AM.

City Hotel

Main St., Columbia, CA (209) 532-1479	$$
Sunday brunch	D

This charming little 1856 hotel provides not only the flavor of Gold Rush luxe, but also fine modern food and California wine, all tendered with aplomb by a staff of seasoned professionals as well as students earning their degrees in the Hospitality Management Program of nearby Columbia College. For drinks (vintage or modern), the original What Cheer saloon downstairs is an inviting place to linger; it still has its original cherrywood bar, shipped 'round the Horn from New England. The second-floor parlor, which serves as a sitting room during the day, doubles as a breakfast room for guests each morning. And the dining room is known throughout the region for its vintner dinners hosted by local wine makers, its "student cookbook" dinners for which Advanced Contemporary Cuisine students prepare four-course meals using recipes from a popular cookbook, and a seasonal menu that reflects enthusiasm for local produce as well as a knowledge of classic cuisine.

Cafeteria-Style Dining

Common in the South and southern Midwest, where most of them can be counted on for a good, homey meal, cafeterias were once known as "California-style" restaurants. Way back in the 1920s, self-service was a modern novelty, and the fact that all the food was out in the open for customers to see (instead of lurking in a germy kitchen) seemed to express perfectly the open, honest nature of the Golden State. Amazingly, there are still a handful of swell cafeterias on the West Coast, but now instead of seeming like the restaurants of tomorrow, they are relics of a culinary past.

☛ Beadle's Cafeteria, Pasadena, CA (p. 314)
☛ Cassell's, Los Angeles, CA (p. 314)
☛ Cole's P.E. Buffet, Los Angeles, CA (p. 316)
☛ Philippe's, Los Angeles, CA (p. 327)
☛ Bakeman's, Seattle, WA (p. 337)

Cole's P.E. Buffet

| 118 E. 6th St., Los Angeles, CA | $ |
| (213) 622-4090 | £𝔇 |

The oldest restaurant and saloon in Los Angeles (since 1908), Cole's is a dark and atmospheric hole-in-the-wall cafeteria with sawdust on the floors. Customers pile trays with hot lunches of days gone by: platters of steamed corned beef and cabbage, beef stew, thick-sliced roast beef. The house specialty is the French dip, a West Coast sandwich that might have been invented here. The story is that shortly after Cole's opened for business in the Pacific Electric Railway station, a customer complained that his gums hurt. He wanted a beef sandwich, but feared he couldn't bite through the crusty roll. Chef sliced the roll as usual, but before he loaded it with beef he dipped each half in the pan of natural gravy where the beef sat. The gravy softened the bread . . . and the French dip sandwich was born. It is a splendid concept, particularly well executed by Cole's carvers. When you request a French dip, the man in the toque forks a slab of hot brisket from the steam box and hand-slices a mound of thick, juicy pieces, then spears each half of the sliced roll and holds it in a pan of natural gravy long enough to fully flavor the soft part of the chewy bread but leave the crust crisp. The moistened bread melds with the mellow beef it wraps, and the result is a delicious mess. At the tables, glass jars hold fierce hot mustard—the tender French dip's ideal complement.

The Diner

6476 Washington St., Yountville, CA (707) 944-2626	$$
Tues–Sun	BLD

The heavenly wine country hash house serves four-star cheeseburgers and shoestring French fries, real cherry Cokes, and fine Mexican dinners. But the stellar meal at this Napa County treasure is breakfast, "served all day." Consider banana-nut pancakes with maple syrup, or buttermilk corn cakes sided by sausage patties seasoned with herbs from the Diner's backyard garden. Eggs and omelets are accompanied by heaps of cheese-draped, onion-laced fried potatoes and toast made from homemade sourdough rye, raisin wheat, or potato bread. The coffee is rich and strong; but if you've got time to linger, you might also favor a Mimosa, made with freshly squeezed orange juice and locally bottled champagne.

Doidge's

2217 Union St., San Francisco, CA (415) 921-2149	$
(reservations advised, especially on weekends)	BL

Doidge's is a storefront café that is a breakfast boodle. Glorious French toast is made from your choice of bread (raisin-nut, honey-wheat, etc.) and heaped with fresh fruit, nuts, and sour cream. Baked eggs are served in cups made from thick bacon. Corned beef hash comes with crunchy fried potatoes, a garnish of sour cream, and a sourdough roll on the side. Omelets are expertly made with all the usual ingredients and plenty of extraordinary ones. We especially like the peach and walnut chutney omelet, but never can resist that French toast and classic eggs Benedict.

Duarte's	
202 Stage Rd., Pescadero, CA	**$**
(415) 879-0464	**BLD**

Regular customers often share tables with traveling strangers in this snug 100-year-old tavern, where the specialty of the house is always artichokes (grown in nearby fields). Artichoke omelets are served at breakfast, artichokes are stuffed with fennel sausage later in the day; and every dinner is served with cream of artichoke soup.

Duarte's offers a whole menu of fine square meals, such as pork chops with mashed potatoes and roast turkey with dressing, all served with good, gardeny salads; but beyond the artichokes, the kitchen's main attraction is fresh Pacific seafood. We've eaten impeccable little sand dabs and rex sole in Duarte's pine-paneled dining room; and plump oysters are baked with plenty of garlic in a buttery casserole. Cioppino, made with Dungeness crab, mussels, prawns, and clams, is a weekend specialty.

Pies are hefty and homey, like the best truck stop might serve, made from local olallie berries, rhubarb, apples, and apricots.

Du-par's

6333 W. Third St. at the Farmer's Market, Los Angeles, CA	$
(213) 933-8446; other locations are	BLD
75 W. Thousand Oaks Blvd., Thousand Oaks (805) 373-8785;	
and 123 Lexington Dr., Glendale (818) 240-5454	

Du-par's is a small chain of old-style coffee shops that specialize in savory pot pies—chicken, steak, or steak and kidney—and a dazzling array of dessert pies including southern pecan, lemon, and coconut custard. It is a three-meals-a-day kind of place: the breakfast pancakes are a Los Angeles legend (you can buy batter ready to take home and pour on the griddle), as is buttered and grilled date-nut bread. Night owls come for fine Welsh rarebit; and there are plenty of regular customers who time their lunch visits according to the immemorial daily specials: Monday fried chicken, Tuesday turkey, Wednesday pot roast, Thursday liver 'n' onions, Friday meat loaf—all accompanied by freshly mashed potatoes.

These hearty foodstuffs are served in spic-and-span surroundings by waitresses who wear tiny yellow hats shaped like cupcakes, white uniforms, and yellow aprons. The West Third Street Du-par's has the added attraction of being at the Farmers' Market, which is a good place to browse among fresh produce and shlock souvenirs and spot the many celebrities who shop here incognito.

El India

3695 India St., San Diego, CA	$
(619) 299-0333	LD

This breezy taqueria along the Interstate serves fresh Cal-Mex food: carnitas and burritos, guacamole-topped platters of chimichangas, quesadillas, hefty tacos and diminutive taquitos. Wait in line and tote your own meal to a jammed-together indoor seat or to an open-air patio just across the street. It's cheap, fun, and tasty; and when you're finished, you can heave your disposable plate into the garbage and get back on the highway in a jiffy.

Far Western Tavern

899 Guadalupe St., Guadalupe, CA	$$
(805) 343-2211	£Ð

Meals at the Far Western Tavern are served on cowboy-theme dishware emblazoned with little images of brands, spurs, and cows' heads, in a dining room that features a spectacular suite of hairy brown-and-white cowhide curtains. All this could be the decor of a campy new-West restaurant, but here in Guadalupe it is the real McCoy. This is ranch country, where the vaqueros once rode and where cattle is still big business, so naturally the best thing to order is red meat. In particular, the Far Western features a "bull's-eye" steak cooked on an open grate over flaming live oak logs. It is accompanied by all the companions required at a traditional beef banquet in central California: a tray of relishes to start, zesty little pinquito beans on the side, salsa to heat things up, and crusty bread for mopping juice.

The Grill

9560 Dayton Way, Beverly Hills, CA (310) 276-0615	$$$
Sun D only (reservations advised)	£Ð

When it opened for business some fifteen years ago, the Grill's straightforward approach to food went against the prevailing winds of fancy-pants gastronomic minimalism. But times have caught up with the Grill, and forthright food is fashionable again. Few restaurants anywhere manage to be so basic, yet with such panache.

The menu is printed every day: a long roster of grilled steaks, double-cut lamb chops, calves' liver steak an inch thick, simply prepared California seafood, eastern oysters, and a grand Cobb salad made with perfect chunks of slippery ripe avocado, strong blue cheese, and crisp nuggets of bacon. We love the Grill's potatoes, from the plain baked one, served erupting from its chewy tan skin, to a wickedly crusty combo of fried potatoes and onions.

People-watching and eavesdropping opportunities abound. Table talk is movie contracts or big real estate deals. Agents sit with casting directors; stars join producers at the bar; rich couples peruse pictures of million-dollar houses; and white jacketed waiters—some of whom you've seen in bit parts and commercials—chatter among themselves about casting calls and backstage goings-on.

Hayes Street Grill	
320 Hayes St., San Francisco, CA	*$$$*
(415) 863-5545	*LD*

Hayes Street Grill has managed to maintain an intimate, small-restaurant feeling despite the fact that it is one of the seminal Bay Area kitchens that has defined modern California cuisine. Leave celebrity-chef dining rooms to their gourmet-club clientele. Reserve a table at Hayes Street and start with a marvelous house salad of beets, Stilton, and walnuts, or with simple cracked crab accompanied by red-pepper aioli; then move on to mesquite-grilled halibut, snapper, or

Old California Cuisine

Much as we appreciate the salubrious influence of "New" California cuisine on American menus, we've got a soft spot for Golden State traditions that pre-date the reign of Alice and Wolfgang, goat cheese, and boutique pizza. An old California meal can be as simple as chicken pot pie at Du-par's or as deluxe as steak and martinis at Musso's. These restaurants are pretty much the same as they were fifty years ago.

- ☛ Cole's P.E. Buffet, Los Angeles, CA (p. 316)
- ☛ Duarte's, Pescadero, CA (p. 318)
- ☛ Du-par's, Los Angeles, CA (p. 319)
- ☛ Far Western Tavern, Guadalupe, CA (p. 320)
- ☛ Musso and Frank, Hollywood, CA (p. 326)
- ☛ Philippe's, Los Angeles, CA (p. 327)
- ☛ Tadich Grill, Los Angeles, CA (p. 328)

scallops with your choice of garnishes that include salsa, lemon-butter, luxurious béarnaise and peanutty Szechuan. Top it off with crème brûlée, and you will have consumed a sophisticated San Francisco meal to remember.

Hitching Post

3325 Point Sal Rd., Casmalia, CA	**$$**
(805) 937-6151	**D**

The Hitching Post's top sirloin is grand—pungent with age, oozing juice, an easy chew—but the filet mignon is even better. Its fibers glow with the flavor of the hard oak wood over which it's cooked, and with the piquant smack of the wine vinegar and oil marinade that is applied as the meat cooks. The beef is served as part of a traditional Santa Maria–style barbecue dinner, which includes relish tray, a cocktail of microscopic pink shrimp in red sauce, garlic bread, salsa, and potatoes.

The Hitching Post is one of the few businesses on the main street of Casmalia, a sleepy little town that seems worlds away from modern Los Angeles. Restaurant decor is cow-country casual: linoleum floors and red tablecloths, a TV always on above the bar, a bison head wearing a Buffalo Bills cap, and wall hangings made of cattle hides.

Hob Nob Hill

2271 First Ave., San Diego, CA	**$**
(619) 239-8176	**BLD**

Eating in so gentle a coffee shop makes us think of mid-century domestic science brochures that offer advice to the eager new bride who wants to create a happy home: set an attractive table, cook wholesome and well-balanced meals, add a pleasant little garnish to every plate to show you care. So it is at Hob Nob Hill.

There are mouth-watering daily specials (Tuesday short ribs and Sunday sauerbraten are delightful), but the everyday entrees are special, too: chicken croquettes with gravy, mashed potatoes, and tart cranberry relish served in half a hollowed-out orange; turkey with sage dressing in the evening; big fruit plates and fiesta salads at noontime.

Hob Nob Hill is a joyous place for breakfast; to start the day with freshly squeezed juice, good coffee, and a wedge of spicy rhubarb sour cream coffee cake or a pumpkin muffin is a taste of California heaven. Amid the rush and crowds, waitresses liven up the room by schmoozing with customers they have served for decades as enthusiastic pastryhounds rhapsodize out loud over the individual bundt cakes and caramel sticky buns and sweet rolls in the glass case that everyone admires while they wait for a table.

Ichiban P.B.

1441 Garnet Ave., Pacific Beach, CA	$
(619) 270-5755	£ D

There are many restaurants around San Diego that serve Japanese fare cheap. Aside from well-made sushi and hot teriyaki at low-low prices, the special charm of Ichiban P.B. is its beachside character. The ocean is blocks away, but Ichiban's counter and booths attract crowds of surfers and a broad assortment of the kind of happy-go-lucky Pacific Beach denizens who give this neighborhood its panache. Japanese though the food may be, the experience of eating a bowl of "stamina noodles" or a platter of California rolls at Ichiban P.B. is *way rad*—a taste of the sun-drenched essence of surf culture.

The Ivy

113 N. Robertson Blvd., Los Angeles, CA	$$$
(310) 274-8303	£ D

Reviewers warn that you have to be a star to enjoy the Ivy, where so many show biz folks come to eat; but we're nobodies and we have been treated nicely (maybe not as nicely as the TV sitcom actor sitting next to us or the hyper-tanned producer who spends half his meal yakking on a cell phone). Anyway, it is neither service nor star-gazing that brings us back to splurge at this casual but perennially trendy establishment whenever we pass through town. It is wonderful food, starting with warm anadama bread, moving on to fiery mesquite-grilled shrimp, elegant pastas, deliriously tender lime chicken, and cool cocktails festooned with fresh mint leaves. And dessert! There are two that make us swoon: the hot fudge sundae, with all ingredients, including a sweet cloud of the finest whipped cream, marshaled for the diner to apply as desired; and a warm, caramel-sopped apple tarte tatin that sets the world standard.

Note: Ivy at the Shore, 1541 Ocean Ave. in Santa Monica, serves big portions of expertly prepared high-fashion food. Like its inland sister, it is a choice spot for celebrity spotting.

John's Waffle Shop

7906 Girard Ave., La Jolla, CA	$
(619) 454-7371	฿£

This happy café is reminiscent of the days La Jolla was just a little getaway-from-it-all village by the sea. Nothing fancy about it; you come to John's in the morning for excellent waffles, pancakes, or eggs, or at lunch for such enduring coffee-shop fare as gentle-tempered chili with beans, an avocado-rich Cobb salad, or our personal favorite, the "smart girl sandwich," made with lots of good bacon, grilled onions, tomato, and cheese. On the side, drink a tall chocolate malt or the salubrious West Coast favorite, a smoothie, which is a health shake made with orange juice or strawberries.

Maurice's Snack 'N' Chat

5549 Pico Blvd., Los Angeles, CA (213) 931-3877	$$
(reservations advised)	£Đ

EAT HERE CHEAPER THAN AT HOME, AND BETTER, TOO, says a sign outside. Inside the friendly, unpretentious soul-food landmark,

Santa Maria Barbecue

❦

Santa Maria barbecue is a unique regional banquet anchored by hefty cuts of red beef slow-cooked over live oak logs. The meal includes little pink pinquito beans, buttered and garlicked French bread, salsa for the beans or meat, plus shrimp cocktail to start, salad on the side, and a baked potato with sour cream or French fries and possibly hot creamed macaroni, too. To wash down this big feed, locals have pinot noir *ordinaire* from one of the Santa Barbara County wineries.

The ritual meal goes back to California's ranch days, when it was served at round-up time to vaqueros from all surrounding ranches; today, it is still a community affair. On weekends, local charities, social clubs, and civic organizations set up open-air cookers and serve barbecue in shopping center parking lots and along the streets of Santa Maria, Nipomo, and Los Alamos to raise money for good causes.

The Far Western Tavern in Guadalupe (p. 320) and the Hitching Post in Casmalia (p. 322) are two restaurants that specialize in the historic feast.

Hollywood celebrities rub elbows with ordinary Angelenos over plates of fried chicken, smothered pork chops, pan-fried fish, short ribs, and meat loaf, all served with heaps of long-cooked, deep-seasoned vegetables. For adventurous eaters looking to get away from fashion-fickle L.A., for homesick southerners in search of comfort food, and for skinny people in search of a serious weight-gain diet, Maurice's is a great place to know about.

Musso and Frank

6667 Hollywood Blvd., Hollywood, CA (213) 467-7788	$$
(reservations advised)	£D

When Musso and Frank opened for business in 1919, Hollywood was young and fresh and Hollywood Boulevard was a magic address. Hollywood is now an institution and the Boulevard has gone to honky-tonk hell in a handbasket, but step inside Musso's and go back

Coffee Shops

It is difficult to pinpoint what exactly makes a restaurant a coffee shop (as opposed to a diner, a café, or a lunchroom), but any connoisseur of urban cheap eats knows that a coffee shop is a special kind of place with a soupçon of refinement that always makes for pleasant eating. Some fundamental qualities include three-meals-a-day service, uniformed waitresses wearing name tags, a large and familiar menu (possibly laminated in plastic), a first-come-first-served seating policy, and—of course—hot coffee served before, during, and after any meal.

Nowhere did the coffee shop prosper more than in southern California, particularly in the 1950s and 1960s, when such futuristic Naugahyde-and-Formica shrines as Ship's, Norm's, and Pann's were designed to resemble the offspring of a tail-finned Cadillac mated to a space ship's rec room.

Although no longer the height of culinary modernity, coffee shops still provide a certain basic, casual gratification not available in a diner, a dive, or an ordinary restaurant. Come as you are, eat well and pay little, and walk out with spring in your step.

- ☛ Du-par's, Los Angeles, CA (p. 319)
- ☛ Hob Nob Hill, San Diego, CA (p. 322)
- ☛ John's Waffle Shop, La Jolla, CA (p. 324)
- ☛ Fuller's Coffee Shop, Portland, OR (p. 333)
- ☛ Knapp's Restaurant, Tacoma, WA (p. 340)

to a wondrous time. Ensconced in a plush leather booth in this wood-paneled institution, you dine on immemorial comfort food that includes svelte lunchtime flannel cakes, sauerbraten with potato pancakes, chicken pot pie every Thursday, and a full menu of broiled steaks and chops with eleven kinds of potatoes available on the side. Old-fashioned cocktails are expertly mixed; and as you sip a martini, manhattan, gibson, or Rob Roy, chances are very good of spotting some of the many show biz celebrities who still come to Musso's. Perhaps they crave the powerful sense of normalcy this old grill radiates.

Philippe's

1001 N. Alameda St., Los Angeles, CA	$
(213) 628-3781	BLD

Philippe's is a self-service restaurant that is as comfy as an old shoe: sawdust-strewn floors, communal tables, nine-cents-a-cup coffee, and superb French dip sandwiches with roaring-hot mustard on the side. It is as good a people-watching place as Spago, but instead of movie stars, you see the Los Angelenos Raymond Chandler wrote about—downtowners who include municipal employees from the nearby post office and courthouse as well as Santa Anita touts who frequent the bank of old wooden phone booths, racing forms in hand.

Pink's Chili Dogs

709 N. La Brea Ave., Los Angeles, CA	$
(213) 931-4223	BLD

Beautiful, taut-skinned hot dogs are nabbed in spongy buns, then topped with mustard, raw onions, and a spill of Day-Glo orange no-bean chili. Customers eat 'em standing on the sidewalk, sitting in cars parked in the red zone on La Brea, or strolling along Melrose Avenue. These raunchy tube steaks have made Pink's a preferred dive for decades, but the menu lists lesser-known breeds of pup worth eating, too: the Guadalajara dog, topped with sour cream; cheese dogs; dogs wrapped in tortillas; chopped dogs in a cup of baked beans. There are even hamburgers and tamales, and a pretty darn good warm potato salad. For dessert, true connoisseurs avail themselves of a Pink's candy machine and top things off with a couple of Atomic Fireballs.

Rainwater's	
1202 Ketner, San Diego, CA	*$$$*
(619) 233-5757	*LD*
Sat and Sun D only	

No place for dieters, penny-pinchers, or slaves to fickle-food fashion, Rainwater's is the number one dining room for a serious splurge in San Diego. The beef is impeccable, the fish is as fresh as the nearby surf, and the Caesar salad is monumental. With its thick white table-cloths and suave service, this modern but beguilingly old-fashioned chop house is a rousing joy for times when the sky's the limit. We love the powerhouse dry martinis, glistening raw oysters on the half shell, big boneless sirloin steaks, and supersweet pecan pie. Many San Diego pinstripers come for business lunch and actually eat light, healthy fare, then return to the office. Our favorite thing to do after a Rainwater's meal is to lie down—usually on the beach or in a hotel room with ocean breezes blowing through.

Tadich Grill	
240 California St., San Francisco, CA	*$$$*
(415) 391-2373	*LD*
Mon–Sat	

Formal and first-class, yet democratic (there are no reservations; everybody waits in line), Tadich Grill started as a coffee shop during the Gold Rush. It has grown and moved a few times over the last century and a half, settling in its current clubby location in the Financial District in the 1960s. For perfect Pacific seafood, simply prepared and elegantly presented by white-aproned waiters, it is the best place in town. The cioppino is authoritative, accompanied by good bread; sand dabs, filleted with utmost finesse and presented two at a time on china plates, are exquisite; fried oysters and prawns, accompanied by four-star tartar sauce, are ethereal (and French fried potatoes are huge and tasty); charcoaled swordfish, snapper, and salmon are moist, market fresh, and delicious. A seafood feast in a private booth at Tadich's is a great American meal.

OREGON

☆ ☆ ☆

Andrea's Old Town Café

160 Baltimore, Bandon, OR	$$
(541) 347-3022	BLD

A storefront café that has been an Old Town good-food landmark since the early 1980s, Andrea's is known for breakfasts of blintzes and muffins, for seafood stews and proprietor Andrea Gatov's home-raised lamb at suppertime, and for an eclectic Sunday brunch featuring specialties from around the world. Andrea's is a soothing place to spend time and sate appetite. Decor includes green plants hung everywhere; and the good smells of home cooking waft from the kitchen morning, noon, and night.

Bar M Ranch

East of Gibbon on the river road, Adams, OR	$$
(541) 566-3381	BLD
for ranch guests only	

The Bar M is not a public restaurant, but the meals are so good and it's such a nice place to stay, we can't resist telling you about it. Only overnight guests eat in the dining room of this bucolic ranch by the Umatilla River where, three times a day, the dinner bell above the main lodge rings to signal mealtime. If you are anywhere within a few hundred yards, you don't need to hear the bell to know that it is time to eat because you will begin to smell chicken and dumplings or sizzling pork chops or hot meat loaf and potatoes. In a big room at long, unclothed tables, guests pass the serving platters and practice their boardinghouse reach while various members of the Baker family, who have run the ranch since the 1930s, regale them with stories of bobcats and bears they have seen along the trails. There is nothing luxurious dished out on the El Rancho pattern china, unless, like us, you consider barbecued salmon or fresh-caught trout a luxury. Home cooking is the rule: hot biscuits or cinnamon rolls to accompany morning bacon and eggs, freshly shucked corn on the cob at supper, and bowls of red raspberry jam made from the Bakers' berry bushes just outside. It's a little bit like paradise.

Bread and Ink

3610 SE Hawthorn Blvd., Portland, OR	$$
(503) 239-4756	LD

In this civilized storefront café, you can get a deliciously aristocratic hamburger—on a homemade bun, with cheddar or Gruyère cheese or great guacamole on top and served with top-quality condiments, including garlic aioli to die for. Or you can eat food inspired by the cuisines of Vietnam (spring rolls), Italy (anchovy-and-tomato bread), Mexico (chicken enchiladas with tomatillo salsa), or the Pacific Northwest (broiled salmon). Come on Sunday and brunch is traditionally

Jewish: cheese blintzes, scrambled eggs with lox and onions, schmaltzy chopped liver.

Bread and Ink is a lovely place to linger over coffee. Magazines and papers are provided and the staff seems to enjoy being part of the nicest restaurant in town.

Cimmiyotti's

137 South Main St., Pendleton, OR	$$
(541) 276-4314	D

Eastern Oregon is cattle country, and the beef served in this clubby Main Street steak house—listed on the saddle leather–bound menu under a heading that reads "From the Feed Lot"—is exemplary. There are big New York strips and ladies' tenderloins, filets mignon, chopped steaks and hamburgers, and teriyaki steaks; the specialty of the house is a good-size rib-eye that runs with juice when you slice off a hunk.

Cimmiyotti's Italian specialties are guileless Italian-American fare from an age of culinary innocence: soft white spaghetti noodles topped with chunky, oregano-flavored red sauce; lasagna with onions and sausage, made with three stout cheeses; cannelloni; manicotti; ravioli; and fettucine Alfredo. All come with glistening loaves of gentle-flavored garlic bread.

Circle S Barbecue

210 S.E. 5th, Pendleton, OR	$
(541) 276-9637	BLD

Breakfast is great in this friendly cafe that is loaded to the rafters with western decor, including farriers' tools, vintage saddles, and an inspirational plaque titled CODE OF THE COW COUNTRY ("Always kill a rattlesnake. Never ride a sore-back hoss."). You can eat crunch-crusted chicken-fried steak; a vast platter of pancakes, German sausages, and hash browns, or biscuits and gravy. On the side, many regular customers imbibe a concoction known as red beer, which is a combination of beer and tomato juice.

At lunch and dinner, there is excellent barbecue insinuated with the tang of apple- and cherrywood smoke. We especially like Circle S chicken, which glistens like polished mahogany and is as crisp-skinned as Peking duck, so fragile that you can hear it crackle when you ease a knife down through it and watch the juices flow. Barbecued beef isn't nearly as pretty, but the flat slices have a pleasant smoke flavor nicely complemented by the dark red sauce that comes alongside. You can also get heavily garlicked barbecued German sausage or pork ribs, which are a royal mess to eat and about as porky as a rack can be.

Dan and Louis Oyster Bar

208 SW Ankeny St., Portland, OR	$$
(503) 227-5906	£D

"Oyster Stew" are the only words you need to know if you come to Dan and Louis ancient mariner of an eatery, where the walls are covered, floor to ceiling, with nautical bibelots. The stew is a mild brew of little oysters, warm milk, and melted butter, but can be made brinier by ordering it with a double dose of oysters. Stew has been the specialty here for decades; for a change of pace in winter months, we also like creamed crab—an old-fashioned kind of chafing-dish meal that has virtually ceased to exist as more modern chefs insist on serving seafood that actually looks like fish.

Dory Cove

5819 Logan Rd., Lincoln City, OR	$
(541) 994-5180	£D

Amid marshlands near a clamming beach, this wood-shingled shack is liked by locals for its hefty half-pound hamburgers, available every which way, but especially tasty topped with cheddar cheese and Canadian bacon on an onion bun. Nor do you want to miss Dory

Cove's Oregon-style (ultrathick) clam chowder, and you must save room for dessert. The thing to eat is pie, of which there are nearly a dozen homemade kinds every day, including chiffons, meringues, creams, sour cream raisin, and monumental deep-dish peach or apple, served piping hot.

Fuller's Coffee Shop

136 NW Ninth Ave., Portland, OR (503) 222-5608	$
Mon—Sat	B£

When it's time for breakfast in Portland, find this good, old-fashioned luncheonette among the factory buildings and you can't go wrong: freshly made cinnamon rolls, four-star French toast, and omelets accompanied by classic hash browns. At lunch, count on meat loaf with mashed potatoes, corned beef with cabbage, fresh salmon and halibut in season, plus the locally favored treat, fried razor clams. Fuller's is a simple place, easy to love.

Heaven on Earth

Quines Creed Rd. (exit 86), Azalea, OR (541) 837-3596	$
always open	

Oregon has a high cinnamon-roll consciousness, and along with Iowa, it is where the best and biggest will be found. The bakers at Heaven on Earth outdo themselves. All sorts of ordinary hot breakfasts and a variety of baked goods are available in this round-the-clock café at exit 86 off the interstate; but if you've got a serious appetite, the plate-size cinnamon roll is all you need to know about.

Jake's Famous Crawfish

401 SW Twelfth Ave., Portland, OR	$$
(503) 226-1419	£𝔇

Forget the crawfish. Although crawfish pie and étouffée have been on the menu since 1920, they are not what's good about this ever-popular hangout, where many customers come for no reason other than to drink microbrewed beer and eat raw oysters by the dozen and socialize at the back bar. The great things to eat are salmon, Dungeness crab, petrale sole, and a daily blackboard list of a few dozen sea creatures hauled in fresh from the market that day. Jake's also happens to be a fine place to sample the West Coast specialty hangtown fry, an omelet made with fried oysters.

The setting is Barbary Coast–vintage Pacifica: gold-flocked wallpaper, glittery chandeliers, high-back wooden booths with a patina of decades, and white-jacketed waiters who go about their business with all the efficiency of faro dealers.

Mario's Basque Bar B-Q

3107 Southgate, Pendleton, OR (541) 276-1665	$
open 4 days in Sept on the Pendleton Round-Up grounds; otherwise, call	

Mario Zubiria doesn't currently have a restaurant, but he is well known around Pendleton as a caterer. If you are lucky enough to be in Pendleton during the big rodeo in September, you can sample his robust food; the rest of the year, give him a call and find out where he is cooking, and ask if you can bust in to the event for a taste.

At the rodeo, Mr. Zubiria sets up a big mobile barbecue where he and his men charcoal-grill lamb chunks and chops, beef, and foot-long chorizo sausages, sending mouth-watering smoke signals wafting above the arena. The lamb chunks are chewy and tangy, served in a cardboard boat with charcoal-grilled onions, green peppers, and mushrooms. The hefty chorizo sausage, ground in Boise, Idaho, has an alarming red hue, and is peppery but not very hot. Its crisp skin encloses luscious, coarsely ground and well-garlicked pork, and although it is available on a stick for easy eating, we like it Mario's alternative way: wrapped inside a loaf of French bread and smothered with grilled onions.

The Oasis	
State Line Rd., Milton-Freewater, OR	**$$**
(541) 938-4776	**LD**

The Oasis is like a nice old pickup truck: ramshackle and rugged, but endearingly soulful. Art on the walls includes portraits of John Wayne and Chief Joseph of the Nez Perce; video poker machines in adjacent gaming rooms provide distant boinging background sounds for diners. From our table, we had a good view into the bar. There, perched on stools, were three large X's in a row: suspenders on the broad backs of three gents in cowboy hats having drinks and shooting the breeze. "How-do?" asked one, tipping his hat in our direction.

"Doing fine!" said we as our beef arrived. The sirloins, branded with a neat field of cross-hatch char marks, were mighty slabs of juice and flavor with agreeable tooth resistance. Notify the kitchen in advance and they will cook you a seventy-two-ounce sirloin; if you eat it and all its trimmings within an hour, you get it free. If you aren't interested in consuming four-and-a-half pounds of beef but want something opulent, there is prime rib; the largest one, a ten-ounce "ranch cut," is well over an inch thick, fleshy, and laden with natural gravy.

Otis Café	
Hwy. 18, Otis, OR	**$**
(541) 994-2813	**BLD**

For big, satisfying food, especially at breakfast time, there isn't a happier place to eat between Coos Bay and Astoria. Lush and crunchy hash browns, topped with melted cheese, are what you want on the side of anything, even sourdough pancakes. There are cinnamon rolls the size of Oregon, excellent whole-wheat black molasses bread, and berry pies to die for. At lunch, to accompany your hot plate or hamburger, have a chocolate malt.

Yankee Pot Roast

720 N.W. Sixth St., Grants Pass, OR (541) 476-0551	$$
Wed–Sun	D

Yankee Pot Roast is a name guaranteed to attract the attention of all meat-and-potatoes fans; and this extremely quaint restaurant in the old brick house on Sixth Street does not disappoint. The atmosphere is Victorian, including period costumes for the staff and the aroma of baking breadstuffs in the vestibule. Pot roast is always on the menu, along with other robust entrees like ham steak with sweet potatoes, meat loaf with mashed potatoes, roast pork, and grilled steak. Good as the meaty meals are, what won our hearts was seafood—lovely plates of fresh halibut and salmon, moist and flavorful, with delicious jumbo biscuits on the side.

WASHINGTON

☆ ☆ ☆

The 3 Crabs

101 Three Crabs Rd., Sequim, WA	$$
(360) 683-4264	LD

There is only one crustacean to focus on when you dine at the 3 Crabs. Dungeness crab, in season in the fall and through the winter, is steamed and served "cracked," which means the meat is easily accessible beneath the broken exoskeleton. It is sweet, tender meat, a pure pleasure to savor and a north coast delight all the more enjoyable for the easygoing ways of the pine-paneled dining room of this comfortable old restaurant alongside the Dungeness Spit.

Beyond the crab, the 3 Crabs does offer other tasty shellfish, from raw local oysters and comfortable oyster stew to geoduck chowder. And there are plates of fish, too—salmon, halibut, sole—all simply and expertly prepared, accompanied by creamy cole slaw and followed by high-flavored berry pies.

The restaurant's name, according to a waitress, refers not to denizens of the ocean but to the humans who opened the restaurant decades ago.

Bakeman's

122 Cherry St., Seattle, WA (206) 622-3375	$
Mon—Fri only	£

L isten up: at Bakeman's you want either turkey or meat loaf, on white or wheat, with mayo or mustard; and if you choose turkey, you might want cranberry sauce, too. Make all these decisions before you step down into the subterranean cafeteria known as Bakeman's because the line moves fast and the sandwich makers don't have time to nurse anyone along. The turkey is warm and juicy, sliced fresh; the meat loaf is honest and beefy; the bread is good, too. These simple sandwiches, in this workers' café, are some of Seattle's culinary treasures.

Canlis

2576 Aurora Ave., Seattle, WA (206) 283-3313	$$$
Mon—Sat (reservations recommended, jackets required for men)	D

G od bless it, Canlis hasn't changed in the near half-century since it opened. Here is a taste of postwar gourmet living in all its splendor: a debonair dining room with a spectacular view across Lake Union; silk-smooth service by kimono-outfitted waitresses who toss salads tableside with utmost aplomb; and unrepentant steak-and-potatoes (or stellar sautéed prawns and potatoes) meals that conclude with Grand Marnier soufflés. This classical food is delicious; the setting is romantic; and the whole experience is epicurean Americana at its best.

The Canlis Salad

ound on the back of a souvenir postcard given out by Canlis of Seattle, this recipe epitomizes the style of the fine old cliffside restaurant—traditional, yet with an extra rakish twist of luxury. Here, Canlis does a dizzying gloss upon Caesar salad, adding tomatoes, onions, bacon, and fresh mint to create a powerhouse flavor combo. (If you are a salmonella-phobe, you'd better skip the coddled egg in the dressing.)

    2 peeled tomatoes
    1 large head romaine lettuce
    $1/4$ cup chopped green onions
    1 cup freshly grated Romano cheese
    1 cup cooked and finely chopped bacon
    2 tablespoons chopped fresh mint
    $1/4$ teaspoon oregano

    dressing:
    juice of one lemon
    $1/2$ teaspoon fresh ground pepper
    1 coddled egg
    $1/2$ cup olive oil
    $1/3$ cup croutons

Cut the tomatoes in eighths and put them in a large salad bowl. Wash and dry the romaine, then cut it into 1-inch squares. Add onions, all but a couple tablespoons of the cheese, bacon, mint, and oregano.

Make the dressing by whipping the lemon juice, pepper, and coddled egg in a separate bowl and gradually drizzling in the olive oil, whipping constantly as you add it. Pour the dressing over the salad and toss thoroughly. Add croutons and the remaining sprinkle of Romano cheese.

Serves 4–6

Daly's

2713 Eastlake Ave., Seattle, WA	$
(206) 322-1918	£Đ

Dear to the hearts of grunge-food connoisseurs, Daly's introduced Seattle to the flame-broiled hamburger in 1962. It is nothing but a cheap-eats dive, but the burger it serves is indeed a good one, attended by skinny French fries in a little paper sack, and washed down with a refreshing fruit milk shake.

The Dunes

Just off Hwy. 105, Grayland, WA	$
(360) 267-1441	ß£Đ

Come, gather near the fireplace in the vintage red-cedar hideaway called the Dunes. The view is of the ocean and the sands; the highlight of the menu is crisp-crusted razor clamcakes—a treat for breakfast, lunch, or dinner. Creamy chowder, also made with large chunks of razor clam, is a homey delight. Salmon and crab, oysters on the half shell or in a stew: every kind of local seafood is fresh, traditionally cooked, and delicious. Accompanied by big, airy rolls warm from the oven and topped off by cranberry cake or blackberry pie, this is exactly the right meal for hungry travelers on the Olympic Peninsula west of Highway 101.

Emmett Watson's Oyster Bar

Soames-Dunn Bldg., Pike Place Market, Seattle, WA	$
(206) 448-7721	£Đ

Here are the makings of a carefree Seattle afternoon: a choice from more than three dozen kinds of bottled and draft beer and a half-dozen varieties of oyster on the half shell. That's what's available most days at this pint-size eatery with a scattering of tables in a pleasant off-street courtyard. In addition to impeccably fresh raw oysters, the kitchen makes fine salmon soup, chowder, and spicy fish and chips. For breakfast, it is an ideal place to savor hangtown fry—the West Coast omelet made with oysters.

Hi-Spot Café	
1410 34th St., Seattle, WA (206) 325-7905	$
Wed—Mon, D Wed—Sat	BL

We don't know about lunch or dinner (the menu lists sandwiches, pasta, pizzas), but breakfast at the Hi-Spot is a must-eat Seattle meal. On weekends, you will wait in a line that stretches out the door of the quaint old house in Madrona; once you get a table amid the happy vintage-clutter decor and the fine food starts coming, all minor inconveniences are forgiven. Aromatic cinnamon rolls and fruit-studded scones are the highlights of the baker's yield; off the stovetop come berry pancakes and complex omelets; from the oven emerge swank shirred eggs. Casual but competent service helps make this an easy, fun place to be, whether you are single, on a date, or with the whole family in tow.

Knapp's	
2707 N. Proctor St., Tacoma, WA	$
(206) 759-9009	BLD

It is all too easy to take Knapp's for granted: a middle-of-the-road restaurant, neither deluxe and trendy nor colorfully raffish. When you dine in the vintage neighborhood café, you are served by professional uniformed waitresses, at tables clothed with clean white linen. You eat unsurprising meals of roast pork loin (every Wednesday), liver and onions (every day), corned beef and cabbage (the Tuesday special), or turkey with dressing and mashed potatoes. Start with shrimp cocktail or salad, top it off with homemade peach pie and a bottomless cup of coffee. Expertly prepared meals such as these, at honest prices in comfortable surroundings, are not only delicious; they are good for the soul.

Ray's Boathouse	
6049 Seaview Ave., NW, Seattle, WA (206) 789-3770	**$$**
(reservations are essential)	**£D**

R ay's is the great place to eat seafood in Seattle. Start with oysters galore, steamed clams, or creamy chowder. Exemplary fillets and steaks of all kinds of Pacific salmon are available poached or broiled, plain or fancy; there are tender sautéed scallops, exquisite grilled rockfish strewn with capers and lemon, succulent smoked black cod with wheatberries on the side. The best fish dishes here are the simple ones—neither overdone nor annoyingly undercooked. Meals are deftly served by a helpful staff in the refined downstairs dining room as well as in a more boisterous (and cheaper and easier to get into) upstairs café.

The Spar	
114 East Fourth Ave., Olympia, WA	**$**
(360) 357-6444	**BℒD**

W e love this 1930s-vintage lunchroom for its cinnamon rolls, served hot and fresh in the morning, then made into creamy bread pudding for dessert later in the day. We also like the real milk shakes that accompany good hamburgers; and if you are on the lookout for tasty local seafood, you'll get that here, too: pan-fried oysters, crab Louis, or grilled salmon and halibut.

West Coast Splurges

~◆~

Expensive, fancy, and/or fashionable regional restaurants that are worth it.

- ☛ The Grill, Beverly Hills, CA (p. 320)
- ☛ Hayes Street Grill, San Francisco, CA (p. 321)
- ☛ The Ivy, Los Angeles, CA (p. 323)
- ☛ Musso and Frank, Hollywood, CA (p. 326)
- ☛ Rainwater's, San Diego, CA (p. 328)
- ☛ Tadich Grill, San Francisco, CA (p. 328)
- ☛ Cimmiyotti's, Pendleton, OR (p. 331)
- ☛ Canlis, Seattle, WA (p. 337)

Twin Teepees

7201 Aurora Ave., N., Seattle, WA	$
(206) 783-9740	BLD

Ok, so the food won't soon be featured on the cover of *Gourmet*. But it isn't the extraordinary meals that have drawn customers to Twin Teepees since it was built in 1937. The lure is the structure itself—exemplary West Coast roadside kitsch—that suggests you will dine in some sort of Native American mess hall. In fact, once you enter the pointy-topped place, it looks pretty much like any Naugahyde-booth diner, but with an Indian motif; and the cuisine is strictly paleface fare. That includes a large assortment of burgers, from plain and cheese-topped to a Hawaiian burger with a pineapple ring, and a "chicken breast burger," as well as skillets full of hot turkey and roast beef au jus. Although the Teepee Lounge offers highballs and exotic libations, including fuzzy navels and mai tais any time after 11 am, the meal many devoted customers like best is breakfast, when the place is packed, the coffee flows, and tables are piled high with plates of eggs and potatoes, pancakes and sausage.

Restaurants by Region and State

★ ★ ★

New England

Mid-South

Deep South

Midwest

Michigan

Minnesota

Missouri

Ohio

Wisconsin

West Coast

CALIFORNIA

OREGON

WASHINGTON